MR31 A73-67 banks steeply
away from its escort, over the
vast barren area of Australia's
Northern Territories while on
detachment at Darwin,
demonstrating its manoeuvre-
ability and showing the rather
slender planform of its wings.
In a turn of up to 60° of bank,
the pilot will be needing to
apply considerable back-
pressure on the control wheel to
maintain height. /J. L. Laming

LINCOLN
at War 1944-1966

Thor was used not only for goodwill and liaison visits abroad but also in the more mundane task of providing armament, systems and bombing training for College students, and is seen here unloading a stick of 500 pounders, probably on nearby Theddlethorpe or Wainfleet range./*Ministry of Defence*

LINCOLN
at War 1944-1966

Mike Garbett and Brian Goulding

LONDON

IAN ALLAN LTD

First Published 1979

ISBN 0 7110 0847 7

Design by Anthony Wirkus LSIAD

© Ian Allan Ltd 1979

Published by Ian Allan Ltd, Shepperton, Surrey,
and printed in the United Kingdom by
Ian Allan Printing Ltd.

Corpus Non Animum Muto
'I change my body, not my spirit.'
Motto of 57 Squadron, the first squadron
to have the Lincoln.

Contents

Left: It needs nerve to take a picture like this! With three props feathered and barely eight feet off the deck – less under the H2S radome – the near-30ton RF346 is an awesome sight as she bears down on the cameraman at TFU Defford, September 1949, flown by New Zealander Flt Lt Alan Gibson, DFM. Very low flying (usually on four engines) was part of experiments involving proximity fuse testing. /*Royal Radar Establishment*

Preface

With this book we have attempted to fill a gap in aviation history by telling as fully as space permits the story of the last piston-engined bomber to serve with the Royal Air Force. Whilst the Lincoln, nor any other aircraft for that matter, could ever hope to match the glamour and affection rightly bestowed on its forbear the Lancaster, nevertheless it filled a very important need in its time, and proved a reliable and sturdy work-horse in the reformative postwar years.

The Lincoln was a natural evolvement of the Lancaster but it came along just too late to prove itself in battle, though no doubt it would have acquitted itself just as well as the Lanc under fire. It emerged when the world was trying to forget about wars and everything they meant; when the brave deeds of the bomber crews were already being pushed into the background. Though used extensively in active policing and deterrent roles round the world, the Lincoln was primarily a stop-gap between the Lancaster and the jet age. It played an important part in the field of development of new engines, equipment, and techniques, and was widely used in the training role. Most aircrew who flew the Lincoln look back on it with some affection

for its stability, ruggedness and forgiving ways. It served its users well and rendered sterling service for many years in both the Royal Air Force and Royal Australian Air Force.

We hope we have done it, and its devoted air and ground crews, full justice by again concentrating on the human interest aspect rather more than the technical and general background, which is covered in other books. We have sought to give an insight into not only the normal routine of the bomber squadrons, but also some of the more special-ized tasks undertaken by the Lincoln and its crews serving with small units on which little has appeared in print before. Some details of the Lincolns' work must, regrettably, remain untold, both for security reasons and for another all-too-familiar reason: that of price-less material having been lost or thoughtlessly discarded by companies and official bodies. However, we hope there is something in the book to suit most readers, from the former aircrew (many of whom remained in the service to reach high ranks), to the aviation buff, and younger enthusiast – 'atmosphere', technical, historical, and even markings.

Below: A comparison in speed and age is this formation of Hemswell's No 83 Squadron Lincolns engaging in Battle of Britain day flypast practice in company with Canberras of 139 Squadron. The picture is dated September 1954 and the airfield is Kirton-in-Lindsey. /*M. J. Cawsey*

Acknowledgements

In the preparation of the book we have, as usual, gone to the people with first hand knowledge, the men who flew, operated, and serviced the Lincolns, and who have responded so well to our requests. Their response has enabled us to use, in the main, pictures which have not been published before. Reference to official records has been minimal.

We are especially grateful to the many ex-Lincoln men in Australia who have so trustingly lent their photos and mementos from the other side of the world. Whilst it is not possible to mention by name everyone who has helped us in our many years of research, we must particularly thank the following:

Air Britain; Air Cdre R. M. Aldwinckle, RCAF, (Retd); Wg Cdr R. I. Alexander, DFC, (Retd); Trevor J. Allen, (for proof reading); Flt Lt Stan W. Archer, DFC, (Retd); Wg Cdr Artie Ashworth, DSO, DFC, AFC, (Retd); Sqn Ldr R. C. B. (Chris) Ashworth, (Retd); John Austin (and staff of the Sir W. G. Armstrong Whitworth Aircraft Division of Hawker Siddeley).
Sqn Ldr G. M. Bailey, AFC, AMBIM, (Retd); Wg Cdr S. (Tubby) Baker, DSO, DFC, (Retd); Bryan Bardon; Grp Capt J. J. Barr; Wg Cdr G. Jim Bell; AVM D. C. T. Bennett, CB, CBE, DSO; Dave Birch; Sqn Ldr Peter J. S. Boggis, DFC, (Retd); Flt Lt Alf Bowden, DFM, (Retd); Wg Cdr Ken R. Bowhill, OBE, (Retd); Sqn Ldr A. B. (Paddy) Boyle, DFC, AFC; Grp Capt D. B. Bretherton, DFC, (Retd); E. Brown; Air Cdre B. (John) Brownlow, OBE, AFC; Flt Lt A. W. F. Burge, (Retd).
Flt Lt Denis B. Cassell, (Retd); Flt Lt Michael J. Cawsey; John Chatterton, DFC; Paul Chesterfield, (Royal Radar Establishment); Flt Lt Max E. Chivers, DFC, (Retd); M/Eng Frank Cholerton, (Retd); Alex F. Christie, (for typing); Grp Capt D. Clare, DFC, (Retd); Flt Lt Alan Clarke; Flt Lt Alan W. Clifford, (Retd); Sqn Ldr Leslie F. Compton, C Eng, AMIEE, AFRAeS, (Retd); Wg Cdr N. P. W. Conquer, OBE, (Retd); Sqn Ldr Phil J. Cornwall, DFM, (Retd); Paul Cullerne, (Chief Photographer Avro's); Sqn Ldr Jack A. L. Currie, DFC, (Retd).

Flt Lt Don Dacre, (Retd); Sqn Ldr Fred P. J. L. Dankwardt, (Retd); Capt Peter Davison; Sqn Ldr Leo C. E. De Vigne, DSO, DFC, AFC, (Retd); Wg Cdr Hal L. Derwent, AFC, (Retd); Brian P. Dobbins; Grp Capt Frank E. Doran, OBE; AVM J. C. T. Downey, CB, DFC, AFC.
Wg Cdr Mike H. de L. Everest, MVO, AFC, (Retd); Sqn Ldr Stan H. K. Eyre, DFC, (Retd).
Walter Faraday; Sqn Ldr Peter J. Field Richards, (Retd); Air Cdre D. B. Fitzpatrick, CB, OBE, AFC, AFRAeS, MBIM, (Retd); Flt Lt Leo E. Flatt, DFC, (Retd); Wg Cdr Geoff R. K. Fletcher, AFC, (Retd); Sqn Ldr F. W. John Flippant, DFC, (Retd); Flight Refuelling Staff (including R. Dickinson, DFC; K. F. Collins, D. B. Mackey, A. J. (Ted) Alsop); Grp Capt Don J. Flood, DFC, AFC, AFRAeS; Neville Franklin; Air Cdre Brian J. Frow, DSO, DFC.
Capt Stan F. Gage, DFC; M/Eng Ian Gibson; Flt Lt Peter Gillespie, (Retd); Sqn Ldr Don W. Greenslade, MBE, AFC.
Stan E. Hanson (for proof reading); Eric Harlin; Frank E. Harper; Sqn Ldr D. C. T. (Doyne) Hayes, (Retd); Keith Hayward; Flt Lt Joe A. Hemmings, (Retd); D. S. Hine; Harry Holmes; Capt Pat R. Hornidge; Wg Cdr R. M. (Bob) Horsley, DFC, AFC, (Retd); Harry Houghton (and other former staff of Avro's, Langar); Grp Capt Alan Hollingsworth, (Retd); Sqn Ldr Peter U. Hubbard, (Retd); Sqn Ldr C. W. G. Hughes. Sqn Ldr Ron C. Instrell, MBE, DFC, (Retd); Wg Cdr T. E. (Tiny) Ison, DSO, DFC, (Retd).
Wg Cdr Ron A. Jell, DFC, AFC, (Retd); George A. Jenks; Grp Capt E. A. Johnston, OBE, (Retd); Flt Lt Frank M. Jones, AFC, (Retd).
Flt Lt Joe K. S. Kmiecik, AFM.
Sqn Ldr Alistair G. Lang, DFC, (Retd); Sqn Ldr Kenneth R. Lang; Sqn Ldr Pete G. Langdon, DFM; Flt Lt John D. Langley; Sqn Ldr Frank R. Leatherdale, DFC, (Retd); Sqn Ldr Joe L'Estrange; Sqn Ldr Ken H. F. Letford, DSO, DFC, (Retd); Des Langthorne; Reg F. Lucks.
Wg Cdr Norman A. J. Mackie, DSO, DFC, (Retd); W. A. (Bill) McNeil; Capt Tom C.

Marks, DFC; Wg Cdr Ken M. Marwood, AFM; Grp Capt John R. Mason, (Retd); Flt Lt Roy L. Matthews; Grp Capt Cecil D. Milne, OBE, DFC, (Retd); Staff of MoD AR8, (RAF); Derek Monk; Sqn Ldr Denis Moreau; Douglas Mortimer (and staff of College of Aeronautics, Cranfield); Flt Lt Ian W. Mountain, (Retd); Flt Lt John W. H. Murdin, AFM (Retd); Eric Myall.

M/Plt R. C. (Bob) Nash, DFC; National Gas Turbine Establishment; Wg Cdr Alan E. Newitt, DFC, (Retd); Sqn Ldr Steve A. Nunns, DFC, AFC, (Retd).

J. F. Painter of Hawker Siddeley Canada Ltd; M/Sig Pete G. Palmer, (Retd); Sqn Ldr Tom J. Page, DFM, (Retd); Norman E. Parker; Cyril Parrish (for printing); Sqn Ldr John Partridge; Norman E. Peach; Arthur Pearcy, AFRAeS; Sqn Ldr Keith H. Perry, DSO, AFC, (Retd); Don H. Pickavance; Philip H. Plater; Sqn Ldr H. Ian Popay, DFM; Portsmouth Aviation Co Ltd; Staff of Paymaster General's Office (Crawley); Flt Lt A. V. (Gilly) Potter, AFC, (Retd); Rodney C. H. Poynton; Alfred Price; M/Sig George V. Price, DFC, DFM, (Retd); Flt Lt P. N. B. Pritchett, (Retd).

Sqn Ldr Don S. Richardson, DFC; Mervyn J. Ricketts; Grp Capt A. W. (Tony) Ringer, MVO, AFC, AMBIM; Sqn Ldr Tom W. Rippingale, DSO, DFC, (Retd); Bob Roberts (for printing); Bruce R. Robertson; Flt Lt E. T. Robinson, RAFVR(T); Capt H. Cliff Rogers, DFC; Rolls-Royce.

Wg Cdr R. J. (Bobby) Sage, OBE, AFC, (Retd); Max Scrimshaw; Bill Sharples; Sqn Ldr Harry J. Shaw, (Retd); Frank Shelton (of the Lincolnshire Standard Group); Sqn Ldr W. C. (Bill) Sinclair, AFC; L. Skivington; John C. Smith; Wg Cdr David Smyth, (Retd); Flt Lt Ken P. Souter, (Retd); Sqn Ldr E. J. Spencer, (Retd); Flt Lt Les Spink MBE, (Retd); P. D. Starling (and staff of RAE West Freugh); Ernest Stott, (RAE Farnborough); Ray Sturtivant; Grp Capt Ian C. K. Swales, DSO, DFC, DFM, (Retd); John Sykes.

Sqn Ldr Robert Tate, (Retd); Wg Cdr David H. Tew, AFC, (Retd); Alan Thomson (and staff at Hawker Siddeley (Avro's) Bracebridge Heath); Bruce Thompson; Wg Cdr John E. Tipton, DFC, (Retd); Sqn Ldr A. P. (Tony) Trowbridge, AFC, (Retd); E. H. Turner and E. S. Bateman (and staff of MoD Air Historical Branch).

Grp Capt G. W. W. (Joe) Waddington, DFC, (Retd); Peter Wakeham; Chas S. Waterfall; Sqn Ldr H. (Mike) Watkin-Jones, DFC, (Retd); Herbert Watson; Flt Lt Fred H. A. Watts, DFC, (Retd); Flt Lt Chris M. F. Webster; Sqn Ldr Eric D. Whybray, DFC, (Retd); Ray Williams; Sqn Ldr R. J. R. Williams; George W. Wilson, AFRAeS, MIAeS; Sqn Ldr Don F. Wimble; Wg Cdr Jack H. Woods, DFC, (Retd). Flt Lt W. E. (Bill) Youd, (Retd). Our two 'Secretaries', Pam Golder and Christine Burchall.

From Australia we have had outstanding help from:

Members of Aviation Historical Society of Australia; N. J. Flanagan & Staff of Australian War Memorial; Wg Cdr Arthur Barnes, DFC, AFC; Alan Charnley; E. T. Clifford & Staff of Records, Dept of Defence; Wg Cdr John H. Cooney, BA, (Retd); Air Cdre F. A. Cousins, OBE, BE; Bunny D'Arby (New Zealand); Staff of Director of PR Dept of Defence, Canberra; Wg Cdr W. R. Fisher, MBE; Flt Lt Syd G. Gooding, DFC, (Retd); David E. Johnson; Capt. John L Laming, AFC; K. Llewellyn, PRO, RAAF Melbourne; Grp Capt M. K. Lyons, AFC; Air Cdre Geoff D. Marshall, OBE, AFC, (Retd); Wg Cdr W. Noel Nichol, (Retd); Capt John Pickwell; Grp Capt Ken V. Robertson, DFC, AFC & Bar, (Retd); Sqn Ldr C. S. (Dinny) Ryan; R. F. Smalley, Dept of Defence; Air Cdre C. H. Spurgeon, CBE, DFC; Robert D. Stewart; C. Streten of Queensland Newspapers PTY Ltd (also Courier-Mail); Edward W. H. Ward; Alan Underwood.

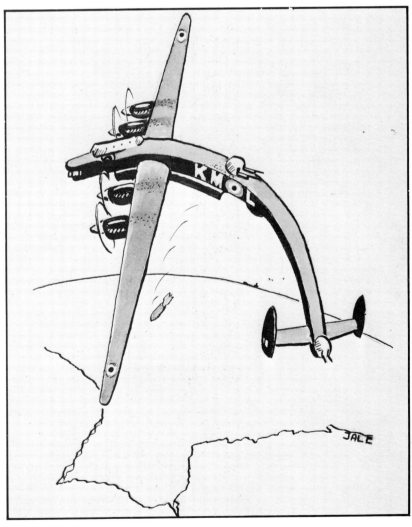

Glossary

A&AEE	Aircraft & Armament Experimental Establishment	IAS	Indicated airspeed
AEO	Air Electronics Officer	IFF	Identification friend or foe
AFB	Air Force Base	ILS	Instrument landing system
AFS	Advanced Flying School	JASS	Joint Anti-Submarine School
AGLT	Automatic Gun Laying Turret	kts	Knots (approx 1.2 statute miles)
AI	Airborne Interception	LR	Long range
ampg	Air miles per gallon	M/F	Medium frequency
ANS	Air Navigation School	MO	Medical Officer
AOC	Air Officer Commanding	MoS	Ministry of Supply
API	Air position indicator	MR	Maritime reconnaissance
ASI	Airspeed indicator	MU	Maintenance Unit
ASR	Air Sea Rescue	NCO	Non Commissioned Officer
ASV	Air to surface vessel	NDB	Non-directional beacon
ASWDU	Anti-submarine Warfare Development Unit	NSA	National Service Aircrew
ATDU	Aircraft Torpedo Development Unit	OCU	Operational Conversion Unit
		POW	Prisoner of war
auw	all up weight	PPI	Plan position indicator
AWA	Sir W. G. Armstrong Whitworth Aircraft Co Ltd	PR	Photographic reconnaissance
		QDM	Request for magnetic bearing to steer
BABS	Blind approach beam system	QFI	Qualified Flying Instructor
BBU	Bomb Ballistics Unit	QGH	Request for descent through cloud for landing
BCBS	Bomber Command Bombing School	QTE	Request for true bearing from station
BCIS	Bomber Command Instructors School	RAE	Royal Aircraft Establishment
		RAFFC	Royal Air Force Flying College
BDU	Bomber Development Unit	RCM	Radio counter-measures
C of A	Certificate of airworthiness	R & D	Research and development
c of g	centre of gravity	RRE	Royal Radar Establishment
CFS	Central Flying School	R/T	Radio telephone
CGS	Central Gunnery School	SABS	Stabilising Automatic Bomb Sight
CNCS	Central Navigation and Control School	SAR	Search and rescue
		SASO	Senior Air Staff Officer
CRT	Cathode ray tube	SBAC	Society of British Aircraft Constructors
CSIRO	Commonwealth Scientific and Industrial Research Organisation	SD	Special Duties
D/F	Direction finding	SNCO	Senior Non Commissioned Officer
DME	Distance measuring equipment	S of TT	School of Technical Training
D/R	Dead reckoning	TFU	Telecommunications Flying Unit
DRC	Distant reading compass		
EAAS	Empire Air Armament School	TI	Target indicator
ECM	Electronic counter measures	T/O	Take-off
ETA	Estimated time of arrival	TRE	Telecommunications Research Establishment
ETPS	Empire Test Pilots School		
FEAF	Far East Air Force	u/s	Unserviceable
FTS	Flying Training School	VHF	Very high frequency
GCA	Ground controlled approach	VNE	Velocity not to exceed
GHQ	General Headquarters	VSI	Vertical speed indicator
GPI	Ground position indicator	V/T or VT	Variable time
GR	General reconnaissance	WO	Warrant Officer

The Die is Cast

Prototypes

From the date the Lincoln prototype (then named Lancaster IV) first flew on 9 June 1944 it was to be a relatively long time before any production lines were set up and before there were sufficient aircraft available for delivery to the squadrons. The second prototype did not fly until five months later (9 November 1944) which rather indicates the lack of urgency with which the Lincoln was treated. The factories were at that time still very much preoccupied with the well established and smooth running production of Lancasters which, even in 1944/5, were still proving quite adequate for the needs of the European war in which the Allies were getting well on top. There was certainly no pressing need for a new type so it was accorded low priority.

On the design side, too, development of the Lincoln was slow, because in 1943/4, with the tide of war beginning to turn and peace possibilities becoming more than a vain hope, Avro's were already turning their thoughts to other things, such as the York and Tudor, and from 1944 onwards the minds and efforts of the designers were turned quite positively towards an anticipated postwar air transport boom.

From the outset the Lincoln had been designed for longer range operations, initially with Eastern Europe in mind; but the Russian advance from the east had eliminated that particular need. Then the project was again revived because of a likelihood that the war against the Japanese was likely to be prolonged, but by 1944 with the Americans, too, beginning to turn the tide in the Pacific, the need for more Allied bomber participation receded, so the Lincoln's design and production priorities fell even further down the scale.

Contingency plans for Allied heavy bombers to be switched from Europe to the Pacific war theatre had been drawn up at quite an early stage, and a certain amount of training got under way in the UK as the European war ended using the name Tiger Force. Even by that stage however it must have been known by those in high places that the atomic bomb was imminent, and would surely bring about Japan's early submission. At least the Tiger Force training prevented too sudden a run down of the operational bomber squadrons and served to demonstrate certain intentions of unity to the Americans.

A paper produced in September 1944 summarized discussions which had taken place between Allied and US Chiefs of Staff on a projected need for 40 squadrons of British heavies to join in the long-range bombing of Japan from US air bases on Pacific islands, half to be bombers, half tankers, divided into three Groups; British, Canadian and mixed British, New Zealand and Australian. The Lincoln, it was calculated, could achieve a 1,150-mile operational radius carrying 4,000lb of bombs at a take-off auw of 75,000lb, operating from the much shorter, more advanced bases than the B-29. With a 1,000-gallon saddle tank fitted, or refuelled in flight, it could achieve a radius of 1,500 miles with 7,500lb of bombs, the figures being based on the theories of Flight Refuelling Ltd. The Lincoln was designed with provision for in-flight refuelling in mind, but the Americans did not like the idea because of vulnerability to night fighters, unreliability of the weather, and, in particular, the training timescale problems, and the need to accommodate so many additional squadrons which the tanker fleet would involve (perhaps also the fact that the idea was not their own had a bearing).

As an alternative it was put forward that, at an 'overload' auw of 83,000lb using existing long runways, the Lincoln's radius of action could be stretched to 1,500 miles with 4,000lb of bombs, thus enabling it to be used against the less distant targets. But these were early days to be talking of extending the Lincoln's performance, and if the hopes did not materialize Lancasters were to be used instead. It was planned there should be two special squadrons to carry 12,000lb Tallboy bombs using the Lincoln in overload configuration, to be flight refuelled en route to the target. As an added protection against fighters, it was planned that the Lincolns should have an FN88 or Redwing ventral turret in place of H2S which would have been relatively ineffective for the long over-sea stretches in any case.

Left: Still bearing masking tape and lacking armament, PW925 the prototype (then named Lancaster IV) stands on a rain soaked apron at Ringway before delivery to Boscombe Down on 13 June 1944, five days after her initial flight on 9 June in the hands of Captain 'Sam' Brown./*Avro*

Below: Few hangars could take the 120ft wingspan due to a 100ft prewar limitation and pictured is PW925, with side-tracking skates in place at Kelstern, Lincs, on 10 February 1945./*L. J. Hakes*

Bottom: Dressed in full prototype finish of dark green and dark earth with yellow fuselage P in circle and yellow under surfaces is PW929 second of the three prototypes, pictured over the Wiltshire countryside during Boscombe Down trials. Fully armed, she was five months to the day later than PW925 taking to the air, while PW932 the third prototype did not fly until 6 November 1945, giving a fair indication of the low priority afforded the type./*British official*

Lancaster production was to be reduced from 284 per month in November 1944 to 124 per month by June 1945, phasing out altogether by November 1945, with Lincolns increasing to 66 per month in March 1945, 123 per month by May 1945, peaking to 200 per month from August 1945 to June 1946, a projected total of 2,254. In the event, of course, even the initial target was not achieved and the dropping of the atomic bomb in August 1945 and the resulting capitulation of Japan curtailed all Tiger Force plans, it being declared officially disbanded on 31 October 1945, just a month or so after the first few Lincolns had reached RAF squadrons.

Lincoln production lines were set up at Avro's Chadderton, Metrovick Trafford Park (both using Woodford for final assembly and test flying), and Armstrong Whitworth at Baginton and Bitteswell. It was also planned to build some large batches at Yeadon, but only six Lincolns were eventually built there before the plant closed down in the postwar recession in the industry. The approximate cost of a Lincoln appears to have been £69,100.

Deliveries of Mk Is commenced from late February 1945, in small numbers, gathering momentum in April-June. These early aircraft with Merlin 85s were delivered mainly to specialist trials units, the rest to MUs or direct into store at Woodford and Langar.

The Lincoln airframe, based largely on the tried and tested Lancaster, was sound enough, but the engines and certain items of new equipment gave problems, mainly vibration and surging, with the powerplants tending to display a definite 'nodding' mode which caused extreme vibration, to which the Lincoln's longer, more flexible wing may have contributed.

Some of the first production Lincolns went to TFU at Defford for radar equipment installation and trials, including RE229 as early as March 1945. They were regularly grounded, TFU boffins being as puzzled as Wing Commander R. M. Trousdale, DSO, DFC, (a New Zealander in the RAF) and his flying crews as to the repeated engine failures, flaps creeping down while selected 'up', and even undercarriages doing the same. The TFU men, although mainly radio/radar specialists, were concerned that their airborne radar work was being put so far behind, so put their brains to helping solve the problems. One of the theories put forward was that the vibration pattern of the engines, or the harmonics of it, corresponded to that of the airframe, and it was decided to try one of the Lincolns with 4-bladed propellors in place of the existing 3-bladed type. The installation appears to have been made on RE229 at TFU in mid-July 1945: the result, instant success, with the excessive vibration prob-

lems completely cured. Whilst both Avro's and Rolls-Royce had no doubt been working to solve the troubles, it certainly appears that the TFU men must claim some of the credit.

The first production Lincoln, RE227, was delivered to A&AEE Boscombe Down in April 1945 for handling trials, by which time RE228 and RE230 were with Rolls-Royce at Hucknall for engine trials. The Bomber Development Unit at Feltwell was the first RAF unit (other than a pure research or maintenance unit) to receive the Lincoln, taking delivery of RE240 on 21 May 1945. This early batch was fitted initially with twin 0.5in guns in a Martin dorsal turret and FN121 (4 x .303in) tail turrets, the intended types not being available at that stage.

Coastal Command expressed early interest in the Lincoln, and ASWDU was allotted an early Mk I; and though nothing came of it directly, Coastal Command subsequently getting Lancasters as an interim type instead, they were followed by the Shackleton which can be said to be a direct maritime development of the Lincoln. Other Mk Is used on trials included RE231 which, after tests with '8,000lb' (bulged) bomb doors, passed on to torpedo development work, while RE281 went to the Aircraft Torpedo Development Unit at Gosport (later at Weston-Super-Mare). By VE-Day, between 45 and 50 Lincolns had been built and test flown, and

Above: Employees of the Victory Aircraft Factory at Malton, Ontario, watch as FM300 is rolled out for the first time on 20 October 1945. Designated Mk XV, she was, in the event, the sole example to fly, company test pilot Ernie Taylor taking her aloft for the first time on 25 October for one of her few flights. Along with the remaining part-completed initial batch of six machines, FM300 ended up on the scrapheap, summer 1946./*Hawker Siddeley Canada*

by then the Merlin 68 was becoming available from Packards in America, and which, when fitted with the DH 4-bladed propellers proved a significant step towards getting the Lincoln into squadron service, though certain engine problems still persisted.

The official prototype BII was RE289 with Merlin 68s, delivered 6 July 1945 to Langar, complete with B17 dorsal turret, Boulton Paul Type D rear turret and IIIG H2S radar. The first production BIIs had already left the AWA factory by VE-Day. RE230 was the first Lincoln actually converted to BII standard by Rolls-Royce who had also earlier fitted Merlin 68s outboard in PW925, the prototype. The first tropical trials were undertaken at Khartoum with RF370 in August 1945, by when the order had already been given for two Lancaster squadrons to each receive three Lincoln BIIs in full tropical form. No 57 at East Kirkby received the first, RF385, on 22 August 1945, followed by RF386 and 387 on the 27th. Less than a week later, 75 (NZ) Squadron at Spilsby received its three, RF383, 388 and 389. Both squadrons were somewhat restricted due to poor serviceability, including unusable dorsal and rear turrets lacking certain items to complete them. These early aircraft had no heating either!

Service trials on AGLT were put in hand by BDU using BII RF393 in September 1945; in November, the Airborne Forces Experimental Establishment at Beaulieu re-

Among a number of machines attached to the Rolls-Royce 'Fleet' at Hucknall were RE228 (*above*), and RE290 (*right*). The second production Lincoln, RE228, is shown during handling trials at Boscombe Down soon after delivery in March 1945. Clearly visible are the one inch wide red jacking positions but she is devoid of the white underwing serials introduced on all military aircraft shortly after the European war ended. A sharp contrast in war paint is RE290 in Far East markings.
/*Ministry of Defence; Rolls-Royce*

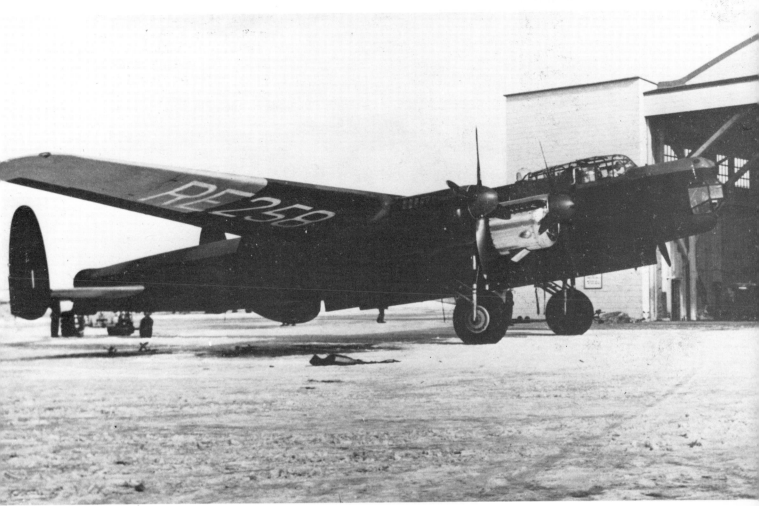

Two Lincolns were sent to Canada for winterisation trials, both new aircraft. RE258 was the first, leaving Pershore in early November 1945, fitted with Merlin 102s inboard, a Merlin 68A port outer and Merlin 85A starboard outer. After operating from No 1 Winter Experimental Establishment at Edmonton, Alberta, in temperatures below −45 C, RE258 returned to the UK in July 1947. Not so fortunate was SX924 (Merlin 621s outboard and 68As inboard) flown out in October 1947, and destined to meet an untimely end on 10 November 1948 (*right*). After a summer lay-up SX924 was on delivery from Edmonton to Watson Lake in Yukon Territory when Flt Lt Jimmy Fewell, RCAF, experiencing fuel flow problems in severe weather, successfully ditched in Watson Lake itself. /*B. Thomson*
Above: RE258 at Edmonton in January 1946, clearly showing red arctic survival markings on wings and tailplanes./*B. Thomson*

Right: The need for a production Lincoln in Australia for continuing type trials under tropical conditions provided seven Australian veterans with the unique opportunity to fly home on release from service in the UK. Sqn Ldr Ed Pickles and crew collected RA648 from Pershore and are seen before final departure on 15 March 1946 for an 11-day flight to No 1 Aircraft Performance Unit, Laverton, Victoria. The Lincoln, whose crest was designed by the crew, was a Mk I with Merlin 85As and Rotol propellers. Left to right: Sqn Ldr Ed Pickles, DFC (pilot); Flt Lt John Henry, DFC (second pilot); Sqn Ldr Phil Cornwall, DFM (flight engineer); Sqn Ldr Les Parker, DFC (navigator I); Flt Lt Doug McDonald, DFC (navigator II); Flt Lt Jim Grahame (wireless op); Flt Lt Bill Brookes (rear gunner)./*P. J. Cornwall*

ceived a BII, RF445, direct from Armstrong Whitworths for glider towing and parachutist trials which do not appear to have progressed very far. The Lincoln was stressed for glider towing, with certain attachments built in at the rear end, but, like the Lancaster, never became involved in it. As for parachutists, it was totally unsuitable because of the close proximity of the tailplane to the rear door. The initial Lincoln trials ended at the close of the year 1945, by which time 75 Squadron had disbanded and 44 (Rhodesia) Squadron had taken its place as the 3 Group trials outfit, based at Mildenhall. On 26 November 1945 the order was passed that all Lincoln BIs were to be fitted with fully modified Merlin 85s for use in the training role, though as far as can be ascertained, no Mk Is reached either squadrons or training units, and merely remained in store until scrapped. By the same order, all BIIs in store were to be modified by contractors as a result of the trials. The main problem lay in delays in supplies of modified engines, so whilst a large stockpile of new Lincolns existed by late 1945, none were up to the required standard, the trials having shown above all else that at an auw of 75,000lb, the Lincoln compared unfavourably with the Lancaster at 68,000lb – but the die was cast. English Electric were to fit the latest

radio and radar, and other modifications to update to full Far East standard were undertaken by Short Bros and Harland (RA serials, Metrovick-built), Avro's Langar (RE serials), and Armstrong Whitworth (their own RF batches).

Service Entry

The first Lincoln Trials Flight of 57 Squadron was specially formed at East Kirkby with Flight Lieutenant Frank M. Jones, AFC, in command. The most lasting impression he and his crews had, seems to have been the considerable flexing of the Lincoln's wings, particularly at the tips, shown in the manufacturers' destruction tests to be capable of an eight-foot movement before breaking. The aircraft was found to be gentle enough, with no tendency to drop a wing in the stall, and with wheels and flaps down, still capable of being flown down to 68-70kts. The crews had little difficulty converting, though pilots with considerable operational experience on Lancs were unwilling to concede its pride of place to any other aircraft whether from the same stable or not! The service trials included flying the Lincoln in all configurations, day and night on two and three engines, at all flight levels, on fuel flow and consumption tests, etc. On 30 November 1945, Flight

Bottom left: Glossy black under surfaces gleaming, RF385 is put through her paces by Flt Lt Frank Jones, AFC, OC the Lincoln Trials Flight, on 25 October 1945 during a press visit to East Kirkby. Codes were originally grey, but soon changed to black. Those on the first three Lincolns delivered to No 57 Squadron were initially painted wartime dull red by East Kirkby's paint and dope section but changed within a few hours. The squadron's work up period on the Lincoln was sadly marred by the loss of RF385 when Flt Lt M. G. Horton and crew crashed at Queniborough near Leicester during a violent thunderstorm on 20 February 1946./*The Aeroplane*

Above: RF389, first of three Lincolns delivered to No 75 (New Zealand) Squadron at Spilsby only a few days behind No 57. RF389 was to survive in Bomber Command until 1960. /*H. B. Mackinnon*

17

Lieutenant Jones took 'DX:F' (RF387) up with only one other crew member aboard for a test flight lasting 14¾ hours – there were no union rules in those days!

Initially, take off weight was limited to 75,000lb, but progressively increased to the theoretical safe limit of 82,000lb. One of the first take-offs at this weight was by Flight Lieutenant Gill in RF407, but it was a frightening experience, with the wheels only just clearing the hedge beyond the end of the runway. At these sort of weights the early Lincolns just about reached 23,000ft, though sometimes having to jettison the dummy bombs to do so.

From 26 November 1945 the Lincoln Service Trials Flight, as it became known, continued the flight testing from a new base, 'sunny' Scampton, still under the aegis of 57 Squadron, and commanded by Squadron Leader R. J. (Bobby) Sage, AFC, from January 1946. The squadrons were tending to move round the Lincolnshire area quite frequently at that time as grass airfields which had sufficed during the war years, had new concrete runways laid, and former tarmac runways were strengthened. By then the Trials Flight had four Lincolns on strength, all BIIs with Merlin 68s. A number of the flight engineers were men who had gained their pilots' wings at the end of the war, but, finding themselves surplus to requirements, elected to remuster as engineers in order to remain on flying; they continued to wear pilots' wings and as engineers were kept fairly busy with the problems still being experienced in 1945/6 with the 68s – blowbacks of superchargers, plug fouling, etc.

There were some hectic moments, caused mainly by the positioning of the electrical control panel carrying all the circuit breakers and overload cutout buttons, on the starboard side of the main cabin. Anyone squeezing along the fuselage behind the navigators almost invariably caught the panel with parachute harness or Mae West, cutting out many or all of the instruments and control circuits. This could cause great panic on a night approach, so movement within the cabin had to be banned until the panel was resited.

A lot of the electrical rectification work was done by English Electric who undertook two major programmes of modifications to Lincolns from late 1945 to the end of 1948, the aircraft flying into the company's airfield at Samlesbury, near Preston, some from storage at Langar, etc, others straight from new. The work involved the fitting of Loran navigation equipment, Rebecca homing gear, Gee Mk 2, provision for H2S radar and radome (though not the radar itself), fitting of automatic gun laying equipment for the rear turret, consoles with cathode ray tube displays, and extensive mods to wiring, generators, etc. Early kits of parts were supplied by RAF St Athan, but later kits were made by Short Bros & Harland under subcontract to EE. Altogether, the company dealt with 350 Lincolns at various times, many of them passing through Samlesbury twice.

Below: RF388 (also delivered to No 75 Squadron initially) seen in the colours of No 44 (Rhodesia) Squadron on 27 February 1946 at Mildenhall, the crew of six under Flt Lt John Chatterton, DFC, posing for his camera. White upper surfaces ('Far East' scheme) were intended to reflect heat, particularly from wing fuel tanks./*J. Chatterton*

The Squadron Round

Gradually, the modified BIIs started to appear, the first three from Armstrong Whitworth going to 44 (Rhodesia) Squadron for continuing trials at the end of February 1946, RF405, 406, 407, taking part in March in Operation Sinkum; the disposal of surplus wartime stocks of incendiary bombs in Cardigan Bay. By July 1946 all three had found their way to 57 Squadron for further trials in general squadron service. No 57 itself received its first three fully modified Lincolns from Avro's in March 1946, RE377, 379 and 380, and Bomber Command finally accepted the Lincoln for full squadron service on 2 April 1946, 101 Squadron at Binbrook being the next to get them, in June, closely followed by 97 at Coningsby.

Suddenly, it seemed, after a false start, re-equipment of No 1 Group was getting under way, but it was not an easy path. Corrosion problems were added to engine and armament setbacks, and several Lincolns were stripped for detailed analysis only a year after being built, a special study group being set up in December 1946. By then, the much improved Merlin 68A with automatic charge temperature control was just beginning to appear. The end of 1946 saw the conversion of the 1 Group squadrons from Lancasters completed, all still bearing well known wartime identities. The postwar No 1 Group was a combination of the former 1 and 5 Groups, the latter having been disbanded in December 1945. The 'new' No 1 Group, with its HQ at Bawtry in Notts, was based wholly in Lincolnshire, so its prior claim to the Lincoln was, perhaps, fully justified. The squadrons reflected the general contraction in the RAF, each being only half the size of a wartime unit, with eight aircraft each, commanded by a squadron leader instead of a wing commander, and in some cases, having only six aircraft under a senior flight lieutenant, more like a wartime flight, in fact, than an actual squadron.

The squadrons continued to play an important part in the development of the Lincoln, including the pioneer, No 57 Squadron, and by late 1946, the crews were already becoming involved in what was to become the more or less standard postwar routine of high level bombing, both visual and radar, air-to-sea firing, occasional formation flying, day and night cross-countries, regular circuit work (continuation training) instrument approaches, Rebecca/GCA, etc.

From late 1946, however, several of the 1 Group squadrons, including 50, 57, 61 and 101, were allotted a new task which was to last through 1947 and 1948 – the gathering of meteorological data for weather forecasters, the sorties named 'Seaweeds' and 'Pampas', for which a specialist eighth crew member was added. Given the rank of Sergeant with an 'M' brevet, they were installed in the nose with special sampling and pressure monitoring equipment from which half-hourly reports were passed back to Group by the signallers, thus supplementing the work done by the Met Halifaxes, the complete task later being taken over by the Met Hastings of 202 Squadron. Each of the 1 Group stations shared the task on a rotational basis.

A Seaweed took the crews northwards, past the Shetlands, out over the North Sea past Fair Isle, east towards Norway, to the fringe of the Arctic Circle, turning south nearly to Bergen, and back to base; a long, hard flog, day and night, $7\frac{1}{2}$ – $8\frac{1}{2}$ hours at varying levels up to 20,000ft. Seaweeds were regular daily/nightly commitments, but the Pampas were flown when specially called for, there being several routes, either well out into the Atlantic, flying north of Ireland outbound and returning to the south of Eire: others down over France, and out into the Bay of Biscay.

It was on the Seaweeds that a serious fault came to light during the particularly cold winter of early 1947. The sorties involved full-power climbs from sea level at certain geographic points north of the Shetlands, to as high as the aircraft could be coaxed, for the met observer to take pressure readings, etc, at various levels on the way up. For what was believed to be the first time, plastic fuel piping had been used extensively in the Lincolns, some of the piping being in quite long sections. On the climbs, the rapid reduction in temperatures caused considerable shrinkage, pulling ends of pipes off connections, in some cases causing loss of two engines on one side and of half the fuel,

Above: Upwood-based Lincolns in stately formation over patchwork West Country farmland on 13 March 1950. While RE348 'MG:C' and RE301 'MG:F' from No 7 Squadron carry standard code letter presentation, RE296 'QN:AW' has the unique double identity letters of No 214 (Federated Malay States) Squadron allocated under a 3 Group system introduced in 1947 and necessary with several squadrons sharing the base. Both RE301 and RE348 appear elsewhere in later style markings./*Flight International*

miles out over the inhospitable North Sea. Fortunately, the crews were able to divert to such bases as HMS Fulmar (Lossiemouth) which, with other coastal airfields such as St Mawgan, were to become welcome refuges to Lincolns when home bases were fogbound, these sorties taking place in all weathers.

The long-range flights north in the depths of winter also taught the crews how cold and uncomfortable the Lincoln could be at high altitudes, particularly for the gunners who had the most boring of tasks, and the most uncomfortable of seats. Some pilots took thick blankets or rugs to wrap round themselves in an effort to make the long trip a little more bearable; and flight engineers discovered the knack of inadvertently making holes in the lagging of the heating pipes at certain strategic points, causing a welcome increase in hot air, though ground crews would insist on patching up the holes. The outstanding recollection of all Lincoln crewmen is, in fact, of long, cold, boring, night exercises, on which the autopilot invariably went 'on the blink'; and of egg sandwiches, apples, and tepid coffee.

In 1947, the Lancasters were really starting to disappear as the 3 Group squadrons' conversion to the Lincoln also got under way. No 44, (which had already operated Lincolns on a trial basis from 10/45 to 5/46, then reverted to Lancasters) started the 3 Group ball rolling again by getting modified Lincoln BIIs in late December 1946, followed in February 1947 by 15 Squadron, then 90 in April, and 138 in September, thus completing the Wyton 'Wing'. As in No 1 Group, the Lincolns were filtered in amongst the Lancasters to start with, full replacement and crew conversion (still on the same informal basis at squadron level) usually taking a few weeks. The year had started badly with the heaviest snowfalls and freeze up for many years, especially on the Lincolnshire Wolds where Binbrook, the home of Nos 9, 12, 101 and 617 Squadrons, was snowbound for a month, with no flying possible, and supplies of food having to be dropped on the airfield by RAF Dakotas.

Though each of the three or four squadrons on a station maintained their separate identities, and aircraft bore squadron code letters, there was a degree of 'pooling', interchanging and borrowing of machines. Servicing and overhauls became more centralized at each station, and even crews were not of quite such regular make up as in the immediate past. Bomber Command exercises involving the Lincolns were beginning to get under way, with such names as Rufus, Hat-Box, Lightup; and overseas tours by squadrons, small groups and single aircraft were becoming a feature. No 3 Group's squadrons took part in Operation Wastage, the continued disposal of surplus bombs and ammunition in Cardigan Bay. Flying tended to be only spasmodic, due to general economies and a fuel shortage. Generally, however, it was very similar to the later Lancaster days, with little change in tactics, or equipment, though with more emphasis on radar bombing with H2S. Sunrays to Shallufa commenced in 1947.

In February new designations for the Lincoln were announced: BII/IIIG and

BII/IVA, depending on the type of H2S radar fitted (later becoming B2/3G and B2/4A when Arabic numerals were introduced from 1950). It was hoped to equip 1 Group with the IVA Lincolns (originally to be known as the IIa) and 3 Group with the IIIG by the summer of 1947, but the programme was repeatedly put back and it was to be two years before the first IVA-equipped Lincolns entered squadron service with No 9, whose updated aircraft were also the first with the more advanced Gee-H Mk II.

Though the work of the Lincoln squadrons tended to be humdrum and routine a good deal of the time, revolving as it did round training and more training, long cross-countries, which progressively extended further afield over western Europe, every crew had its moments, and its stories: one very experienced crew on a day cross-country got themselves hopelessly lost over France, finally getting a 'fix' by flying along a railway line and circling the first station they came across at extreme low level to read the name (shades of World War I almost!). Another Lincoln (from 61 Squadron) was among the French Alps in poor visibility, with the engineer in the left-hand seat with no dual controls. The rest of the crew became alarmed, donned their parachutes, stood in line and threatened to bale out unless the skipper and engineer got into their proper places, upon which the pilot burst into tears, pulled the engineer out of the seat and resumed control. A flight lieutenant of 100 Squadron took off one day in 1947 from Hemswell for an exercise and found himself

with half an hour to spare before setting course. To fill in the time, he flew to nearby Gainsborough and put the Lincoln into a series of very tight turns round the spire of his favourite pub, the Rising Sun. A policeman standing opposite the pub took the aircraft number and reported the incident, but to the relief of all, nothing came of the subsequent enquiry; the old wartime spirit of the locals was obviously on the wane!

Sometimes the Lincolns flying the Pampas down to the Bay of Biscay would land at Gibraltar, giving the crew a welcome day off before returning. A Waddington Lincoln arrived back from one such trip minus two of its crew members (one of whom was the met observer). They turned up six weeks later, having spent the intervening time in a Spanish gaol; after a rather liquid night out in La Linea sampling the wine, they had been caught by the police relieving themselves into the local bull ring and were promptly arrested. Again in 1947, one of 100 Squadron's Lincolns on a cross-country over France diverted to Paris for some obscure reason. A week later another Lincoln was despatched to find the crew of the first one, and it was a week after that before both returned to Hemswell.

An interesting by-product of the new training methods set up from 1948 for conversion and standardisation of Lincoln crews was the Bomber Command Instrument Rating and Examination Flight, based at Scampton with two Lincolns coded WB – inherited from BCIS. The role of the flight was to examine all aircrew roughly twice a year,

Above: Lifting off the Binbrook runway is SX958, fitted with Mk IVA H2S in enlarged radome. Lincolns thus equipped were known as BII/IVA (later B2/4A when the RAF changed to Arabic numerals) and No 9, closely followed by No 12, (sharing Binbrook with 101 and 617) received the first machines during June/July 1949. No 9, operating Lincolns since July 1946, converted to Canberras at the end of April 1952 and broke an Avro link dating back to 1942./*B. Brownlow*

Top right: Sqn Ldr Alan Butcher and crew of No 12 Squadron Binbrook dropping poppies from special bomb bay panniers over the Alamein Memorial, 22 October 1950, while on detachment at Shallufa. Clearly seen is the larger, unpainted cupola of the Mk 4 H2S, whose size may be judged by comparison with the 48in underwing serials. Less than two months after this picture RE344 was to come to grief during a night continuation training exercise./*N. A. J. Mackie*

Centre right and below: Two views of RE344, liberally covered in foam, among the young trees of the spinney just beyond the Binbrook perimeter following a 3-engined overshoot by New Zealander Flg Off 'Windy' Blows which went slightly wrong, 12 December 1950. The crew escaped unhurt, some by merely walking through a gaping hole in the nose.
/*Both N. A. J. Mackie*

checking on standards, procedures, renewing instrument ratings etc.

During the late 1940s – early 1950s Lincolns continued to pass between squadrons – some quite regularly, others remaining with the same unit for several years. As more squadrons were re-equipped in 1949/1950, a large number were brought out of storage, modifications updated at MUs or Avro's at Langar, with final preparation for squadron service usually taking place at Binbrook by Bomber Command Aircraft Maintenance Squadron (BCAMS). A Lincoln would normally average 15-20 months on a unit before major overhaul, either at Langar, an MU, or on the station itself in some cases. Some squadrons would also have facilities for up-dating modifications and carrying out 'special fits' of equipment, but generally the work seems to have been spread round.

During its service life, a Lincoln would usually top the 1,000 hours of flying, the most being about 1,700, others less than 500. Some, of course, were scrapped as surplus to requirements with less than double figures of hours flown, but showing signs of corrosion after a few years in open storage. There was no set pattern.

From February 1949 a system of pairing of squadrons commenced – never popular and somewhat meaningless to the crews. It enabled certain old-established squadrons to maintain their identities and unbroken runs of service in order to qualify for standards; for example 44/55, 83/150, and 57/104 lasting into the mid 1950s. The squadrons were almost invariably known by their first numbers only.

Unit Miscellany

It was in September 1949 that one of Bomber Command's worst postwar tragedies was to happen, during Exercise Bulldog, a full-scale test of Britain's air defence system lasting three days, its purpose being to give experience to bomber crews in day and night attacks on defended targets. In addition to the RAF, aircraft of the USAF, Dutch, French and Belgian Air Forces were to participate for the first time. The whole of the RAF fighter defence system, including Royal Auxiliary Air Force air and ground units, was mobilized. It was a full-scale operation under simulated wartime conditions with virtually every RAF bomber taking part, Lancasters, Lincolns, Mosquitos, plus USAF B-29s and B-50s. The defending fighters, mainly Hornets and Meteors, were supplemented by aircraft of Training Command carrying out special roles – Mosquitos, Lancasters, Harvards, and Prentices. Also involved were the Royal Observer Corps and both Regular and Territorial units of the Army's Anti-Aircraft Command.

The attacking bombers used the same stream tactics as in wartime, with main force led by target markers, controlled by a master bomber. On the night of 26 September there were several hundred aircraft engaged: no lights, complete radio silence, with air gunners keeping a sharper-than-usual look-out, and reporting shadowy shapes to their pilots, some probably imaginary in the murky, pitch black conditions. There were regular bumps and jolts from other people's slipstreams, not surprising with separations of only 50ft vertically and 30 sec horizontally. Some aircraft had actually 'bombed' the selected target when suddenly a huge flash lit up the sky, right in the midst of the main stream, and the blazing wrecks of two Lincolns fell away, watched by hundreds of pairs of eyes in cockpits, turrets and astrodomes, the glare visible to other aircraft as far away as London. The pilot of one Lincoln switched on his navigation lights, and immediately everyone else followed suit so that within seconds the sky resembled a Christmas tree with coloured lights everywhere, gently bobbing and swaying.

The two doomed Lincolns which had collided fell in open countryside at Averham and Staythorpe, on the outskirts of Newark, their 14 crew members having stood no chance. Both aircraft, RF407 of 61 Squadron and RE374 of 57 Squadron, were from Waddington.

Another double tragedy occurred on the night of 15 March 1950, not a collision this time, but two totally unrelated incidents. RF472 'HW:B' of 100 Squadron, Hemswell, crashed on the approach in mist at its home

Below: An early requirement was for one squadron to be equipped with Lincolns specially adapted with enlarged bomb doors for internal carriage of 12,000lb Tallboy deep penetration bombs. The unit chosen – No 15 Squadron – had already carried out trials with the 22,000lb 'Grand Slam', using Lancaster B1 (Specials) taken over from No 617 Squadron. Here, RF514 of No 15 Squadron Wyton displays its more bulbous outline./*D. H. Newton*

Right: Service aircraft soon lost their factory fresh appearance; this is RF445 from No 44 (Rhodesia) Squadron Wyton in 1948, showing a weathered finish and the ever-present exhaust stains. Note the dinghy position in starboard wing root, clearly outlined with red oxide masking tape and which turned pink in due course. Originally one of the Lincoln trials squadrons, No 44 was a combined Lancaster/Lincoln unit until June 1947. Washingtons replaced the latter from January 1951. */Sport & General*

Below: Sporting the large 42in high white serials introduced late February 1952 is WD148 from Waddington-based No 49 Squadron, pictured on a cross-country stooge in April 1953. No 49 flew Lincolns from October 1949 until disbanding on the first day of August 1955, pending re-equipment with Valiants. Lincoln WD148 was in fact the last but one delivered – first week of April 1951 – and later saw service with CSE becoming a familiar sight at Battle of Britain displays until relegated to Watton's dump for fire fighting duties. */A. E. Newitt*

base, while RF511 of 230 OCU Scampton, on a night cross-country, flew into the 2,000ft Carnedd Llewellyn in Wales. Except for one survivor at Hemswell both crews were lost.

Nos 83 and 97 Squadrons were to remain the Flare Force for some years, well into the early 1950s. They specialised in radar bombing and navigation, using the Mk 4A H2S exclusively, their war role being twofold: to drop flares for the visual target markers flying Mosquitos (109 and 139 Squadrons) and blind sky marking, using radar, when weather conditions prevented visual marking. The squadrons also had to complete a quota of visual bombing, usually on the Theddlethorpe, Saltfleet, or Wainfleet ranges.

On one visual night dropping session, in marginal conditions, a bomb aimer identified Wainfleet's circle of lights, or so he thought, and let go a 10lb practice bomb, right on target, which, however, proved to be not the Wainfleet range, but a similar circle of lights at a traffic roundabout just inland. The bomb demolished the small outside toilet of a garage at the island, and in the press a few days later, an Air Ministry spokesman explained it away as 'a flash in the pan'.

On exercises, the Marker Force consisting of 12 Lincolns normally carried 12,000lb of flares and target indicators of different colours,

flying ahead of the main force in what was in theory a wide box, each crew navigating individually, forming four waves of three aircraft. Separation was $\frac{1}{4}$ mile between aircraft and 300ft in height between waves, calling for very accurate flying. Some 30 minutes before reaching the target the Flare Force leader would check by radio on the serviceability of the H2S in each aircraft, then replan the formation to get the serviceable aircraft in the front wave. Each pilot would be advised by radio of his new station, and then on the order 'Shuffle, Shuffle', everyone would move simultaneously: all this in the dark with no navigation lights, and often in cloud, sometimes seeing nothing but other exhaust flames very close. How did they survive! Many look back and wonder.

One of 97's Lincolns, SX939 was nearly lost on the night of 29 November 1951 when, on a night bombing exercise over the ranges, it got into a spin in thick cloud over Mablethorpe, falling from 9,000 to 5,000ft, then spinning in the opposite direction until being pulled out at less than 2,000ft. The fuselage was so badly twisted it was declared a write off, and in December, was transferred to No 2 School of Radio at Yatesbury, allotted the 'Instructional' serial 6943M. The radio and technical training establishments received a

Above: Lincoln Cathedral, a towering sentinel and welcome landmark for returning Lancaster crews provides a majestic backcloth to RF394 of No 50 Squadron, based at nearby Waddington, flying low over its namesake city in 1949. Currently (1977) flying Vulcans, and again at 'Waddo', No 50 has an association with Avro bombers dating back to 1942 and broken only by a seven year spell on Canberras at Binbrook and Upwood./*E. Beswick*

Above: Waddington's RF518 written off at Wittering and displaying No 61 Squadron's Red Lincoln Imp, a figure reflecting the unit's long association with the Lincoln area. The incident occured on the night of 8/9 July 1948 when, after completing a radar bombing 'Ding-Dong' exercise, Flg Off Eley and crew burst a tyre on touching down at Waddington but diverted to Wittering for a safe belly landing. The origin of the name *Khomahsott Tiger* is unknown./*L. Skivington*

Centre right: First of the Lincoln units to be axed pending introduction of the Washington was No 35 (Madras Presidency) Squadron based at Mildenhall and equipped with Lincolns for a mere six months before disbanding in 23 February 1950. A very rare picture of a No 35 Squadron Lincoln staging through Luqa, Malta, January 1950./*I. W. Mountain*

Bottom right: Another relatively short-lived Lincoln squadron was No 90 based at Wyton, Hunts. Using Lincolns from April 1947, the squadron disbanded on 1 September 1950, scheduled to re-equip with Washingtons. The picture was taken at Castel Benito in 1948 on return from a Sunray. Centre aircraft is RF451 'WP:N' with RF447 'WP:P' beyond./*L. C. Jealous*

number of Lincolns withdrawn from flying duties.

During 1951, 83 and 97 joined a number of other squadrons in 1 and 3 Groups on an experiment over the London radar defences. At least 50 Lincolns flew in a pre-designed staggered box formation, with 400ft vertical and 400yd horizontal separations. The idea was to create a large 'block' on radar screens rather than a number of individual blips, so preventing singling out of aircraft. The idea was the brainchild of an armaments officer from Upwood. To enable pilots to keep the correct station in the formation, each one wore a headband from which protruded a wire about 12/18in long. On the end was a sighting loop, rather like a ring sight, with which the pilot was to line up the aircraft in front and slightly offset. It was tried out about six times, but was not a success and after a while, merely sent the pilot crosseyed. Later, as an alternative, the front gunsight was used and suitably modified for the bomb aimer but the whole thing was soon abandoned.

From August-October 1949 the last of the 3 Group 'Wings,' comprising Nos 35, 115, 149 and 207 Squadrons at Mildenhall at last exchanged its Lancasters for Lincolns, some years later than planned, and followed in January-February 1950 by 148 and 214 at Upwood, bringing the number of Lincoln squadrons in Bomber Command up to 22, with about 200 or so aircraft including reserves. Again the changeover was achieved by filtering in the Lincolns among the Lancasters, each crew converting on the squadrons. But the Lincolns' reign with the Mildenhall wing

was to be short-lived, a period of only six months or so. The machines issued to its squadrons were either brought out of store or were ageing specimens which had already served their time on other units, and the rate of unserviceability was chronic.

It had already become apparent that because of its known limitations the Lincoln was not suitable for the nuclear deterrent role. Whilst the Lincoln could undoubtedly deliver a nuclear weapon, it had neither the height nor speed to ensure that it could get away quickly enough from the explosion, making each drop a potential suicide mission. By the late 1940s it was becoming a dire necessity to find a replacement, highlighted by the Berlin blockade, and heightened by the Korean War which suddenly made Communist intentions very clear indeed. With the jet-bombers still some time away from entering service, the decision was taken (after much controversy) to order 70 Boeing B-29s under the Anglo/US Mutual Defence Aid Programme as an interim nuclear bomber. Perhaps because No 3 Group had been rather left behind in the Lincoln queue, and also because its bases were nearer to existing USAF bases in East Anglia, it was the Mildenhall squadrons (with the Lincoln B2/4A) which were selected to receive the first B-29s, or Washingtons as they became known in RAF service. The first to receive the new type was 115 at Marham in June 1950, followed soon afterwards by Nos 90 and 149 in October-November of the same year and 15 in January 1951. The other squadrons to use the Washington were Nos 44, 57, 207 and

Above: A much travelled aircraft was RF529 with the interior specially fitted out for use by VIPs, typified by Air Chief Marshal Sir Hugh Saunders' visit to the USA during August and September 1947. Here she is seen at Northolt, 7 February 1948, still in the markings of No 97 (Straits Settlements) Squadron Hemswell but soon to join No 9 Squadron. Note rear fuselage windows and nose pennant. */L. S. Vowles*

Left: The first Lincoln IIs went to No 101 Squadron at Binbrook in June 1946; five years later, in June 1951, the squadron was the first to re-equip with the Canberra. Shown is RE424 sporting a striped fin (colours uncertain) to indicate her role as Binbrook leader for the mass flypast in honour of the King's birthday in 1950. Though never a widespread practice, similar high visibility markings were occasionally adopted for large scale exercises. Lincoln RE424 was the last to be built by the parent firm and was delivered on 24 April 1946./*B. Brownlow*

35, the bulk of the crews again being former Lincoln men.

The contrast for them was striking. The B-29 was a considerable advance over the Lincoln in armchair comfort, adequate heating, pressurisation, cooking facilities, sound proofing, range (4,000 miles), ceiling (over 30,000ft) speed (350mph) and auw (140,000lb). The B-29s were to remain with Bomber Command for three years and following their withdrawal, quite a number of the crews converted back to Lincolns for operations in Malaya and Kenya.

While the B-29 squadrons were pre-occupied with re-equipment and working up to operational status, the remaining Lincoln squadrons continued in their training and conventional bomber role, with regular flights over western Europe exercising with Allied fighter and radar defences, bombing on the Heligoland range, etc. In fact, the squadron 'round' continued very much unchanged. It was from March 1950 that the Malayan commitments started, and which were to continue on and off for five years, with Kenya added from late 1953, thus ensuring the Lincoln squadrons of plenty of work yet.

In the early 1950s the Waddington squadrons were allotted the special task of providing a Lincoln and scratch crew at very short notice 24 hours a day, all the year round, to ferry urgent brain cases from the nearby RAF Hospital at Nocton Hall to Abingdon for transfer to a local specialist hospital. A normal stretcher would not go through the rear door of a Lincoln, so a special rubber mattress was designed into which the patients were virtually 'rolled'. A number of lives were saved as a result of the prompt response by the Lincoln

crews. During this period, the OC (Flying) at Waddington was Wing Commander J. B. ('Willie') Tait, DSO, DFC, well known wartime Lancaster pilot, leader of the *Tirpitz* raids, and highly respected by the Lincoln men.

It was at Waddington that a reserve fleet of 12 Lincolns was maintained, known as the Reserve Holding Unit (RHU), and which remained until 1954, supplying replacements for the squadrons following accidents, or as regular aircraft were withdrawn for overhaul, etc. Updating of mods to the RHU aircraft was undertaken by working parties from Avro's at Langar and Bracebridge Heath, and one of the tasks of the Wing Commander Flying was to test fly each of the reserve pool of Lincolns every so often to exercise systems and keep them in flying trim.

In 1951, the Canberras began to arrive on the scene to signal the beginning of the end of the piston-engined bomber. The first of the sleek new jets to enter squadron service were allotted to 101 at Binbrook in May 1951, the first Lincoln squadron to go all-jet; then followed 617 (January 1952), 12 (April 1952) and 9 (May 1952), leaving Waddington, Hemswell, Upwood and Wyton as the remaining main bomber bases still with the Lincoln, still very much involved in Bomber Command exercises, etc. There were numerous overseas detachments by the Lincolns, with Sunrays continuing at squadron strength, and Rangers by individual aircraft as shows of force and to continue to exercise certain flying rights in deteriorating political situations, particularly in the Middle East.

In January 1952, with the Nasser/Neguib coup brewing in Egypt, and with the safety of British subjects in doubt, No 148 Squadron's Lincolns were called out at very short notice. While out in Shallufa, the activity tended to be spasmodic, with little flying once the initial crisis had receded. General Ironside visited the bombing range for a display of live bomb droppings, intended primarily for the benefit of the Egyptians, but the General insisted on watching from a distance of only 500 yards as the 500 and 1,000 pounders rained down from the Lincolns whose navigators, fortunately, were on their best form.

No 148's aircraft were taken over by a mixed bag of replacement crews from Upwood, who themselves were replaced from June by 100 Squadron which took its own aircraft out, but did even less flying before eventually returning home, bringing the Lincolns with them, in August 1952. From May to July 1952, Upwood's Lincoln crews did the flying for the film *Appointment in London* starring Dirk Bogarde and Dinah Sheridan, and for which four Lancaster 7s were brought out of storage. Some Lincolns also took part in the distance to bolster the formation and taxiing scenes. Two years later the same Lancasters were used in the filming of *The Dam Busters* at Hemswell, Scampton and Kirton-in-Lindsey, again being flown by Lincoln crews, this time of 83 and 97 Squadrons.

During the latter half of 1952, the number of NATO and Bomber Command exercises was stepped up considerably: King Pin, Ardent, Mainbrace, Window Box, etc, with Lincolns fully involved at home and abroad.

The Flare Force units, 83 and 97, still soldiered on from Hemswell, still employing

Bottom left: This picture of armourers preparing 4,000lb 'Cookies', could almost be a wartime setting. The squadron is No 138 Wyton in 1948, a 'cloak and dagger' outfit until converting to Lancasters two months before the end of the war in Europe. Lincolns took over in September 1947 and stayed until disbandment on the first day of September 1950. No 138 subsequently became the first V-Bomber squadron. /*Syndication International (Odhams)*

Above: Three of No 148 Squadron's eight Lincolns on the loose from Upwood, Hunts, soon after taking over from Lancasters in January 1950. The squadron's Lincolns, forming part of the Upwood wing, carried the 'AU' codes for only 12 months, being allotted the individual letters S to Z before changing to the large serial identity style. The last Lincoln squadron to operate in Malaya, No 148 disbanded 1 July 1955, scheduled to receive Valiants. Shown here are SX975 'AU:U', SX976 'AU:V' and SX983 'AU:X'./*Mrs B. D. Graham*

much the same tactics, and still involved in continual radar and visual bombing training exercises, Pinplots, Backchats and Bigshots; this situation and routine continuing into 1953 which was another year of quite hectic activity for the remaining Lincoln squadrons, with frequent Command Exercises, regular Rangers over Germany to establish Allied flying rights in the Berlin corridors following the loss of RF531 of CGS (related in another chapter); plus Sunrays, and, most notable of all, the substantial involvement of the Lincoln squadrons in the Queen's Coronation Review at Odiham on 15 July with 45 taking part in the flypast. For three months, there had been intensive formation practice and rehearsals, and on the big day, the make up of the Lincoln contingent was as follows: from Upwood 9 Lincolns led by Sqn Ldr E. P. Landon, DFC, and 9 led by Flt Lt P. N. B. Pritchett; from Waddington 9 Lincolns led by Sqn Ldr A. P. Huchala, DFC, RCAF, and 9 led by Sqn Ldr R. I. Alexander, DFC; from Hemswell 9 Lincolns led by Sqn Ldr W. C. Sinclair, AFC.

During 1953 Lincolns were still being called upon for a variety of special duties: RA672 of 83 Squadron carried out television interference tests in May, and the following description by a young 97 Squadron flight engineer, Michael J. Cawsey illustrates the sort of situations in which the crews found themselves on occasions:

'On 7 August 1953 we were called out in the night for an Air Sea Rescue search out over the Atlantic to look for a missing American

B-36. We took-off from Hemswell at 06.10 for Aldergrove. The aircraft was my old favourite RA713 (in my log book as B) and the captain was Flt Sgt Graham Smith. After refuelling at Aldergrove, we took off again at 10.45am and after reaching the search area we went down very low, with everyone keeping a lookout. The sea was rough and the chances of survival minimal. It was well into the afternoon, 3.15pm, with me flying the aircraft from the right-hand seat when suddenly Norman Peach, the signaller in the nose said "we've just passed over a dinghy!" Graham Smith, the captain leapt into action like a big spring just released: "Time me nav – 30 seconds then a turn 45 degrees starboard for one minute, and a rate one turn port onto reciprocal: all crew look out: sig make contact with HQ. Now, eyes down!", and there it was, a grey dinghy, with what looked like a body in it, there and gone in a flash. We fixed our position and went into a holding pattern, acting as a control centre. Eventually a ship arrived and picked up the dinghy and we had to make for home at minimum-drag speed finally landing back at Nutts Corner (Belfast) after 12hr 40min in the air, (the last 1hr 55min at night), just about as far as the endurance could be stretched on the normal 2,850-gallon fuel load. What an end to the day.

'My most frightening moments were when we were on a photographic sortie over Turkey, having flown from the Canal Zone to Nicosia (Cyprus) and taken off from there on 21 March 1953 during Exercise New Moon.

Right: Attempting a 3-engined overshoot at Waddington on 3 September 1952, No 61 Squadron's RF343 developed an uncontrollable swing and crashed on the edge of the airfield. Flg Off Frank Hercliffe and crew escaped unharmed but tragedy struck two days later. The customary guard had been removed and two adventurous small boys entered the partly burned Lincoln to play. Somehow they set off some pyrotechnics – thought to be verey cartridges – which set fire to the wreck and one of the boys lost his life before help arrived./*R. C. H. Poynton*

Left: Many who served on No 1 Group Lincoln squadrons will vividly recall the bitter winters spent on the Lincolnshire Wolds. Savage winds and heavy snowfalls were an occupational hazard and periodically stations were snowbound and cut off from the outside world. Pictured are two views of Binbrook in January 1951, showing 'KC:F' of No 617 Squadron standing on a partly cleared hard stand, and a case of many hands make light work as an overnight fall of snow is cleared. In the background is No 9 Squadron's RA675 'WS:J'.
/*A. P. Trowbridge*

We were due to do some fighter affiliation with the Turkish Air Force. The local terrain is very mountainous but we had not been briefed to expect anything untoward, and as it turned out we were the only ones to suffer this terrifying experience.

'We were cruising at about 15,000ft when the speed started to fall off, so we increased power by pushing the throttles forward. The speed still fell, and the Lincoln was descending. The throttles reached the "gate", and the revs were by this time up to 2,850, which was our normal maximum except for take-off. Still the speed fell and the descent continued, the mountains getting closer and closer. We went to plus 12 and 3,000rpm, Graham Smith grim faced and me speechless. No effect. So "through the gate" they went with another surge of noise and power. But it did no good at all and still we drifted down at the minimum airspeed we dared fly at. In desperation I had my hand on the "tit" (the emergency boost override lever), with the mountains now looming up. I think we all had visions of our past life flashing before us. Surely it was only a matter of time. We had parachutes aboard but it did not seem right to even think of deserting a fully serviceable aeroplane and the thought was not even mentioned.

"Pull it" said Graham. I heaved it down, and the Merlins roared louder. I looked across at the pilot's panel – we didn't have much time, but the VSI was now indicating level, the speed had steadied and the colour was returning to the boss's face. Slowly the speed built up, the mountains slid by only just below, and we reduced to climb power, the aircraft now responding more normally, and eased back up to 15,000ft. We talked about it a lot. I don't think the powers that be believed us and there it ended. Of course there is a lot more known now about Standing Waves, which is no doubt what we had encountered. It was a nasty 'do'.

'When Binbrook went over to Canberras I was detailed to fly RF569 to Waddington with a Sgt Harrington as Captain. On arrival at the ship we discovered the end of one of the props was bent back about 75° for about 8in or so. After a quick discussion we called for two large metal objects ie sledge hammers. Bob held one and I set to and did the blacksmith act. Well it looked OK and – well – it flew OK. Who ever knew after all – and the bird was going to her retirement!'

It was during 1953 that the corkscrew was officially discontinued as a fighter evasion tactic. The Lincolns were getting older, their crews younger, the fighters faster, and the manoeuvres more violent, resulting in a number of cases of twisted fuselages and wings and 'Cat 5' write offs.

Above: Pilot portrait; a view from the engineer's position of Bill Youd at the controls of a Lincoln. The cockpit 'greenhouse' could be an uncomfortably hot and sticky place and though in shirt sleeves he wears gloves to protect hands from the hot wheel./*W. E. Youd*

Pilot Portrait: The Youd Story

To give some idea of the life on a Lincoln squadron in the 1950s we have included here the story of a pilot who modestly describes himself as typical of the period. The details as related to us will, it is hoped, convey to readers some of the atmosphere and happenings in which the air and ground crews found themselves caught up.

Pilot Officer W. E. (Bill) Youd was posted to 230 OCU Upwood in January 1954, after 18 months of basic and advanced flying training, starting on Prentices at 3 FTS Feltwell, progressing to Harvards at 1 FTS Moreton-in-Marsh, and finally doing 90 hours on Varsities at 201 AFS Swinderby. At 27 he was a little older than average, having previously served in the Parachute Regiment and as a sergeant radar fitter.

With a total of only 305 flying hours in his log book, the prospect of flying a Lincoln was exciting, but at the same time somewhat frightening. Yet, after only six hours of familiarisation and conversion flying, he and his newly formed crew went solo. The young crew, all newly trained in their various tasks, had come together on meeting at the OCU, on the usual hit or miss informal basis, just as in wartime. The pilot's initial Lincoln conversion was by Sqn Ldr Keith Perry, DSO, AFC, then by Flt Sgts Appleford and Warwick; it was quite common to find NCO flying instructors in those days. On the three month course, the crew completed 86 hours in Lincolns approximately half day and half night. The crew itself was to remain together, almost as a small family unit, until December 1955.

Having successfully completed the Lincoln course the crew was posted to No 7 Squadron at Upwood (May 1954) and after brief initial day and night flying acceptance checks of 1hr 15min each by the Squadron QFI, Flt Lt Ian Popay, DFM, became immediately involved in the home-based squadron routine of continuation training, air-to-sea firing, visual and H2S radar bombing (Bigshots), cross countries, gradually completing the mandatory number of exercises, day and night flying hours, instrument flying, etc, to 'white' rating standard, in order to achieve combat status.

During this working up period the main element of No 7 Squadron had been out in Malaya operating against the Communist terrorists as part of Operation Bold, returning to the UK in April/May 1954. In July it was to return to Tengah for a further three – month tour, this time the newly trained contingent accompanying the older hands. For Bill Youd and his comparatively inexperienced crew came the chance of their first long range overseas flight. The crew departed from Upwood on 12 July 1954 in RE348, each Lincoln of the detachment taking off within a few minutes of the others, the intention being to fly out as a loose gaggle. The crews were to experience the strange, but regular phenomenon of seeing no sign whatever of another Lincoln for seven hours or more until shortly before reaching the overnight staging posts, when quite suddenly and rather surprisingly, the other Lincolns would all appear in the sky around from various directions, as they homed in together.

The route taken was the (by then) well established one with first class RAF servicing facilities down the line, via Idris (7hr 30min), Habbaniya (8hr 55min), Mauripur (7hr 35min), Negombo (6hr 50min), finally arriving Tengah (7hr 50min) on 17 July.

The only en route incident for the crew was the discovery a couple of hours out from 'Habb' of an unfastened wing top fuel filler cover. As a precaution, in case the filler cap itself was off, and fuel was being lost, a short stop was made at Bahrain to check, but all was well.

After a three day rest and settling in period at Tengah the crew were set to work, with a 3hr 20min round Malaya cross country, followed by practice time and distance runs, simulated strikes, formation flying and continuation training in the circuit, on BABS, GCAs, etc. There was also some fighter affiliation with the Vampires of 45 Squadron during which the fighter pilots were distinctly heard to ask the Lincoln pilots to ease off a little to give them a chance to get their sights lined up occasionally.

On 3 August 1954, Flt Off Youd and crew carried out their first live strike in SX982, dropping 14 x 1,000lb bombs under the watchful eye of the flight commander, Flt Lt David H. Tew, and the squadron navigation leader, flying with them as a screening exercise to check they were up to the required standards. Their first solo strike was on 16 August in RE301. This time the load was 14 x 500 pounders. On 30 August came the crew's sole night strike, again in RE301 and again with Flt Lt Tew acting as 'screen'. On this operation, 14 x 500 pounders were dropped individually at 15-minute intervals on army marker flares, the idea being to keep the CTs awake and on the move all night.

After each day strike came the far more satisfying and exhilarating experience of emptying the front and rear turrets on low level strafing runs. Altogether, the crew was to complete nine day strikes, usually as part of a five or six aircraft loose formation, dropping 11 x 1,000 or 14 x 500lb of bombs from medium height (3,500-6,500ft depending on height of terrain) flying any one of the squadron's pool of eight Lincolns. It was also to participate in the Battle of Britain Day flypast and the large united RAAF/RAF formation strike. On 11 October 1954, No 7 Squadron left Tengah for the UK, the Youd crew bringing back SX983 on a 'shared' basis with Flt Lt Tew, following the same route as on the outward journey with the exception of the Bahrain stop. On 15 October, the final leg from Idris was started in loose formation. Just south of Paris, however, low cloud was encountered, so the Lincolns closed up into tight vics of three in line astern, roaring all the way back to Upwood at extreme low level, provoking many complaints about noise, etc. Exciting flying indeed.

Back in the UK after a welcome spell of leave it was on with the round of training and minor exercises for several months. Having achieved combat status the crew was qualified to undertake a single-leg Lone Ranger flight of approx eight hours, usually direct to Idris, Malta or Gibraltar, with the crew making all its own arrangements, flight plans, etc, as a demonstration of its independence and operational capability. Having already flown to Malaya and back this was something of an anomaly for Youd and his men. However, their first Lone Ranger was duly undertaken on 10 March 1955 from Upwood to Idris, returning two days later, 8½ hours each way, in SX925. Shortly afterwards the pilot and crew were recategorised as 'Select' – ie a 'Select pilot' in a 'Select crew', thus qualifying them for the next step – a multi-leg, long duration Lone Ranger in SX983, starting from Upwood on 12 July, routing via Idris, Abu Sueir, Khartoum, Eastleigh, Khartoum, Fayid, Luqa, to finish back at Upwood on the 18th, with only one day's rest down the route, and totalling 42 hours flying time.

On the Khartoum-Fayid leg, 983's radio gave trouble. The crew was unable to transmit the ½ hourly position reports, but was able to communicate with civil aircraft flying the routes. Two of the airline pilots brought stewardesses to the flight deck to chat over the radio to the Lincoln crew to keep up morale!

On the final return leg from Luqa, No 1 engine started to vibrate rather badly and it was observed that the spinner was out of true (later found to be cracked). On nearing the south coast of France, the engine was feathered and the last 750 miles to Upwood flown on three, the crew by then being determined to get home at all costs. All went well until the artificial horizon packed up in thick cloud near Paris, but the pilot coped and landed safely at base.

Nearly 50 hours of flying in a week, with one day's rest required some stamina. Add to the noise and vibration and normal strain of flying the extremes of temperature, unfamiliar conditions, time changes, strange food, planning, etc, and it will be appreciated that the crew was placed under some stress, purposely so, the test of a select crew being to remain operational under all conditions, almost anywhere.

The following month (August 1955) came another Lone Ranger, to Khormaksar in Aden, the round trip taking seven days. SX982 was flown out, probably for delivery to the 7 Squadron detachment out there, and RE340 was brought back, possibly for major overhaul. A month later the crew took 348 to Gibraltar for a weekend, 7hr 10min each way.

Between these more exotic tasks were the everyday chores of continuation training, day and night, practice bombing, etc, with the occasional exercise, such as Sky High in April 1955, which involved laying mines in the Kattegat off the Danish coast. Two parachute sea mines were dropped at night from low level, the idea being that a NATO unit should firstly plot, then sweep the mines, but nobody ever got to know the outcome. In September followed Exercise Beware on a pitch-black night, with taxying and take-off carried out in strict radio silence, using green Aldis signals. On the climb out, the crew suffered its first live engine failure, when No 2 lost oil pressure rapidly and had to be feathered. The crew returned to base still in strict R/T silence, and again exchanged Aldis signals with the ground for landing clearance. A quick change to the reserve aircraft, 348, and the crew was off again on a long, cold, 7½-hour night 'flog' shadowing a fleet in the far north of the North Sea. Shortly before this last incident, the crew had managed one other brief but pleasant two day detachment to Germany. There had been complaints from local residents about noise and disturbance from the bombing range at Heligoland, so the Lincoln dropped numerous bombs of varying sizes while scientists on the ground took seismic readings. The crew was chosen for this particular task because the pilot's SD cap was considered by the squadron commander as unfit to be seen on the AOC's parade to be held at that time!

The next event was in November 1955. Having just landed back at Upwood one Friday afternoon from a 'cross-country navex' (to drop off a colleague at Merryfield, near home, for leave) the crew was called into the CO's office to be told they were off to Aden on the Monday morning. The pilot was given the weekend off to get married, leaving him less than 24 hours to arrange the wedding. Briefing was at 7am on Monday 4 November. Two aircraft were to go out, Bill Youd and crew in RE398 and Sergeant John Merry and crew in the other Lincoln. Tailwheel oleo trouble delayed 398's take-off, and despite a very low level pass over Peterborough in the hope of provoking an immediate recall for an enquiry, Idris was reached safely, but in the dark. The crew were unanimous in their opinion that it was their pilot's best-ever landing, attributing it to his new family responsibilities. The next day Fayid was reached in 5hr 15min, and on 8 November the last leg to Khormaksar took 6hr 50min. The two Lincolns completed the 7 Squadron detachment in Southern Arabia which included four Lincolns over at Bahrain.

The following two weeks were spent patrolling the Yemeni border, showing the flag by flying round all the British forts and posts at low level on general protection and surveillance work. On Monday mornings, the Sunday newspapers (brought out by Comet) were dropped to the forts, a good morale booster. During this phase, the crew flew RE398 exclusively. On 24 November 398 was flown to Bahrain to reinforce the local detachment of Lincolns for patrols of the Saudi/Trucial border. It was suspected that the Saudis were about to attack the Buraimi Oasis, an important oil development centre. From Bahrain the crew carried out numerous 3/4-hour patrols in RA664, all at low level in very hot, bumpy conditions. All side windows had to be kept closed, and when taxying, or when take-offs were delayed, coolant and cockpit temperatures were a problem. On 4 December, a six hour search for some missing Aramco oil men was undertaken. They were eventually found and after some very careful flying on dead reckoning, were established as being the wrong side of the border. By a lot of wing waggling and hand signals, the oilmen were persuaded to move back into friendly territory.

Most patrols were at dawn and dusk, which was when any potential attackers were most likely to move, rather than in the scorching heat of the day. Carrying a parachute was eventually discontinued altogether because there were no packers available, and they had all been soaked in water in any case. Aircraft flown on the detachment were RA664, RE398, RE322, SX982, most of which were to pass to No 1426 Flight which was soon to take over No 7 Squadron's duties in South Arabia. On 22 December, only 10 minutes after take-off in 322 for the dawn patrol, Flg Off Youd was suddenly recalled because of his mother's death. On landing, his aircraft and crew were immediately taken over by another pilot to fly off on the patrol. Flg Off Youd flew home by civil airline to England, the Constellation taking-off from Aden as the Lincoln was landing. He was never to see his crew again as a unit – it was a sudden and unexpected end to a tour of 20 months. They did meet up individually by chance as their Service paths crossed on odd occasions, but that was all. The crew remained behind in Aden for several months, becoming part of 1426 Flight when No 7 Squadron disbanded on 2 January 1956.

Bill Youd's flying must have been more than satisfactory or average, as he was chosen to attend a Flying Instructors' course, firstly on the 'jet retread' phase, flying Vampires at Oakington, then passing to CFS at South Cerney on piston Provosts. On graduating as a QFI in July 1956 he was to have gone to one of the ab initio flying training schools, but suddenly Bomber Command found itself short of Lincoln instructors, so a quick change to CFS Little Rissington for the asymmetric course, followed by a posting in September 1956 to the Lincoln Conversion Flight at Hemswell to join the two other resident instructors, Flt Lts Mick Morrissey and 'Johnny' Johnson, renewing an acquaintance with the latter dating back to Varsity days at Advanced Flying School when Johnson had been his instructor! The three Lincolns flown regularly and exclusively on instruction and conversion duties were RF575, RF569 and RF444.

Hemswell was in the throes of change, however, in the winter of 1956/57, with the Lincoln well and truly on the way out as the Canberras moved in to take over the RCM/ECM role, and with the V-Force becoming established elsewhere. In March 1957, with the impending departure of the Lincolns, the Con Flt was closed down and the instructors posted to nearby Lindholme, where Bomber Command Bombing School had the largest remaining contingent of Lincolns in the RAF, with 14 of them on B Squadron. On arrival at Lindholme, the instructors were asked by the Station Commander if they had ever flown Viscounts, as it was proposed to buy six as replacements for the Lincoln in the V-Force Navigation Bombing System training role. In the event, the purchase of the Viscounts fell through on cost grounds, and instead BCBS got some of the RAF's oldest Hastings, a number of which are still flying with the unit's successor, now at Scampton, at the time of writing.

At Lindholme, the job of QFI and Instrument Rating Examiner was full time, with only occasional relief in the way of Bomber Command exercises or an overseas flight. On 29 July 1957 there was a night trip to Gibraltar in SX944, and on arrival at dawn the airfield was covered in fog, with only the top of the famous Rock visible out of a white carpet. The planned diversion was Port Lyautey in North Africa, but it, too, was fogbound, so the Lincoln diverted instead to a USAF B-47 base, Sidi Slimane, 200 miles south of Gib. As the Lincoln completed its landing run, it was surrounded by three jeeps full of Yanks armed with sub-machine guns pointing menacingly at the aircraft. The young 'lootenant' in charge took some convincing, and he explained after a while that it was thought to be some trick to upset the airfield security as 'you limeys gave us no prior notice that you were coming'. After a good breakfast, the Lincoln and its crew were permitted to leave on condition that the Americans were treated to a beat up. The whole base seemed to turn out with cine cameras to record the most impressive of displays by the rather old looking aircraft which they were convinced was a Lancaster.

Display flying became something of a speciality for Bill Youd who performed his 4-3-2-and 1-engine flying routines at the last two Battle of Britain displays to be held at Lindholme, in September 1958 and 1959. The one engined flypasts were always watched in some awe by the crowd, but it was perhaps not as difficult as it seemed, though the pilot and his flight engineer (Flt Sgt 'Larry' Parkes) needed to know what they were doing. For the single engined runs, the routine was to approach the airfield in a shallow dive on four engines, at 250kts, feathering the two outboards in the dive, then feathering one inboard just before the boundary, levelling off at 220kts, flying past on the one, with speed falling to 150kts at the far end of the runway, then unfeathering the three to climb away. The feathering drill was 'fiddled' a little, because when the last of the three engines stopped, all ignition switches were left on, pitch levers put back up through the feathering gate, throttles set, booster pumps off, and master fuel cocks left on so that as soon as the feathering buttons were pressed, at least one other engine would start up almost immediately.

Otherwise the flying at Lindholme remained fairly routine, apart from one more overseas trip in RA674 in February 1959, when at short notice, a V-bomber crew had to be ferried out to Idris from Finningley for an exercise, and a number of ground crew brought back. On arrival back over the UK the whole country was covered by fog, and 674 and its crew spent two days at St Mawgan.

Bill Youd was to continue as an instructor at Lindholme until April 1960, when he was posted to 242 OCU at Dishforth on Hastings. By then he had attained the very high A2 QFI category, and had amassed over 1,600 hours on Lincolns. A man of humour and skill, a fairly typical Lincoln type, he has now retired from the RAF and works for an oil company based in Sussex.

Winding Down

On 4 August 1953 the whole of the Waddington Wing, comprising Nos 100, 61 and 49 squadrons moved to Wittering lock stock and barrel to enable Waddington to prepare for the V-bombers. It was at Wittering on 14 August 1953 that Wing Commander Hal Derwent, AFC, briefed the squadrons for what was to prove the last participation by Lincolns in a major Bomber Command Exercise – Momentum, the briefing being attended by HRH the Duke of Edinburgh.

The following year, however, in September 1954, No 148 Squadron took part in a NATO Exercise, Morning Mist, flying to Norway, landing at Vaernes to refuel and rearm, its ground crews setting up a Eureka beacon to help the Lincolns negotiate the treacherous approach up a fjord. During 1954 148 alternated with No 7 Squadron on detachment to Tengah, until 148 carried out the final RAF, Lincoln sortie in Malaya in April 1955 returning to Upwood to join No 7 for a short time before disbanding on 1 July 1955 to convert to Valiants a year later. (Many of the early V-bomber crews came from the ranks of former Lincoln men). No 49 Squadron, returning from Kenya also disbanded a month later.

This left only one true Lincoln bomber squadron, No 7, to carry on, it being called upon regularly for 'flag-wags' and ceremonials, including, on 29 April 1955, a fly-past over The Hague to celebrate the 10th anniversary of Operation Manna (dropping of food supplies to the starving Dutch people as the war ended). No 7's Lincolns dropped a million daffodil heads and 50,000 good-will leaflets. Participation in NATO and Command exercises continued, though in minor supporting roles, such as mining in Sky High in April 1955. On the very verge of disbanding and giving up its Lincolns, however, No 7's ageing warhorses (the aircraft that is) were unexpectedly called out again – this time to Aden as described in the 'Pilot Portrait' story. They could not quite do without the old Lincoln yet!

Nos 83 and 97 continued for a short time with Lincolns in a new role of training V-Force navigators, and 199 on ECM work. In January 1956 (2nd-13th) the former 83 Squadron, by then known as Antler, provided an aircraft (RA711) and crew for an inspection tour of the route planned for the Queen's visit to West Africa: via Tripoli, Kano, Kaduna, Lagos, Accra, Freetown, Bathurst, Gibraltar. The small detachment was commanded by Wing Commander A. A. N. Nicholson, the Wing Commander Flying at Hemswell, who was subsequently appointed Deputy Force Commander for the actual tour by the Queen. Captain of the Lincoln was Flight Lieutenant D. P. Davison.

By the end of 1955, however, the Lincoln had been almost completely overtaken by the jet age, and most of them were going for scrap in large numbers, both straight from the squadrons as they disbanded and out of storage from the MUs. So closed a chapter in Royal Air Force annals.

Below: Fresh out of the shops, and positively the last of the line, WD149, the final 'New Build' (RAF) by the Sir W. G. Armstrong Whitworth Aircraft Ltd factory at Baginton, near Coventry. She was delivered to No 20 MU, Aston Down, on 28 March 1951. The last Lincoln actually delivered to the RAF was WD147 which left Baginton a few days later – 4 April 1951 – for CSE Watton. A number of the flight shop personnel pictured here are still with the former 'AWA Division' of Hawker Siddeley at the Bitteswell factory.
/Armstrong Whitworth (Hawker Siddeley) via John Austin

Bomber Crew

The Lincoln, like the Lancaster, carried a standard operational crew of 7, comprising pilot, flight engineer, navigator/plotter (who acted as visual bomb aimer and front gunner), nav/radar (acting as H2S bomb aimer), signaller, mid-upper and rear gunners.

In the early squadron days of the Lincoln, until the late 1940s, there was an ample supply of pilots and aircrew with wartime experience on Lancasters, with the exception of navigator radars who were in short supply for a time. For most crew members, the transition to Lincolns was a natural progression. Gradually, however, many of these wartime stalwarts left the Service for 'civvy street', and the newer, younger men started to appear, though a number of the ex-wartime types were still to be seen round the Lincoln units until the very end.

When the Lincolns first appeared on the squadrons, they would be filtered in, by twos and threes to operate alongside Lancasters, and pilots and crews already well used to four engined bombers, would convert fairly easily on an informal basis to the new type, with the minimum of ground instruction, and only the briefest of check-outs with another pilot. With the gradual withdrawal of the Lancaster, however, it became necessary to train crews ab initio on the Lincoln, and No 230 OCU gave up its Lancasters for Lincolns to cope with the new, postwar influx of crews.

Pilots and Flight Engineers

Some of the new pilots would be slim young lads of no more than 19 or 20, fresh out of advanced flying training school with 250/300 hours in their logbooks, which would include 70 hours or so on a heavy twin, usually a Wellington, later a Varsity. Within only a mere six hours or so of dual conversion, the young pilot would be flying the Lincoln solo with his crew.

A number of pilots would, however, be older, more experienced men from other types, perhaps with wartime tours on Spitfires, and other non-bomber types. For them the rather lumbering four engined heavy was a new venture, not always relished at first after the independence and exhilaration of fighters; but in most cases to become a satisfying and cherished experience.

There were others who had been POWs, shot down during the war, and returning to resume flying, in some cases becoming squadron commanders.

The method of crewing up at the OCU was very much a hit and miss affair, just as in wartime. A group of new entrants would be put in a room together with instructions to sort themselves out into crews within half an hour; some of the younger, very new boys would look for an older, obviously experienced flight lieutenant pilot, while others would prefer to be 'all new together'. One or two might have met before, in the Service, or perhaps even on the train to Lincoln, and decided to stay together. The system (or lack of it) seemed to work very well.

On any Lincoln squadron, the majority of flight engineers appeared to be ex-wartime men, often the elder statesmen of the crews, even in the last days of the Lincolns. Many had served during the war, not only on Lancasters, but also on other 4-engined heavies such as Stirlings, Halifaxes and Sunderlands: knowledgeable men of vast experience with large, well-worn hands; reliable, sometimes appearing a little taciturn, not ready sufferers of fools or 'sprog' pilots. To the older ones, flying always appeared something of a bore, yet secretly they were undoubtedly proud of their skills and expertise, and would not choose to do any other job. Many engineers had, in fact, left the Service after the war, but had soon elected to rejoin.

If a new young pilot had any sense he would soon learn to rely implicitly on his flight engineer who had often 'forgotten more about flying', as they say. After a brief shake-down period at the OCU pilot and flight engineer would soon begin to establish a working relationship, each learning quickly the other's likes and dislikes, such as throttle handling, or operation of pitch levers. Some pilots preferred to handle the throttles for both take-off and landing, others for take-off only, or not at all, leaving them entirely to the 'eng'.

It was usual for the pilot to open the throttles initially on the take-off run, and for the engineer to follow him through to hold the throttles against the gate, leaving the pilot with both hands free for the control wheel for lift off and climb out. The engineer would generally handle the four pitch (or propeller) levers at all times, one of his main jobs being to synchronise the engines by lining up the propeller 'strobes' visually, a particularly difficult task at night when it had to be done by ear. The engineer also managed the fuel system, kept a comprehensive log of power changes, fuel states, estimated weights etc, and would spend a good part of any Bomber Command exercise shovelling bundles of window out of the nose chute; as well as dispensing rations to the rest of the crew. Engineers were also expected to do a certain amount of flying in case of emergency and to give their pilots a welcome break from time to time. Some were even permitted to have a go at take-offs and landings, and most became reasonably accomplished at straight and level flying.

By the end of the OCU course, the relationship between pilot and flight engineer would have settled into one of implied mutual reliance and quiet efficiency, where few instructions needed to be given, only the briefest of check calls and acknowledgments, with each becoming satisfied that the other knew his job. Many a young pilot had his experienced engineer to thank for nursing him through OCU, and early squadron days.

By the end of a squadron tour, after nearly two years of sitting shoulder to shoulder for up to 750 hours of flying, sharing monotony, excitement, fright, and many other sensations, pilot and engineer would have become firm friends, nearly always on first-name terms between any rank from sergeant to flight lieutenant, and often above when in the air.

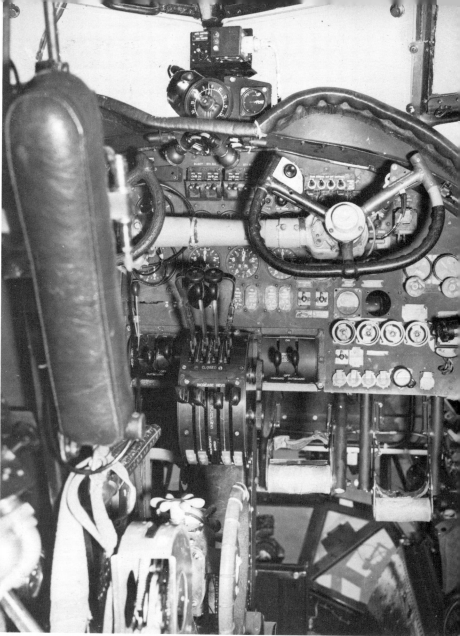

Two cockpit views showing a dual control RAF BII and the ultimate Lincoln development, an MR31 of the RAAF (with control column and seat removed for clarity), pictures spanning 10 years. While it is not the purpose of this book to draw a direct comparison and list all the instruments and equipment visible, close scrutiny reveals a number of additions and rearrangements on the MR31, the most notable being the auto-pilot controls on the extreme left hand side of the cockpit. Note also the civil call sign painted above the blind flying panel.
/Ministry of Defence; J. L. Laming

Most engineers were NCOs, often warrant officers, men not to be trifled with, men whose 'Union' was just as strong a freemasonry as that of the other closed shop – the navigators' union.

Some pilots and flight engineers would have the quietest of working relationships, with hardly a word spoken, yet with a strong bond between them, developed to such a high degree of mutual perception that even when performing pre-take-off and landing checks and drills, few words needed to be exchanged, each knowing instinctively what the other was thinking, and exactly when to perform each specified task or operation. A beautiful dawn, sunset, or moonlit cloudscape could be mutually appreciated in total silence.

Others would have a boisterous, joke-a-minute liaison, with constant backchat during the whole flight. From personal experience, it was most amusing to have listened to some of the older hands who flew the Lincolns at Lindholme, pilots and engineers who had flown together for some years. They inevitably and almost constantly enjoyed their 'beef and bind' or 'eff and blind', usually about some aspect of service life which they were finding tiresome, like duty rosters, or preparations for AOC's inspections. From well before leaving the crewroom to entering the aircraft, they would be animatedly discussing some problem or subject totally unrelated to flying, putting the world to rights. The discussion would continue without any apparent pause, during pre-start checks, engine starting, taxying and pre-take-off checks, with only the briefest occasional reference to the job in hand, never once referring to a check list, yet missing nothing. They knew their job inside out. It was equally amusing to a young Royal Observer Corps member, who regularly 'begged' flights in the BCBS Lincolns, to listen over the intercom to two old friends, each with many thousands of flying hours, Master Pilot Tom Connelly, and Master Engineer Tom McCartney singing the pre-landing checks to a tune from a well-known opera.

In the early 1950s retirement from the RAF and the expansion of Coastal Command, with the appearance of the Shackleton in large numbers, led to a shortage of engineers on the Lincoln squadrons, and a number of National Servicemen and short service NCOs were recruited as engineers.

For the young National Servicemen who were lucky enough to get the chance to become flight engineers in the early 1950s, it was, indeed, a unique experience. After the usual few weeks of basic service training there followed an intensive 12 weeks course at No 4 School of Technical Training, St Athan, then a posting to 230 OCU to crew up. Some

were fortunate enough to go straight to a squadron to fill pressing vacancies.

Eric Myall was a National Serviceman who became a flight engineer, and he tells his own story:

'June 1950 saw the commencement of my National Service with the Royal Air Force, shortly after the outbreak of the Korean War, and the consequent rapid expansion of the Service.

'After initial traumas at Padgate lots of young hopefuls travelled down to Hornchurch to the Aircrew Selection Centre and the successful few ended up in every current aircrew category from pilots to air gunners. To my surprise, as I was not exactly a mechanical genius, I was offered the chance to become a flight engineer, and accepted this with alacrity.

'Eventually 12 of us arrived at No 4 S of TT St Athan, where we formed No 3 NSA course. Looking back it seems that we were

Above: A flight engineer (or 'airborne plumber') at his panel checking a fuse. Above the fuse and circuit breaker panel (here shown with cover removed) are the fuel flow, or 'gallons gone' meters and oil and coolant temperature gauges, while above the engineer's head on the main cockpit panel are the four engine fire extinguisher buttons, panel lighting switch and flash jettison button. Behind his back is the elevator trim wheel, and in right foreground, flexible oxygen supply tube./*Ministry of Defence*

very lucky, since we were some of the first National Service aircrew and nobody really seemed to know what to do with us! We suffered a lot of cheerful abuse from the Regulars at St Athan but the square-bashing part of the course must have been mild compared with the rigours of such bastions as West Kirby and Hednesford, etc.

'We were at St Athan from July to November 1950 and in that time were introduced to the aerial delights of the Avro Lincoln B II of which there were two on the Unit – RF462 and RF484 [ex-*Crusader*]. Some of the flights were from nearby Llandow and my log book records that there were two basic flying routines. We also had numerous sorties in Anson 12 PH804 and Oxford HN309 which were enlivened by the pilot calling us up front one by one, handing over control to us, and then chopping one engine. My right leg is still more powerful than my left as a consequence!

'We flew a total of 16 hours, a lot of which was spent over the beautiful North Wales countryside. We seemed to spend most of the trips stopping and starting the engines. On one of the early flights the pilot spent some time practising his Battle of Britain display party piece which was to fly the Lincoln round with three out of four stopped. Some time later we learned that this had caused some consternation on the ground at that time, since it would have been well nigh impossible to have landed it on one, if the other three hadn't restarted!

'Flying, of course, was the highlight of our time at St Athan where most of the day was devoted to lectures on engines, airframes, propellers, and systems, airmanship and meteorology. Our billets were seemingly relics from the war; the weather was at its South Wales best, and it was very, very wet.

'We were promised, if successful, not only Lincolns as possible future mounts, but Lancasters and Sunderlands as well, but although all 12 of us passed the course, only one went on to Lancasters and the rest of us went on to Lincolns at 230 OCU, Scampton. The course, although apparently somewhat haphazard, must have worked well enough, since eventually 11 out of the 12 reached the squadrons. During the course at St Athan we were known as aircrew cadets, with the appropriate laurel wreath badge worn on the sleeves. We would presumably have become Engineer IVs but they changed the system yet again and we became sergeants instead.

'It was during the OCU course at Scampton that I was to make my first ever night flight and it turned out to be more memorable than any that were to follow. The date was 12 March 1951.

'Officially it was "Exercise X111" – night familiarisation. We had a squadron leader instructor for the captain, and for me, still an "engineer u/t", a screen engineer.

'The weather looked pretty grim: low heavy cloud, strong winds and occasional rain. However I was very much the junior on this flight and comment from me would have been superfluous and probably received with ribaldry.

'My most vivid impression of the flight was, and still is, the astonishing variety of lights which seemed to make the appropriate patterns and sense to everyone else, but not to me. There were all sorts of lights, both inside the aircraft and outside. The control panel had its fair share and so did the nav's area. There were lights on the hangars, on the taxiways and the runways. The airfield beacon was flashing, other aircraft lights appeared and disappeared all over the sky, it seemed.

'Before I could orientate myself in any way we had bounded down the runway and into the fast gathering murk. It was no better up there! There were now vastly greater numbers of lights which came and went as we flew around and into and out of clouds and rain.

'There is little else I remember of the flight itself, which must have been a success since we didn't have to repeat it despite the sudden ending! At some time I must have gone up front to do my bit under the watchful eye of the screen engineer. The latter was a pleasant soul who seemed to have a remarkable ability for doing very little – and taking his time over that.

'Some two and a half hours after take-off we all seemed to have done well enough to go back to base and land. There were probably a lot less lights 'out there' now, but the real significance of this did not then hit me.

'However, I was soon aware that my skipper was having trouble with the approach. *I* was still having trouble with orientating *myself*, and how he even found finals I still don't know. Twice we approached the runway and twice we overshot; and then the instructor took over. I recall that I was probably standing in the navigator's area, with the skipper still in the driving seat and the squadron leader in the normal engineer's position, to his right. The screen engineer was sitting where the signaller would have been, if we had carried one.

'Suddenly we arrived on the runway with an almighty crash that very obviously did the undercarriage no good at all. We then seemed to be sliding along the runway, roughly in the right direction accompanied by loud metallic noises, sparks and even more lights. I never did see the exit of my "placid" screen engineer but was reliably informed afterwards that before we stopped sliding he was up through the astro-dome, and down on to the wing, complete with fire-extinguisher and was running alongside until we stopped! So much for his inactivity.

'I think I must have got a slight knock on the head, as it all seemed quiet after a while. None of the others seemed to be there at all, but they all appeared to have left items of kit about, so I dutifully started gathering my kit and theirs until somebody shouted through the front end (not very politely) that a hasty retreat was desirable as the fuel tanks had ruptured. At this point I leapt out of the aircraft with some alacrity, only to go base over apex on the black ice which covered the runway!

'My facetious remarks (probably prompted by shock/relief) about "arriving in style" did not seem to go down well with the rest of the crew, least of all the instructor, but I was gratified by the response of the other "engineer u/ts" when they viewed the wreckage the following day. Their interest and concern must have lasted all of two hours or so.

'RA721(SN-O) was a sorry sight, undercarriageless and with obvious twists and bends to wings and fuselage. It must have been at least Cat 4, and probably Cat 5 when I last saw it, still on its belly "round the back" at Scampton, and I think they dismantled it there [RA721 was indeed written off].

'After Scampton I went on to No 148 Squadron at Upwood and spent some 15 months on operational service on the Lincoln. It wasn't the most exciting bomber of all time, but 25 years later I'd dearly love to have another go at it.'

Below: A typical nav plotter, Flg Off Colin Palmer, nav/op to the flight commander, Flt Lt David H. Tew, at his table in a No 7 Squadron Lincoln out on a strike from Tengah in 1954. He wears a lighter-weight canvas headset, so essential in the tropics. Tools of the trade include his Dalton Computer, chart, dividers and anglepoise lamp. */Douglas Pike*

Navigators

The introduction of the Lincoln saw the end of the specialist bomb aimer/front gunner of the Lancaster days, and the adoption of the two navigator system as developed by Pathfinder Force during the war, which became known as the Nav 1 and Nav 2, or Nav and Set-Op. In the Lincoln they eventually became known as the Nav Plotter and Nav Radar, the former being responsible for the basic position navigation of the aircraft in the conventional sense, using the navigation charts at the navigation table fitted with air speed indicator, a master compass unit, air position and ground position indicators.

The two navigators worked alongside each other, both sharing the same bench seat facing to port with the nav radar to the right, his job being to operate the Gee or Gee-H and H2S with its cathode ray tube display (known as PPI), complementing and aiding the plotter. He would also operate the Rebecca/BABS homing and landing aids. The nav's compartment could be blacked out with a large curtain for daylight operation.

The nav/plotter also maintained a check on compass accuracy, his gyro indicator being linked directly to the master unit which hung just inside the main rear door of the aircraft. He could wind in the variation on the pilots' DRC (Distant Reading Compass) and in later years with the G4 units fitted, could synchronise all the compass display units in the aircraft. The nav plotter was also mainly responsible for visual bombing, and on nearing the target would vacate his seat and man the bombsight in the nose. This involved climbing round the nav radar, sliding along the metal floor under the engineer's seat and foot rest, past the dual control rudder pedals if fitted, and down two steps into the nose, an exhausting business in full flying kit and off oxygen for a few minutes when at height. The oxygen system in the Lincoln was fairly basic, and the rules were that it was always kept on for night flying at whatever height, and used above 10,000ft for day flying.

The visual bombing system used the T3 bombsight and bombing computer which basically converted the manually set inputs of target pressure setting, target height, bomb terminal velocity and wind speed/direction, together with the continuous and automatic inputs of air speed and altitude to the bombsight. These inputs provided the bomb aimer with a continuous indication of drift and bombing angle, presented to him on a small gyro stabilised glass bombing platform with a cross illuminated on it to determine the release point. The bomb aimer on the bombing run directed the pilot to fly the aircraft so that the target came down the centre line, ordering bomb doors open, selecting the bomb (or bomb stick) and

Left: An early production Lincoln 'bombing office' clearly shows the excellent, if somewhat ugly, view, though the post was often a draughty one. Left foreground is the computer box with the oxygen and air supply control panel above. Top centre, on bulkhead, is the interior light. Above the bombsight are the front gun control handles and triggers, while the course setting bombsight (CSBS) itself is shown in the stowed position. From the seat the twin .5in Browning machine guns mounted in an electro-hydraulically operated Boulton-Paul Type F nose turret were fired. The turret rotated 45° each side of the centre line and 40° above or below the horizontal. Each gun was supplied by a detachable ammunition box with 230 rounds capacity./*British Official*

pressing the bomb release button when the target reached the cross on the display.

The blind bombing H2S system worked out electronically the forward throw of the bomb to be dropped and presented the information to the nav radar on his H2S screen by a radar-painted line and circle representing the track of the aircraft and the forward trajectory of the bomb. The nav radar directed the pilot to fly the aircraft so that the target came down the track line illuminated on the radar screen, and in this case, the nav radar would order the opening of the bomb doors and the making of the release circuits before pressing the bomb release button situated by the side of the H2S equipment. Usually, the visual bomb aimer would follow the nav radar through the target area from the nose, cloud cover permitting of course. During co-ordinated attacks when a bomb had to be dropped visually or blind, the visual bomb aimer would be in the nose directing the pilot with the nav radar providing assistance on the H2S, and if during the last stages of the bombing run the target could not be seen visually the nav radar would try to get the bomb away blind using the H2S.

Many of the early Lincoln navs had flown in Bomber Command during the war and converted easily and quickly to the Lincoln, some of them still with their complete former Lancaster crews. Most of the wartime men had trained in Canada but the postwar ones would probably have done the 'all through' course at 2 ANS, Middleton St George, which included initial training school, (five months) and then the basic and advanced phases (lasting six months and five months respect-

Bottom left: A Lincoln navigator (radar) seated facing his array of sensitive equipment. Bottom right of picture is the Mk 4A H2S console, clearly showing its circular cathode-ray tube, known as the Plan Position Indicator tube, while almost at eye level above the H2S is the G-H Mk 2 set, also having its own display tube. Top centre of picture is the selector which determined the spacing of the bombs released, depending on the time interval set. This navigator has an individual seat; usually Lincolns had a bench seat on which the navigators sat side by side, with the nav (plotter) on the left./*Ministry of Defence*

Above: The same machine looking forward with the main spar and oxygen supply in immediate foreground left. Beyond the wireless operator's station is a bench seat for the two navigators, with the flight engineer's 'dickey' seat shown in the down position on the flight deck. Crew comfort was secondary to function, though the w/op did enjoy warmth for his seat was beside the hot air system outlet. Both his T1154M transmitter and R1155E receiver (the former on top of the latter, both Marconi) were exactly as fitted to RAF bombers during the war and survived in the Lincoln to the end. At the right hand edge of the table is the morse key. /*British Official*

ively). The basic flying training was in Ansons, the advanced in Wellingtons, the total course about 180 hours, before passing to 201 AFS Swinderby for another 60 hours or so of more advanced navigation on Wellington T10s.

All navigators were given the same training which included bombing, gunnery, and wireless operating, but they were not introduced to H2S until arrival at OCU. In the late 1940s/early 1950s newly qualified navigators would usually be crewed with an experienced partner who invariably claimed the plotter's slot. On the squadrons, however, the two did interchange on occasions in order to keep their hands in on both jobs, but rarely did so on operational exercises. Where the two navs were of equal experience (or lack of) the one with the better training record would normally get the plotter's job.

With the removal of the mid-upper turrets from the Lincoln, and the consequent reduction in numbers of air gunners, the job of firing the front guns also fell to the navigators, whose training at the ANS included gunnery theory, gun-stripping, and sessions on the ground-gunnery school trainer which involved firing a few rounds on static mounts on the range, plus about half an hour practical handling in aircraft on the squadron before first firing any guns in anger, such as in Malaya.

Navigators were a mixture of NCOs and officers on each unit, from sergeant to flight lieutenant, representing a wide spread of prior experience and first tour men.

The squadrons had two bombing leaders: one responsible for visual bombing and the other for blind bombing. As part of their duties both leaders maintained records of bombing training tasks and results, keeping visual displays of ranges and target details up to date in briefing rooms and in conjunction with the flight commanders, planning the flying programme. They, of course, also analysed bombing results, organised calibration of bombsights and briefed the navigators for squadron exercises arranged by the wing bombing staff.

Signallers

Signallers on Lincolns fell into three basic categories: Direct entry, ex-tradesmen and National Service. For the full course, the training took about 18 months, with initial radio work and morse done at Compton Bassett, near Calne, Wilts. The secondary and airborne phase might be at Swanton Morley, flying in Ansons and Proctors. Graduates then dispersed to the appropriate OCU for type conversion and then to a squadron.

The signaller was primarily used as a safety radio watch in case of emergency, ready for IFF and SOS. On exercises, during radio silence he would listen out on the allotted frequency and receive the half-hourly Bomber Command broadcasts of target information weather at base, and diversion airfields. They operated the standard fitted jamming equipment (eg Mandrel, Dinah, Tinsel) and on cross-country navexs supplied the navigator with fixes. The 'Fishpond' rear-facing radar for picking up other aircraft was also the signallers' responsibility, but was rarely used, the general opinion being that it was fairly ineffective anyway, and no instruction was given on it at OCU.

On the long range Pampa and Seaweed met flights the signaller would transmit the information passed to him at regular intervals by the met observer who sat in the nose. With the job of sending batches of up to 60 Group messages, plus assisting the navigator, and sending normal position reports, they were the only trips on which the signallers were fully occupied, except for overseas flights.

Even in the mid/late 1950s the basic radio equipment remained the Marconi T1154/R1155 exactly as first fitted to Lancasters in 1942. It was manually tuned and low-powered, and could make an overseas flight hard work for the signaller putting out mandatory half-hourly position reports to foreign Flight Information Regions, and RAF Air Traffic Control Centres. Each transmission could involve several attempts to establish contact on the old and outdated equipment, on which the transmitter had first to be tuned to the receiver, which was time consuming. If, as sometimes happened on overseas flights, the H2S went on the blink then the signaller would, in addition, need to supply his navigator with frequent QTEs (true bearings) obtained from, say, the French Fixer Service. It was not unknown for Lincolns to fly non-stop from the UK to Shallufa, 13½ hours, without once making R/T contact.

During the Malayan campaign, the lead signaller of each formation strike would send to Singapore ATCC take-off time, and Firedog number, then revert to the operational frequency to listen out for target information, etc. The Army Auster spotter/marker planes would communicate direct with the Lincoln pilots on VHF in the target area.

Signallers were also carried by the Lincolns operating in Kenya and Aden, and used to much the same purpose. Gradually, however, as the Lincoln was withdrawn from front line service in the mid-1950s, fewer signallers were needed, much of the radio work becoming all VHF and handled by the pilots, though signallers continued to be carried on overseas flights. Many of the signallers were retrained on development and use of radio and electronic listening and countermeasures equipment, and a large number went into the V-Force as AEOs, and to Coastal Command.

Air Gunners

In the immediate postwar years there was a surfeit of fully trained gunners, many with actual operational experience on a variety of 'heavies'; but gradually, with the obvious decline in needs, and with the new jet-bombers imminent, many retired from the Service. It was clear that the trade of gunner would soon be redundant. However, various unexpected factors revived the need for air gunners: the Korean War, communist activity in Malaya, delays in development and deliveries of jet-bomber replacements, (both Canberras and the Vs) plus the declining political situation in the Middle and Far East, which prolonged not only the life of the Lincoln but also maintained the need for gunners. Indeed, the skills of gunnery were carried right through into the mid 1960s as the Shackleton replaced the Lincoln on colonial policing duties.

To meet the sudden shortage in the early 1950s a number of National Servicemen were recruited as air gunners, signallers and flight engineers. The term of National Service had

then recently been increased from 18 months to two years. This was about as far ahead as the planners were prepared to look in the more obsolescent aircrew trades, so it suited them to use the two year men.

Typically, a National Service aircrew recruit called up in the usual way would report to No 1 Reception Unit at Padgate for initial kitting out, etc. During the first week, those sufficiently interested would be invited to attend aircrew recruiting lectures in the camp cinema (The Astra), and those volunteers with a reasonable academic record were sent to the Air Crew Selection Centre at Hornchurch for five days of intensive medicals and aptitude tests, returning afterwards to Padgate for two or three weeks in Reserve Flight to await results, the waiting period being spent on a variety of interesting duties such as moving coke, potato peeling, painting kerbstones white, or helping to clean floors in the camp hospital.

Successful gunnery applicants would then be posted to the aircrew transit unit at Driffield for two or three months during which a little time might be spent on basic service training, though with an absolute minimum of square bashing, before moving on to the ab initio course at CGS Leconfield (East Yorks.).

Ground school was in a series of bleak Nissen huts and aerial training was in Wellington T10s (until the latter were gradually replaced by Lincolns, the two types operating side by side for a time). During the three month course the student gunner would complete 20/25 hours flying, nearly all by day, fire up to 2,400 rounds of ammo (.303in in the Wellingtons) and 55 feet of camera

Above: Armed with twin Hispano 20mm cannons the Bristol B17 electrically-operated mid-upper turret was a fine piece of engineering but dogged with a troublesome mechanical feed system, causing frequent stoppages. It could rotate continuously through 360° and incorporated an interrupter gear to prevent damage to the aircraft. Ammunition was held in two boxes positioned below the gunner's seat (which was like a cycle saddle) and totalled 361 rounds per cannon (310 in boxes and 51 in lead-ins). The picture shows LAC Ron McGowan cleaning the barrels of a No 1 Squadron RAAF machine at Tengah, Singapore.
/Australian War Memorial

film, all air-to-sea. The usual number on the course was 12 or 13, of whom a few might be flight engineers on gunnery training.

On qualifying, the National Serviceman would be accorded the rank of sergeant (non-substantive) though paid as a sergeant, with flying pay of 3s 0d per day added, thus meaning he would draw about £6 10s 0d per week net, on which he could live quite comfortably.

After leave, those selected for Lincolns would be posted to 230 OCU where they would crew up on the usual haphazard basis. The OCU course was slanted very much towards the pilots and engineers, and to navigation and bombing, with the gunners having only the odd session or two against a target towed along the sea by an ASR launch off Bridlington. It was not unknown for guns and the enthusiasm of gunners to run away, and for the launch itself to come under fire. There would also be a few camera film sessions with Mosquitos doing sedate travelling attacks, always by day to exactly the same pattern, far removed from reality.

Following the OCU Course on which 75/80 hours were flown (roughly half day, half night) and with only 15 months or so of his two years left to serve, the gunner would be posted with his new crew to a squadron.

There the gunner was caught up in the usual round of long cross-countries, night exercises, bombing practice and continuation training with little to do. On the normal bombing or flying training work the gunners would merely sit, read, and often sleep, occasionally (having first obtained the Captain's consent) leaving the turret for a walk-about to stretch cramped limbs, and for natural purposes. Any such movement when the aircraft was over 10,000ft would be with the aid of a portable oxygen bottle. On Bomber Command night exercises, however, with minimal separation between aircraft showing no navigation lights, it was the duty of the gunners to stay wide awake and to keep the pilot advised of the position of other Lincolns and (when possible) of the attacking night fighters.

For the mid-upper gunner it was a particularly uncomfortable task. His seat was a bicycle saddle and a very narrow one at that in the earlier mark of turret. He sat with his legs straddling the ammunition tanks, with feet on the ranging or elevation pedals, and with head and shoulders up in the perspex of the turret, but the rest of his anatomy projecting down into the fuselage was subjected to a continual through draught. Only the inside of the blister was heated and a lot of former mid-upper gunners suffer today from fibrositis.

The mid-upper itself was electrically operated with the current carried on a brass drum on which isolating cut-outs prevented firing into the tail plane, etc, and with electric devices to lift the depressed guns over the fuselage when the turret rotated. When working well, the mid-upper was precise in its action and a pleasure to use, though it tended to be dogged by the inefficient clock-work contrivance which raised the ammo from the tanks to the guns, stripping the links and feeding in each shell singly. The links would come off the belt-feed and cause a jam about which nothing could be done in the air. A certain type of stoppage could cause a lethal explosion in the cannon itself. The cannon were very noisy with ends of breaches right alongside the gunners ears; they also created a lot of smoke which was soon cleared in the continual draught.

Mid-upper turrets were removed from mid-1952 onwards, when it was decided that their weight of almost 1,500lb (including the guns and ammunition) outweighed their efficiency, or otherwise. It was almost equal in weight to a Merlin engine. It is suspected that a number of these turrets were reinstalled in Shackletons as mid-uppers. Their removal from the Lincoln further reduced the need for gunners, immediately halving the number required on Lincolns, leaving the rear turret as the only one manned by an actual air gunner. Most of the mid-upper gunners transferred to the rear turret, which, fortunately for them, was warmer and far more comfortable, though still cramped for the bigger man. It was hydraulically operated with a single control column protruding from the central console. The operation, however, was not as smooth or positive as the mid-upper, and it still had its fair share of jams and blockages. When operating in the UK the rear gunner would usually fly with the heat fully on and the clear vision panel open.

The very last Lincoln air gunners appear to have been those who served with 1426 Flight in Aden until early January 1957.

The 'Erks'

Perhaps at this juncture it is appropriate to include a story from a former Lincoln ground-crew man, Brian P. Dobbins, who, like many, describes himself as 'typical'. There were, of course, many National Servicemen serving on the Lincoln squadrons at the time.

'I served with No 12 Bomber Squadron at Binbrook from November 1949 to April 1951 as an engine mechanic on this fine aircraft.

'12 Squadron, commanded by Squadron Leader A. R. Butcher, was in company with 9, 101 and 617 Squadrons at Binbrook in those days, and I, fresh from eighteen months training as a boy entrant at Weston-super-Mare Technical Training School, was eager to get to my first operational unit and delighted that it was Bomber Command.

'I found the Lincoln to be all that I had been told it was, the king of the big bombers. Standing on the wing ready to receive a refuelling line was like stepping right up to the edge of a precipice and leaning out to grab the line and haul it carefully up until the nozzle appeared and could be taken to a safer point where the fuel tank caps were open. Refuelling a Lincoln, like the Lancaster was a tedious job at a pumping rate of 30 gallons per minute, and in winter the nozzle stuck to your hands if you weren't careful. Replenishing oil for the four Merlin engines was also an awkward operation which entailed standing on a twelve foot ladder and leaning out with the oil can in order to get the stuff into the filler cap. Starting up the engines was a great experience as we had to climb right up onto the undercarriage legs and, when the words "Contact Port Inner" were heard and the great propeller only a few feet in front began turning, we had to prime the fuel system with a Ki-gas pump in order to get the engine to fire, When it did, it seemed that all hell had been let loose and the huge wheel tried to roll forward against the chocks. When that engine was running on all cylinders a flick of the selector switch prepared the Ki-gas

Above: Hinged engine cowlings, here seen on a No 83 Squadron machine (RE415) at Tengah with Sgt D. J. Smith in position, proved an acceptable platform. In hot climates it could be extremely uncomfortable working on the engines and a 'blistered belly' was an occupational hazard. Even if overalls were worn the intense heat from the metal soon burned through to the flesh./*W. C. Sinclair*

Right: Much changed in the world of servicing in the decade after the war. Gone were the once familiar 'personal' ground crews for each aircraft and in their place came centralised servicing. Here RA722, in Germany on a weekend exercise from Lindholme, receives attention in 1958./*C. F. Stevens*

As in the Lancaster each engine could be removed as a complete 'power egg', the Merlin 68, 85 and 102 having the added advantage of being fully interchangeable between engine positions (known as Type MH Universal power plants). The views of engine maintenance in progress on No 15 Squadron Lincolns at Wyton in October 1949 give some idea of the size (and weight – 1,500lb) of a Merlin 68A. Whilst the Lincoln's engines were generally more accessible and easier to service, certain items remained difficult to get at, such as the spark plugs or the inside cylinder block./*Both Ministry of Defence*

pump for the outer engine and the same act was repeated. After the aircrew had carried out ground checks we would stand by the chock-ropes and when the order came, "Chocks Away" we would heave, sweating and cursing until the chock slid out and we could run to the side of the dispersal and watch the kite slowly move forward onto the taxi-track and so onto the runway and eventually into the air.

'One morning, as an engine mechanic with 12 Squadron, I was detailed to carry out before-flight inspections on the starboard engines of one of the squadron aircraft. The bomber was in the hangar at the time and I replenished coolant and oil tanks as necessary, checked everything over meticulously and fastened the cowlings down, finally signing the Form 700. After lunch the aircraft was towed out to dispersal and refuelled for night operations.

'At about nine that evening I was playing snooker in the NAAFI when in rushed one of the night-flying crew to inform me that my aircraft had just had both starboard engines cut dead over Skegness and was returning to base on two; also that the Wing Commander Flying had locked the Form 700 in his safe. I have never been so nervous as I was then and I racked my brains to try and fathom what it was I had done, or not done, to cause such a calamity.

'Next morning at eight I arrived at the hangar to see the aircraft back where it had been the previous day with a fuel-drain barrel in position and all the top brass waiting to see what came out when the fitters turned the fuel cocks on. Almost unbelievably nothing but water came out. The top brass

Until mid-upper turrets were removed crews entered the Lincoln through the nose, in itself an obstacle course with little space to manoeuvre and seemingly endless projections tugging at straps and bags. These comparisons show (*above left*) a seasoned No 138 Squadron crew still wearing battledress as in wartime, emplaning at Wyton in 1948, and (*left*) nervous young hopefuls now dressed in smart grey flying overalls, put on a brave face before boarding a 230 OCU Lincoln at Scampton in July 1952, no doubt including National Servicemen in their number. The flight engineer in the middle is identified by his tool bag. The 230 OCU Lincoln in the background of the second picture is RF347.
/*Syndication International (Odhams); Ministry of Defence*

Above: Detail close up of a 230 OCU Lincoln mainwheel and tyre assembly. Watched by his instructor, Flt Lt Keith Perry, DSO, a pupil checks the valve for tyre creep. Tread was introduced postwar to give added traction in cross winds and slippery conditions. Early machines had to be primed from inside the undercarriage wheel as on wartime Lancs – an uncomfortable task to say the least. Note part/identity numbers on the tyre and chock in true service tradition!
/*Ministry of Defence*

hastily made off next door to the tanker pool to inspect the tanker which had refuelled the starboard tanks. (By the grace of God another tanker had refuelled the port side.)

'The tanker was found to be full of water and a rapid inspection of the bulk fuel installation revealed that huge quantities of sea water were in certain tanks.

'The water had been brought in by the fuel transporting company who in turn had got it from the bulk source. It would appear that no one detected the presence of this water until an aircraft was almost lost through it.

'Meanwhile, on the unit, other aircraft had been refuelled from this contaminated source and no effort was made to cancel operations until the awful truth became apparent later in the morning when engines began coughing and spluttering and one aircraft on take-off run abandoned take-off when almost airborne. The state of affairs became almost desperate and it was said that had it not been for an airframe mechanic over-priming on start-up the bomber would have been just off the deck when the engine failure occurred. Airframe mechanics would often assist in starting engines but would more often than not over-prime the fuel system through lack of experience. Anyway, all flying was cancelled pronto until all planes had been checked and double checked and the con-taminated tankers and tanks purged. The lesson it taught me was that if the tanker driver had carried out his water check he would have discovered it before it got into our aircraft. Later, in 1952 out in Egypt, I remustered to become a driver/mechanic and my first job was on the tanker pool at Kabrit. I never forgot that Binbrook affair and when ever I trained drivers as tanker operators I hammered that lesson home until they were sick of it.

'Another turn of fate occurred to a pilot of 617 Squadron who borrowed one of our Lincolns and had oxygen trouble causing him to collapse at the controls. The bomber fell to two thousand feet before the engineer got it under control. Later, on 18 January 1951 this same pilot, Flight Sergeant Sobszac, [the Lincoln was RA712, "KC:Z" and was on a 3-engine approach] was killed when his Lincoln fell into an air pocket just 100 feet up on his final approach to the runway outside 101's hangar; his tail wheel dropped onto the cockpit of a 9 Squadron Lincoln parked on the ground and this spun the aircraft straight into the hangar doors which were closed. Fortunately for the rest of the crew there was a Lincoln parked outside the hangar facing the doors and so poor old Sobszac pranged right on top of this aircraft after the engineer had cut the throttles, a move which undoubtedly saved the lives of the rest including two radar mechanics working underneath the 101 kite. Fate, it seemed, was determined not to be thwarted.

'I remember that the only evidence left to indicate that two Lincolns had been destroyed were the eight engines complete with twisted propellers which, next morning, were all that remained after the fire which engulfed both aircraft and which, by 10pm that night of the crash had devastated the scene. I arrived shortly after, when the camp cinema show ended. The accident had occurred at about 6.30pm and the fire service had been unable to contain the fire. The hangar had been evacuated with men in all sorts of odd dress man-handling Lincoln aircraft out as there was a grave risk of them being destroyed in the event of explosion.

'I served for twenty years in the RAF ending up at Scampton in 1968 on Blue Steel missiles. Nothing can compare with the sheer magic of four Merlin engines or the sight of a Lincoln (or Lancaster) cleaving the sky in absolute majesty. The Vulcans of Bomber Command may be bigger, better and, of course, faster but . . . the men who worked with Lincolns find on looking back that just as the steam train had a soul as opposed to the modern diesel which has not, the great four-engined Lincoln breathed life as it roared overhead and although now virtually extinct its spirit flies on.

Below: Inside an early production Lincoln looking forward as viewed from inside the rear door. Dominant is the ammunition box for the rear turret, with the twin supply racks running along the roof. Running along the starboard fuselage wall is the hot air supply, suitably lagged, while along the lower port wall are the flying control rods. There are two empty parachute stowage containers, small circular inspection window in rear bulkhead of bomb bay and master compass unit in right hand foreground, beside which, centre foreground is the cover for the H2S Mk 3G./*Avro*

Showing the Flag

The Poor Relations: SAC Bombing Competition 1952

In October 1952 two of Hemswell's Lincolns and crews took part in the annual Strategic Air Command Bombing and Navigation Competition held at Davis-Monthan Air Force Base, Tucson, Arizona, where their hosts were the 63rd Bomb Squadron. The two crews, one from each of the Flare Force squadrons at Hemswell, were selected for their consistently good results, and in particular their performance in the July Lawrence Minot Bombing Competition. Representing 97 Squadron were Sgt K. M. Marwood and crew, comprising Sgt Michael Cawsey (engineer), Flt Lt L. D. (Paddy) Hickey (nav/radar), Flt Lt Denis Moreau (nav/plotter), Sgt Eric Smith (signaller) and

Sgt Peterson (air gunner). They flew their regular Lincoln RA713. The 83 Squadron crew was captained by Sgt John 'Split' Waterman flying RA677, with Sgt Jock Cameron (engineer), Flt Lt McCallum (nav/radar), Flt Lt Bartlett (nav/plotter), Sgt Bernard Steer (signaller) and Sgt McRae (air gunner). The Lincoln detachment commander was the 97 Squadron CO, Sqn Ldr Terry Helfer, and the overall commander of the RAF contingent was Wg Cdr H. N. G. Wheeler, DSO, DFC, AFC, from Marham (later Air Chief Marshal Sir).

Leaving Hemswell on 26 September, the two Lincolns flew first to Marham for special briefing and to link up with the other two participating RAF aircraft and crews, Washingtons, from Marham itself and Coningsby.

Below: RA713 and the two No 15 Squadron Washingtons from the 'rival firm' staging through Keflavik, Iceland on the outward journey, 28 September 1952./*J. W. H. Murdin*

The four aircraft left Marham the next day for Prestwick. For the transit flight the Lincolns carried panniers of spares and supplies in their bomb bays plus 2 x 400gal overload fuel tanks, thus increasing total fuel carried to 3,650 gallons. The tricky part of this installation was that the transfer of the extra fuel from the bomb bay tanks could only start when the wing tanks were getting low, by which time the aircraft were in mid-Atlantic on the crossing to Newfoundland. In the 83 Squadron Lincoln the engineer, Jock Cameron, had problems with the fuel transfer. A valve olive in the joint between auxiliary tanks and main supply had been fitted on the skew and this resulted in most of the contents of one tank being lost overboard, and the Lincoln arriving at Harmon Field desperately low on petrol.

This same machine was to suffer another minor set-back while at Davis-Monthan. During a full ground power run the pannier fell from the bomb bay and, blown back by the propeller slipstream, badly damaged the leading edge of the starboard tailplane. The American ground crewmen immediately set about the repairs; working like Trojans they built a new leading edge from scratch, without drawings, and had it fitted within 48 hours.

The other crew in RA713 also came near to disaster on the Atlantic crossing, and at this juncture, it is appropriate to let Ken Marwood take up the story:

'From Prestwick we flew across the Atlantic via Keflavik to Stephenville, Newfoundland (Ernest Harmon AFB), the two stages being done in one day with some 16 hours in the air, but it was the $10\frac{1}{2}$-hour stage to Newfoundland that was most interesting. From Iceland the first six hours or so were flown at 1,500ft (indicated) on the standard altimeter setting of 1,013 millibars. We had to stay down there to get through a system of fronts, because, unlike the Washingtons, we couldn't fly high enough to get over the top. After about two hours we entered cloud and stayed in it for the next six hours, with only one brief break through which we saw the sea, *very* close. Afterwards we discovered that the barometric pressure at the centre of the depression through which we had flown was only 980mbs which meant that our true height was only 500ft: gave me some idea how Alcock and Brown must have felt!

'From Harmon we flew the next day to Westover AFB, near Springfield Mass, (5hr 20min) and then the following day (30 September) 10 hours direct to Davis-Monthan in clear visual conditions throughout, at no time more than 5,000ft above ground level, a magnificent tour of the USA.

'We spent almost a month in Arizona, but were disappointed with the cowboys: they were all Mexican. We had a very lively social life and established a reputation for ourselves as a singing group. Many of the bars and nightclubs we visited had live music and before long they all used to strike up with "I've Got Sixpence" whenever we walked in. This became our theme song and we really did sing for our supper; we had to do because, with the balance of payments problems which existed even then, we were permitted as NCO aircrew to draw $1.50 per day of our not over generous pay, plus $3 per day in local allowances. We were rather the poor relations and had it not been for the hospitality of the Americans we would have had a dull time.

'Mike Cawsey and I used to have another problem. The minimum age for buying alcohol in Arizona then was 21: Mike was under age, and I was 22 but looked younger than 21, so we used to have a lot of difficulty in persuading them that we should be allowed to buy drinks.

'We did fly as well. We did three practice sorties, bombing at Sathurita Range (Phoenix) on 3 October; a $10\frac{1}{2}$-hour cross-country navex round Kansas and Dallas on the 4th; then finishing with practice bombing at Wilcocks Range on the 7th. Sqn Ldr Helfer flew us back from this one and treated us to a low level tour of the Grand Canyon. We experienced a lot of communications problems. Our VHF radio, newly fitted for the trip, had been borrowed from Oxford aircraft, and it was old Lend-Lease equipment. We caused more breaches of air traffic regulations in a month than most USAF pilots in a lifetime, so many, in fact, that the USAF saw fit to fly some high-ranking air traffic officer 500 miles to Tucson to speak to us.

'The Lincoln itself fascinated the Americans. As one said in Keflavik "You'll never get across the Atlantic in that" But the Americans who flew with us were tremendously impressed with the way in which it could be thrown around in the air, and with the fighter-type approaches we normally flew. It was the sound of the Merlins which usually attracted the most attention. Whenever we were running engines on the ground we always had crowds around, listening to the "music", the distinctive tones of four Merlins running together. We never did tell them they were built by Packard! The Americans also thought we looked much too young to be capable of flying heavy bombers, and they never could quite comprehend how an NCO pilot could captain a crew which included officers.

'On the Competition itself we carried an American major as observer, etc. The route for the bombing and navigation sections was beyond the range of the Lincolns, even with the two extra tanks in the bomb bay (in addition to the two 500lb bombs carried). We

therefore competed only in the bombing itself. Each team consisted of two aircraft and crews, and we each operated three times on alternate nights. The duration of each sortie was between 12 and 13 hours (with only one pilot on board), and we always led the stream, taking off at 9pm. Tucson is in a bowl in the Rockies, 2,500 feet above sea level. The temperatures were in the 90s and we had to orbit for 30 minutes to gain enough height to clear the 15,000-feet mountains all around us. It only took five hours to reach the first target at Kansas City, then a further two and a half hours to the next at Dallas. These were both radar targets and our scores assessed on ground radar were consistent at 250 yards on every run on each of the three nights. These results were quite unprecedented in the UK, but our H2S was so well tuned that it was really like reading from a map. From Dallas another three hour leg to Phoenix for a ground radar-scored simulated visual attack on a drainpipe on the corner of a bank. Finally, another two hours to a desert range near Tucson to drop our two 500 pounders before landing. Our visual bombing results were good, but would have been better had

we been able to calibrate our bombsight after arrival. Had we been able only to equal our average UK visual scores we could have beaten all the USA crews on overall bombing results. As it was we finished first of the RAF crews and fifth overall in the Competition against B-29s, B-50s, and B-36s.

'The homeward journey took three days, routing via Westover (10hr) Goose Bay, Labrador (4hr 20min) then direct to Hemswell (11hr), arriving 24 October. We had flown 120 hours in five weeks and 713's only unserviceability was the autopilot, and that on the final long leg home.

'The trip to the USA was the highlight of my tour. I was very sad when I left 97 Squadron in February 1953 to take a commission. Although I never flew them again other than as a passenger, I have a lasting affection for the Lincoln. It is one of the two aircraft for which I had an immediate affinity as soon as I put my hands on it: the other was the Valiant.'

Ken Marwood left 97 Squadron with an 'Exceptional' rating as a bomber pilot, and was later awarded the Air Force Medal.

Above: At Davis Monthan Air Force Base the No 97 Squadron Lincoln, RA713 is loaded with one of the two 500 pounders to be used in the visual bombing section of the Competition, supervised by crew chiefs Flt Sgt Thomas (No 83 Squadron) and Sgt 'Gillie' Potter (No 97) assisted by USAF groundcrew. Nestling in the back end of the bomb bay above their heads can be seen one of the two 400-gallon auxiliary fuel tanks carried throughout the detachment. /K. M. Marwood

Left: No 100 Squadron was selected to provide one Lincoln and a select crew to accompany the RAF's High Speed Flight to Prague for a special courtesy visit 12-18 September 1946. In overall command was the squadron CO, Wg Cdr Jim Bell, a Canadian in the RAF; the aircraft was captained by Sqn Ldr Dave Bretherton, DFC. Flanked by a Spitfire and a Czech Air Force Pe2 is No 100 Squadron's RE289 'HW:F' (formerly the official Lincoln II prototype) lined up for inspection by the local people. /*D. B. Bretherton*

Centre right: Five weeks after returning from the courtesy visit to Prague, Wg Cdr Jim Bell, CO of No 100 Squadron, was to lead a detachment of three Lincolns to Santiago, Chile. Aircraft and crews were drawn from Nos 100, 83 and 97 (Straits Settlements) Squadrons and left St Mawgan on 27 October 1946, arriving Los Cerrillos, Santiago, on 2 November, for 10 days of local hospitality during which the Lincolns put on several flying displays. Pictured at St Mawgan is No 83 Squadron's RF467 in far from pristine condition, bearing the special codes 'AS' applied to each Lincoln taking part, but changed to 'GB' at the request of the Foreign Office only hours before take-off. The significance of the 'AS' code has not been discovered but the 'GB' presumably signified Great Britain. Detachment commander, Scampton station commander Gr Cpt Peter Lloyd, is thirteenth left; his deputy, and captain of the leading Lincoln (RF463 'GB:A'), Canadian Wg Cdr Jim Bell eleventh left; captain of the 83 Squadron Lincoln (RF467 'GB:B') Flt Lt Freddie Watts, DFC, is far right; Captain of the No 97 Squadron Lincoln (RF468 'GB:C') Flt Lt Derek Shorter, DFC, next to Watts./*G. W. F. Ellis*

Bottom left: It was logical that No 617 Squadron, the Dam Busters, should be called upon to represent the service on a North American tour for which the unit strength was increased to 16 Lincolns and crews, with New Zealander Wg Cdr Cecil Milne, DFC, brought in from No 61 Squadron to command. The tour officially began on 28 July 1947 on arrival at Andrew's Field, Washington, lasting until 2 September when the Lincolns left the USA for a three day visit to Canada, during which displays were flown over the Canadian National Exhibition at Toronto. This photograph shows the welcome by USAF personnel on arrival at Andrew's Field. /ACME/Planet News

Above: A very work-weary RF383 'KC:B' over the barren Rocky Mountains./S. A. Nunns

Right: In October 1947 Binbrook's No 101 Squadron represented the RAF on a goodwill mission to Turkey. Flying direct from the annual Sunray at Shallufa almost resulted in the tour being abandoned due to an outbreak of cholera in Egypt, and on arrival at Etimesgut, near Ankara, the crews were sprayed from head to tow in antiseptic fluid before embarking on a hectic 10-day round of civic functions and flying displays, in which the six Lincolns took part, led by their CO, Sqn Ldr Peter Tunstall. RF512, flown by Flt Lt Pete Langdon, DFM, approaches Etimesgut, 13 October 1947. /J. A. Hemmings

Above: The land of its adoption waited a long time to welcome No 44 (Rhodesia) Squadron, whose six Lincolns arrived at Belvedere, Salisbury, from Wyton on 16 June 1948, led by the CO, Sqn Ldr E. Q. Moody for a 13-day tour codenamed Operation Chessboard. The Lincolns are shown lined-up at Bulawayo, 26 June, with RF419 'KM:H' (Flt Lt Bob Horsley, DFC, and crew) nearest and RF445 'KM:G' (Flt Lt Jack Wheeler, DFC, and crew) next in line. /R. M. Horsley

Sunrays

From mid-1947 onwards, most Lincoln squadrons undertook detachments to Shallufa, continuing the practice established by the Lancaster units, the object being to give all crews some experience of long-range overseas flights and extremes of operating conditions in a foreign country. It also provided the opportunity to continue visual bombing training in clear weather when the British winter could often prevent visual bombing for weeks on end.

The Shallufa detachment was not unpopular with crews; coming as it usually did in mid-winter, it made a welcome break, not only from the weather at home, but also from the somewhat monotonous squadron training routine. The Sunray would usually last a month, and each squadron would go out en bloc. Sometimes a station would send two whole squadrons together.

Departures from base would start at first light, continuing at five minute intervals, the Lincolns flying in a loose stream down over France and the Med to Castel Benito in Libya (taking its name from its builder and founder, Benito Mussolini and later renamed Idris after the King of Libya). Average flight time was eight hours, and the next day, on to Shallufa (6/7hr), midway between Suez and Fayid at the south end of the Bitter Lakes. On occasions, the transit flight from the UK would be made direct to Shallufa for which the Lincolns were fitted with a 400-gallon auxiliary fuel tank in the bomb bay, the trip taking up to 13½hr. Activities during the month at Shallufa would consist of navexs, visual bombing with both live and practice bombs, fighter affiliation. air-to-air firing against drogues towed by Beaufighters and Harvards, and also air-to-ground firing, all culminating in a 'Bullseye' on Khartoum, with one or two aircraft acting as Pathfinders dropping TIs over the range, the rest as Main Force, all landing at Khartoum, about seven hours from Shallufa. After a pleasant two days in Khartoum the crews would depart for Shallufa, with en route fighter affiliation with Meteors or Vampires on the return trip. It was on one such exercise on 11 May 1950 that 148 Squadron's SX957 collided with a Vampire with the loss of all aboard, who included two Air Training Corps cadets.

The weather at Shallufa was in complete contrast to the UK mid-winter variety 120°F, Khartoum even hotter and very sticky. The break was in the main well appreciated. Accommodation at Shallufa was good, and there was an excellent club on the shores of the Bitter Lakes at Fayid for the WOs and SNCOs for whom the 'Stella' beer was always welcome. The detachment would sometimes include a two day visit to another Middle East base such as Cyprus or Habbaniya, which would be used to provide fighter affiliation practice for the local Meteors or Vampires, and on the return journey the Lincoln would act as a raider against the Canal Zone. If a crew was 'well in with the boss' it might even be permitted a weekend Lone Ranger to Malta providing it was done as a night cross country exercise – a 'perk' quite highly sought

Bottom left: Final overseas goodwill tour by a Lincoln unit was a visit to Pakistan by 9 Squadron whose, six Lincolns, led by Sqn Ldr Pete Ostle, arrived at Mauripur on 17 October 1949 direct from a Sunray at Shallufa. During the 12-day stay, the Lincolns took part in fighter and naval affiliation sorties and live bombing practice, during which 4,000lb 'Cookies' were dropped on Churna Island off Karachi the first time that bombs of such capacity had been used in that theatre. It was during these exercises that certain centre of gravity problems were discovered in the new BII/IVA Lincolns, and on return to Binbrook, Flg Off Tony Trowbridge and crew carried out trials to determine handling characteristics. Shown is SX978 'WS:B' at Peshawar on 23 October./*A. P. Trowbridge*

Below: Clear blue sky forms a backcloth to No 7 Squadron's Lincolns lined up at Shallufa in September 1950. Following the example set by No 61 Squadron in 1949 it became the practice for squadrons to fly non-stop to Shallufa, for which the Lincolns were fitted with 400gal auxiliary fuel tanks in the bomb bay. Note elevator and rudder locks in position on RE310 'MG:D'. Temperatures at Shallufa could reach upwards of 120°F in the shade. /*G. R. K. Fletcher*

after when 'The Gut' in Malta still had character and was receiving the full attention of a large Mediterranean Fleet!

On some early Sunrays the Lincolns were called into action from Shallufa to operate against rebels in Aden in support of the ground security forces. 101 Squadron was unexpectedly asked to send several of its Lincolns down to Khormaksar in late October 1947, followed a week or two later by 138 Squadron from Wyton, also out on a Sunray. The operations consisted of a week of live bombing in the Wadi Wahida against the Qutebi Tribe, dropping loads of 14 x 500lb on the rebel positions. Several of the Lincoln crewmen also flew in the locally-based Ansons which dropped warning leaflets the day before the actual bomb drops took place. No 57 from Waddington also took its turn for two weeks in Feb/March 1948 while on a Sunray at Shallufa, again flying down to Aden, this time to chastise Bel Harith tribesmen in the Yemen with 1,000lb bombs and full turret armament.

Right: EII Chatten, a flight engineer, poses in 'well tailored' KD tropical kit at Shallufa, May 1949, in front of the usual clutter of oxygen bottles for topping up oleos, ground starting equipment, etc. In the background stands RF423 'KM:K' of No 44 (Rhodesia) Squadron. The unfamiliar rank EII is a reminder of an unpopular NCO aircrew grading created postwar, with numbers ranging from I to IV preceded by the trade (eg P – pilot, N – nav, S – Sig) within the ranks of cpl/sgt/flt sgt. At the top end of the scale, warrant officers became Master Aircrew, still in use today./*J. A. L. Currie*

Centre left: Over the Suez Delta, No 100 Squadron's RF472 on a practice gunnery sortie during a Sunray. With only one gunner firing sideways a slight yaw occurred; with two firing together the effect was considerable, particularly with the mid-upper in action. In a 45° banked turn positive back pressure was required on the control wheel, while the instrument panel was quite badly affected by 'the shakes'. RF472 was later to be destroyed in a night flying accident at Hemswell./*I. Walker*

Bottom left: A graphic view of the Suez Canal wending its way through an unfriendly expanse of desert, as seen from the tail turret of a No 9 Squadron Lincoln during an annual Sunray detachment, October 1949./*A. P. Trowbridge*

Not all Sunrays were routine or without incident. On 22 October 1948, three Lincolns of the No 9 Squadron detachment were briefed to fly from Shallufa to Khartoum range for a live drop, each aircraft to carry 6 x 1,000lb and a 1 x 4,000lb 'cookie'. Flt Lt Peter Boggis, DFC, (a wartime Stirling pilot) and his crew due to take-off first in RF369 'WS:D' were a little apprehensive as this was the heaviest bomb load yet tried in a hot climate, and the first time a cookie had been included. The dusk take-off was accomplished without incident, and the Lincoln climbed out on course over Suez (six miles or so from the airfield) when at about 2,000ft the crew suddenly saw flak bursting in the evening sky. They could hardly believe their eyes. Someone said 'Christ, skip, they're shooting at us'. Another said 'It'd shake 'em if we dropped this lot on them'. No one knew or could guess why the Egyptians were shooting: possibly to warn the Lincoln away from something. The flak was not too accurate, fortunately, and no evasive action was taken, but nevertheless the crew felt a little

Above: Changing the port undercarriage of No 617 Squadron's RF396, 'KC:G,' at Shallufa, June 1948, showing the special jack in position under the inboard wing section. In the foreground is the replacement oleo leg assembly. Such tasks were usually performed soon after dawn or in the cool of the evening./*J. A. Cook*

Left: Framed by another of the breed is RA665 at rest in front of the old control tower at Castel Benito (later renamed Idris) near Tripoli, Libya, during an annual No 97 (Straits Settlements) Squadron Sunray outing. The two crewmen are a reminder of an era when NCOs formed a large proportion of Bomber Command crews, including in their ranks civilians called up for National Service. /*R. C. H. Poynton*

vulnerable at that height, with the Lincoln still labouring in the climb. A strong sigh of relief was breathed as Suez was finally cleared. The two following Lincolns also got shot at, and whoever was doing the shooting only had heavy ack-ack, as there was no tracer, perhaps just as well.

Some two hours after take-off the Lincolns ran into cu-nim cloud in the dark and experienced a most violent electrical storm, with heavy icing. The storm was so violent that 'George' the autopilot would not stay in, and the wings were seen to be flapping in the most alarming manner. Eventually, the Lincolns battled out of the storm, and at 2300 hours, arrived over the bombing range at Jebel Ba'asham. They were cleared to bomb, and each dropped their 6 x 1,000 pounders in a stick. Then followed the 'cookies' which went off with tremendous flashes.

After landing at Khartoum, almost six hours after take-off, the crews were driven to the RAF mess and were surprised to learn that feeling was running high among the natives: no one had prepared them for the shock of the 'cookies' which must have seemed like the end of the world to them. Because of this hostility, the crews were not allowed into the town for the usual shopping and sightseeing expedition, which was somewhat disappointing after coming all that way. Most of the officers had a high regard for the Sudanese, many of whom were batmen in Egypt, naively imagining that all Sudanese were equally friendly and pro-British. All three crews were pleased to be airborne again for Shallufa a couple of days later.

Whilst the outward journey from the UK to Shallufa was nearly always routine, the return flights often seemed to run into trouble. Departures from Shallufa were early – 0600, in the cool of the morning, the best time for the Lincolns heavily laden with fuel, panniers of spares, duty free, etc. The overnight stop was again at Castel Benito. It was from there on the final long haul to the UK that the Lincolns almost inevitably ran into adverse winter weather, with severe storms, icing and turbulence. Strong N – S headwinds over France could stretch the flight time to 11½hr resulting in tired, cold crews arriving back at base for a night landing, low on fuel, and sometimes with the prospect of having to divert at the last minute due to fog. Several Lincolns were lost on these transit flights, due to icing and in one case after being struck by lightning.

On 30 April 1948 No 9 Squadron's eight Lincolns were homeward bound from a Sunray and ran into very bad weather over southern France, flying into severe turbulence and icing conditions. Two of the Lincolns got into very heavy cu-nim. cloud: one, RF474 'WS:C' failed to make it and crashed: the other, RE305 'WS:F', in the same cloud, lost several thousand feet before the pilot regained control, and turned back to Istres (Marseilles) where it made a forced landing. After heavy repairs which took several weeks, 305 was flown back to Binbrook for major overhaul, becoming the first Lincoln on the station to be turned out in the new black/grey colour scheme, in 617 squadron's markings.

The Shallufa detachments continued until 1953, though with decreasing regularity, as from the early 1950s, the political situation in the Middle East was deteriorating, and the squadrons were becoming increasingly preoccupied with other duties such as Malaya, Kenya and Aden. In the latter days, the Sunrays appear to have been used as a flag showing exercise prior to the British withdrawal from the Canal Zone.

Below: Leaflet issued to aircrew on detachment to or staging through Egypt and the Middle East (eg on Sunrays); commonly known as a 'Goolie Chit'.
/*Loaned by Sqn Ldr G. M. Bailey, AFC*

الحكومة البريطانية **BRITISH GOVERNMENT**

الى كل عربى كريم

To All Arab Peoples — Greetings and Peace be upon you. The bearer of this letter is an Officer of the British Government and a Friend of all Arabs. Treat him well, guard him from harm, give him food and drink, help him to return to the nearest British soldiers and you will be rewarded. Peace and the Mercy of God upon you.

The British High Command in the East.

SOME POINTS ON CONDUCT WHEN MEETING THE ARABS IN THE DESERT.

Remove footwear on entering their tents. Completely ignore their women. If thirsty drink the water they offer, but DO NOT fill your waterbottle from their personal supply. Go to their well and fetch what you want. Never neglect any puddle or other water supply for topping up your bottle. Use the Halazone included in your Aid Box. Do not expect breakfast, if you sleep the night. Arabs will give you a mid-day or evening meal. Always be courteous.

REMEMBER, NEVER TRY AND HURRY IN THE DESERT, SLOW AND SURE DOES IT.

A few useful words.			
Euglish	**Arabic**	**English**	**Arabic**
English	Ingleezi	Day	Yome
American	Amerikani	Night	Layl
Friend	Sa-hib, Sa-deck	Half	Nuss
Water	Moya	Half a day	Nuss il Yome
Food	Akl or Mungarea	Near	Gareeb
Village	Balaad	Far	Baeed
Tired	Ta-eban		
Take me to the English and you will be rewarded.		Hud nee eind el Ingleez wa tahud Mu-ka-fa.	
	English Flying Officer.	Zabit Ingleezi Tye-yara.	
	How far (how many kilos?).	Kam kilo ?	
	Enemy.	Germani, Taliani, Siziliani.	

Distance and time: Remember, Slow & Sure does it.

The older Arabs cannot read, write or tell the time. They measure distance by the number of days journey. "Near" may mean 10 minutes or 10 hours. Far probably means over a days journey. A days journey is probably about 30 miles. The younger Arabs are more accurate.
GOOD LUCK.

5581/PMEB-4/43

Special Duties and Odd Jobs

Radar Reconnaissance Flight

Generally known as Radar Recce Flight the RRF was a small unit formed to provide a library of target information for the new V-Force, and to continue the development of radar for general reconnaissance, though it had no operational reconnaissance role as such.

Its origins lay in No 58 Squadron at Benson, which from late 1950 had operated two Lincolns – SX991 'OT:C' and RF331 'OT:B' – alongside a Mosquito on H2S and F24 photography trials. It was decided to exploit the apparent potential of H2S photography for reconnaissance purposes and to bring radar recce up to the same standard as photo recce; so on 2 October 1951, Radar Reconnaissance Flight was formed, its nucleus being the two 58 Squadron Lincolns and their crews. Its CO was a newly promoted Sqn Ldr, Ron C. Instrell, DFC, a wartime navigator in Bomber Command.

Sqn Ldr Instrell was to prove the driving force behind the development work of the next few years, during which tremendous strides were made. He had already displayed his practical prowess with radar when, after completing the Weapons Course at Manby, he had been posted to Wyton as Senior Weapons Officer in mid-1951. There he teamed up with Sqn Ldr. A. R. (Sandy) Galbraith, DFC, Senior Navigation Officer at Wyton, and together they had the idea of fixing up a blind bombing system based on the H2S Mark 3G (with Bomber Command's blessing provided it was on a spare time basis). A flight sergeant with an engineering degree manufactured the mechanical device which was based on a modified SABS computer. After successful trials on the station static bombing trainer in one of the buildings it was fitted to a Lincoln without the authority of any senior officers, who did not seem to be too interested in what was going on in any case. Trials on Donna Nook range were encouraging and so impressed Sir Hugh P. Lloyd at Bomber Command, that he personally gave the go ahead for the allocation of a Lincoln for further trials. RE369(H) was the first with H2S Mark 3G, followed soon afterwards by RF347(Y) with the Mark 4A. The blind bombing trials using the new electro/mechanical device were highly promising, with average errors from 15,000ft of 375 yards on the 3G and 480 yards on the 4A (odd, as the 3G was considered so inferior). Thus was born the tachometric blind bombsight, later known as TBS and widely used by specialist units such as BTU and RAE after further development.

Soon after completion of the trials in June 1951, Instrell (then a flight lieutenant) was posted to Waddington as No 1 Group Senior Weapons Officer, the sudden promotion to squadron leader only a few months later and posting to Benson coming as a complete surprise. Included in the takeover of the two Lincolns from 58 Squadron were 10 aircrew and a ground crew chief, a prewar type who had little time for new fangled ideas like H2S, but who was a genius at keeping Lincolns serviceable. The two pilots were Sgt Gill and Flt Lt G. F. Cruickshank, a huge, rugby-playing 6ft 4in New Zealander, known as 'Garth' after a well known cartoon character of the time, and with hands so huge they virtually covered the whole of the Lincoln's control wheel. The two Lincolns continued on the H2S photography development work with some help from the boffins at Defford, and there were numerous weekend trips to Germany on radar sorties (the opportunity to load up with cut-price liquid refreshment never being missed).

On the night of 20 December 1951, Gill had an unfortunate accident in SX991. A special duty had been ordered by no less a person than Winston Churchill himself, the Prime Minister at that time. Details must still remain secret, but due to its extreme importance, Gill had taken off in the worst possible weather, so bad, it would have prevented all normal flying. On return to Benson shortly before 11pm Gill joined downwind in thick fog, but before turning finals, one wheel had touched the top of a 1,000-foot high hill on Christmas Common, near Nettlebed, slewing the Lincoln round, and collapsing the undercarriage. It then slid backwards down the hill for a $\frac{1}{4}$ mile, through some trees which tore off both wings at the root (preventing fire), finally coming to rest

with the tail end broken off aft of the main spar. Incredibly, the crew were unhurt after this 120mph 'prang' but on jumping to the ground the wireless op. ricked his ankle. Then, blowing their whistles in the fog, the crew found a farm and with the aid of the farmer's home-made grog were well away by the time the rescue party arrived.

Facilities at Benson were not entirely satisfactory and on 27 March 1952, the unit moved to Upwood, lock, stock and barrel. Shortly after the move, Cruickshank left to return to New Zealand to be replaced as flight commander by Flt Lt Bob Tate. Gill was posted away on promotion and replaced by Flt Sgt Emmanuel and crew from 49 Squadron at Upwood, bringing SS716, their regular Lincoln, with them. The crew had been engaged since June 1951 on trials with map-matching overlays produced from H2S photographs using the techniques pioneered by 58 Squadron. It was thought appropriate this task should be incorporated in the work of the new RRF set up and was to form an important part of its function for the next year or two.

Emmanuel's navigator, Flt Lt Les Spink was one of several 'above average' operators entrusted with the task of producing the transparent overlays for use by squadron navigators. The RRF Lincolns would fly all over the UK and many parts of Europe, particularly Germany, while their highly qualified navigators photographed 'targets' on the H2S radar screens. It required great accuracy, as it was from these pictures that the overlays were produced by WAAF personnel, often working on a 24-hour shift basis, eventually building up a library of target information for the forthcoming jet-

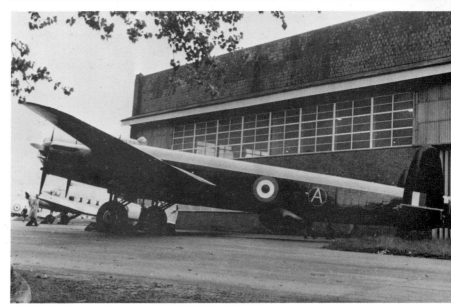

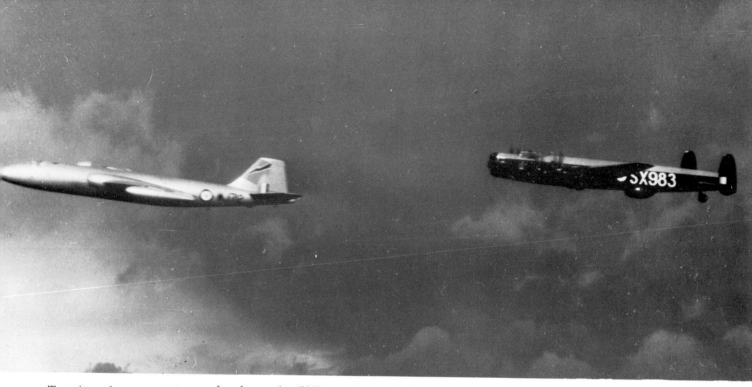

Two views of non-standard Radar Recce Flight Lincolns, appearing almost anonymous in standard dressing. *Centre left:* RE319 waddling round the perimeter track at Wyton, Hunts 1955 with two eagle-eyed military policemen patrolling the boundary fence in the background. *Bottom left:* RF576 at the College of Aeronautics Cranfield, Beds, early in 1956, shortly after retirement from RRF, where she had been latterly for air-to-sea homing missile trials. Though the unit's Canberras sported a green fin flash, the Lincolns carried no unit identification. Spinners were usually grey. */R. C. B. Ashworth; R. C. B. Ashworth Collection*

Above: A classic study in atmosphere is this view of RRF's Blue Shadow Canberra WJ712 (pilot: Flt Lt John Sexton; navigator: Flt Lt Harry Shaw) and Lincoln SX983 (pilot: Flt Lt Roy Matthews; navigator: Flt Lt Dave Mills) in the circuit at Wyton in November 1956. From a series of pictures taken that day one was selected to illustrate the station's 1956 Christmas card. Worthy of mention is the Canberra's green fin flash, and ops score on the nose of the Lincoln, a left-over from service with 148 Squadron in Malaya./*H. J. Shaw*

bombers, the V-Force in particular. The overlays were used by main force or squadron navigators who placed them on their own radar tubes for target identification and pin-pointing, thus ensuring greater accuracy. Eventually this task was taken over by Hastings and Varsities from Defford; they had fuselages spacious enough to incorporate not only the target photography equipment, but also a processing unit, enabling the overlays to be produced by the time the aircraft had landed back at base.

Alongside this work the Lincolns and their crews carried on the development of Sqn Ldr Instrell's side-scan radar ideas. He had conceived the idea of holding the H2S Mark 4A aerial sideways at right-angles to the Lincoln's fuselage and then running a film across the face of the display tube at a speed equivalent to the ground speed of the aircraft. By this means it was possible by the striations across the film to paint a picture of the ground below. Following some spectacular results obtained over Beaulieu airfield by Emmanuel and Spink in RF331, Instrell was ordered to push ahead at all speed and was given carte blanche on any equipment needed.

The unit expanded rapidly, more crews and specialists were posted in, and the Lincoln complement was increased to four aircraft. On 15 July 1953 came another move, this time to Wyton, which was to remain RRF's permanent base. Among those posted in was Flt Lt Ken Letford, DSO, DFC, a former wartime Hampden and Lancaster pilot who had done 96 ops, and who had won a Bar to his DFC when, flying a Sunderland, he had escorted HMS Amethyst down the Yangtse river in April 1949. He was later to return to fly the Valiants which eventually took over

the radar recce work, and later still, he was to transfer to 543 Squadron which, flying Victors, was set up to undertake the radar recce role. Letford and Tate left RRF in 1955. Tate was replaced as flight commander by Flt Lt Noel Ashcroft, and two more very experienced Lincoln men had by then been posted in: Flt Lt Steve Nunns, DFC, and Flt Lt Roy Matthews, bringing their crews with them from their former squadron, No 214 which had disbanded at Upwood on the last day of 1954.

Before RRF had left Upwood the first Canberras had arrived. English Electric were closely involved and Flt Lt John Sexton had been brought in as the first of several pilots to fly them. RRF was given the job of keeping its two Canberras in the air for 22 hours a day on engine and systems proving for a whole month. One was fitted with the (then) top secret radar 'Blue Shadow' of which only one set was available and in which Ron Instrell had a hand with TRE on its design and development. Later were to come other names such as 'Sky Shadow' and the side-scanning 'Green Cheese' and on whose trials Lincoln RA656 was used in 1954. At one point, RRF was scheduled to become 138 Squadron and was actually allotted the Squadron silver etc, before the order was cancelled.

The Lincolns and Canberras operated alongside each other on different aspects of the side-scan radar development. There were thousands of flying hours and much hard work expended on the perfection of Sqn Ldr Instrell's ideas. To further develop the potential of radar photography he had also devised improved systems of photography, film cutting, etc, and of taking pictures at different angles and intensities to overcome

H2S tube light intensity problems. The systems were eventually linked to Instrell's own tachometric bombing ideas and were brought to such a degree of perfection that from low level radar side-scan pictures, it became possible to build up accurate models of ground objects such as power stations, ships, etc, and even to identify different types of aircraft at dispersals. The radar pictures and maps became virtually as good as visual photos.

RRF aircraft performed other duties such as a special Lincoln sortie flown by Flt Lt Tim Bradbury on 30 June 1954 taking a party of scientists from the Royal Observatory up to the north of Scotland to photograph an eclipse of the sun. In October 1953 RRF also covered the England to New Zealand air race which was won by a Canberra (not from RRF) flown by one of the unit's own crews, Flt Lt R. L. Burton, with Flt Lt D. H. Gannon as navigator. It was also engaged in the training of USAF personnel as radar photo interpreters.

Other research undertaken by the Lincolns was into the effect of snow on H2S returns, involving a lot of flying over the Continent and far north of Scotland during the winter of 1955 to photograph by radar terrain under different depths of snow. A considerable amount of flying was also done by the Lincolns on research into ship measurement and identification by radar (A-scope trials). These involved not only RN vessels, but also, in July 1956, the *Queen Elizabeth*, the latter unfortunately without prior arrangement, which caused a few red faces in higher

Bottom left: RF562 'SN:N' of 230 OCU Scampton at Farnborough during the Royal Air Force Display, 7-8 July 1950. Sole survivor of a once large number of heavy conversion units, 230 OCU was based at Scampton from February 1949, with Lincolns supplanting Lancasters. Soon after a move to Upwood on 15 April 1952, the OCU split into separate entities due to a falling demand for Lincoln crews as a result of rapid re-equipment with Canberras. A Lincoln conversion flight was set up at Waddington to cater for No 1 Group's needs, while Upwood housed the equivalent for No 3 Group, until the emergencies in Malaya and Kenya gave the Lincoln a new lease of life. Consequently, 230 OCU was reformed at Upwood on 1 August 1953 by amalgamating the two flights, and remained in being until the crisis was over./*A. J. Jackson*

Above: Debden housed a number of less glamorous but none-the-less important back up units, one of which was the Armament Division of Technical Training Command who operated three Lincoln 'flying classrooms' from August 1950. Pictured are RF443 'S:F' and RE416 'S:G' snapped at Debden in September 1953 and bearing the new style coding (in white) introduced a year earlier, replacing the three letter system (TDE in this case) applied soon after the war. /*C. Davies*

authority as the passengers and crews were somewhat alarmed by the sight and sound of a large, black, 4-engined bomber keeping station at low level.

In July 1955 one of the flight's Lincolns, RF576, was specially adapted for air-to-sea guided weapon trials with HMS *Cumberland*, both the Lincoln and the ship operating out of Malta for some weeks in company with a team of civilian scientists from EMI. The centre-front glass panel of the Lincoln's bomb aimer's nose was replaced by a metal plate carrying a special homing aerial. During the Malta detachment, Vesuvius erupted and Flt Lt Roy Matthews and crew were detailed to fly as close to the crater as was possible to photograph the rather awesome sight. Shortly after this exercise, in November 1955, RF576 was flown to the College of Aeronautics, at Cranfield, by Flt Lt Matthews, where it was used by Fairey Aviation on further trials. SX983, an ex-148 Squadron Lincoln, still wearing her Malayan ops tally on the nose, was collected from Upwood as a replacement.

For the varied tasks some highly specialised radar operators were carried, these including civilians at times. The Lincoln crews needed to fly to the highest standards of accuracy, often with no tolerance whatever on headings. The Lincolns were fitted with the early type of Decca navigation equipment, with the arrowhead aerial mounted at the rear end of the bomb bay doors.

Of the Lincolns, SS716 was flown into retirement at 15 MU Wroughton, by Bob Tate on 12 January 1954; RF331, one of the

two originals inherited from 58 Squadron left in May 1956 to be put into retirement at 38 MU, with SX983 and RE319 continuing until August 1957, RE319 being the last of all to leave for Hullavington on 25 August. Soon after withdrawal of the last Lincolns, No 543 Squadron using Valiants, and still based at Wyton, took over the work.

Ron Instrell himself became so deeply involved in the development work that he was frequently away for a month at a time without apparent authority or prior warning, usually flying with the Americans from Sculthorpe in RB-45s on top secret 'one way' missions, in company with Bomber Command's Chief Scientific Officer. On returning from one prolonged absence he was placed under arrest for a day by the station commander who knew nothing of the very secret nature of the Sqn Ldr's work! After a visit by the station, commander to Bomber Command HQ however, Sqn Ldr Instrell was not only quickly released, but was provided with a staff car and driver to facilitate his duties. He was also often away flying in American RB-36Fs from Fairford (Glos).

On the 5 September 1955, he handed over command of RRF to Sqn Ldr Peter A. H. McKeand, DSO, DFC, AFC, and went to Wright Patterson AFB in the USA on exchange posting, doing a lot more flying with the Americans in B-47s and B-66s before eventually returning to join the staff of the Royal Radar Establishment at Malvern, where his genius was put to continued good use.

The MIG Incident (CGS)

On Thursday 12 March 1953, two routine NATO liaison sorties were scheduled for the Lincolns of CGS Leconfield. These regular fortnightly training flights over Europe provided radar tracking and fighter affiliation practice for both the RAF and other Allied forces, and a reasonable simulation of a 6/7-hour operational sortie at high level for the Lincoln crews, in particular the trainee gunners on the senior course. A crew of seven would normally be carried: staff pilot, engineer, navigator and signaller, plus gunnery instructor and two trainees.

The first Lincoln, 'H' (RF503), captained by Flt Sgt Denham got away on time at 0900 with the CO of the Free Gunnery School, Sqn Ldr F. E. Doran, in the mid-upper turret. By the time the Lincoln crossed the German border at 22,000 feet it had already been 'attacked' several times by friendly fighters such as Dutch Air Force Thunderjets, Belgian Meteors and RAF 2nd TAF Vampires. It was nearing Kassel (well inside the British Zone) when suddenly two swept-wing MIG 15s appeared close on the port beam, no more than 100 yards away, having climbed up unseen from directly below – the Lincoln's blind spot.

After taking a close look they peeled off and executed some menacing high quarter approaches as if to attack. They did not open fire, neither did the Lincoln crew, of course, but the gunners recorded it all on their cine cameras linked to the guns. The Lincoln was turned abuptly from its northerly heading on to west just in case its position in relation to the Russian Zone border could be questioned. It returned to Leconfield without further incident, its crew knowing nothing of what was happening in their wake.

The following Lincoln, some two hours behind, was RF531 'C-Charlie', captained by Flt Sgt T. J. Dunnell. Acting as second pilot was Sqn Ldr H. J. Fitz who had taken over the command of No 3 Squadron (Lincolns) only a few days previously, and who was using the trip for familiarization.

At 1.20pm GMT, 'C-Charlie' was entering the 20-mile wide corridor from Hamburg to Berlin at about 10,000 feet when it was attacked without warning by MIG 15s which opened fire with their cannons from point blank range on the unsuspecting crew. The Lincoln went into a steep dive, followed down by its attackers, still firing. The Lincoln's starboard wing caught fire and the bomber broke up in mid-air. The main part of the wreckage plummetted to earth with four of the crew still inside, crashing into a wood near Bolzenburg, three miles inside the Russian Zone; the remainder fell on the British side, near Bleckede only 15 miles SE of Hamburg on the edge of Luneburg Heath.

Three of the crew managed to get out of the doomed Lincoln, but one parachute failed to open and the two who landed (one in the British Zone) both died of wounds and injuries soon afterwards. German eye witness reports seem to confirm that the attacks were made by two pairs of MIGs, and suggest that one of the fighters also attacked the descending parachutists, which would explain certain features of the medical reports.

Whilst the Lincoln had undoubtedly strayed close to, and perhaps even slightly over the Zone border, the aircraft was flying to a well established pattern which must have been as familiar to the Russians as to NATO and the RAF. In the House of Commons the Prime Minister, Mr Winston Churchill, described the incident as a 'wanton attack'.

Below: The Central Gunnery School, reorganised postwar and based at Leconfield, was responsible for the training of all air gunners in the RAF. Ironically it was a CGS Lincoln which was to fall to the guns of Russian MIG-15s on 12 March 1953. The ill-fated machine, RF531 'C' (not RF345 as previously reported) is seen here in more pleasant circumstances at Leconfield, August/September 1952. CGS became the Fighter Weapons School on 30 November 1954, though a small free-gunnery element remained for a while, entitled the Coastal Command Gunnery School, which moved to Kinloss February/March 1955 to cater for Shackleton crews. */N. Franklin*

Quite predictably the Russians answered the strong notes of protest by claiming the Lincoln crew had fired first, but the House was told that on such training flights, the belt mechanisms were removed from the cannons in the mid-upper, and the rear turret carried guns but no ammunition. The Russians did express regret over the loss of life of the seven crew and they returned the bodies and wreckage to RAF Celle shortly after the incident.

A week previously a USAF F-84G Thunderjet had been shot down; fortunately its pilot ejected safely. Shortly afterwards a BEA Viking was fired at by MIGs while on a scheduled flight in the Berlin Air Corridor; and two weeks later, MIGs also attacked an American B-50 on a routine met flight. This time, the B-50 fired back, without damage, but the MIGs sheered off. For several weeks, all NATO aircraft were on a fully-armed 'fire back' basis, including the Lincoln squadrons at Upwood which went onto an armed standby immediately following the shooting down of the Lincoln. For a few days, the situation looked highly dangerous, but the advent of the East Coast floods rather cooled the ardour of the Lincoln crews who were taken off standby to fill sandbags, and gradually the heat was taken out of the situation.

Flight Refuelling: The U5 Programme

The company was involved in two interesting Lincoln projects: conversion for use as airborne refuelling tankers, and as pilotless drones or target aircraft.

Flight Refuelling had successfully converted some Meteor 4s to Mark 15 drones and the MOD had sent a Lancaster to Tarrant Rushton to be 'droned' as a target aircraft development project, but this had to be abandoned after an over-enthusiastic electronics engineer had cut through the main wiring loom in the rear fuselage in a vain attempt to locate a wire to pick up a circuit. A Lincoln, RF358, was delivered in its place and from February 1954 undertook certain preliminary trials in conjunction with RAE Farnborough. Results were encouraging and the company was given a contract to convert two prototypes to the drone configuration, to be followed if successful by a contract to Avro's to convert 20 Lincoln B2 3Gs to pilotless drone targets. Designated U5, they were to be capable of normal flight with standard crew (minus gunners) plus 'remote controlled crewless flight covering both in sight and out-of-sight conditions'. Performance was to be standard Lincoln in all respects with the remote control to be capable of all normal phases of flight, including landings and take-offs, and operation of brakes, flaps and undercarriage. Certain safety devices incorporated an instantaneous pilot-controlled override cut out and a self destruction system which would enable an unmanned Lincoln to be 'grounded' within 1,000 feet horizontally for each 1,000 feet of height. At each wing tip was to be mounted a cluster of five cameras to record behaviour of the Lincoln, and of the missile in the final approach phase.

Two Lincolns were flown to Tarrant Rushton from Langar to serve as trials prototypes; RF395 on 10 March 1955 and RE366 on 27 May. The various modifications and installations of equipment were made on RF395 and it was first flown as a 'drone' on 29 February 1956. It flew intensively, as many as seven and eight flights daily, mostly captained by Pat Hornidge, flying with finger poised on the 'disconnect' button when it did

Below: RA657 was loaned to Flight Refuelling in September 1949 for continued development trials of the company's 'Probe and Drogue' system and during 1950 was directly involved in the record-breaking first non-stop east-west jet crossing of the Atlantic by the USAF on 22 September. Photo shows the Lincoln refuelling one of the two F-84s used in the successful record attempt, flown by Colonels Dave Schilling and Bill Ritchie, the Lincoln flown on this occasion by Pat Hornidge. The record-breaking flight was fully reported in *Flight* of 7 December 1951. RA657 was next engaged in refuelling trials with the prototype Comet G-ALVG, five contacts being made in December 1950; then the following April came RAF trials from Horsham St Faith with the Meteors of 245 Squadron, before 657 was converted back to B2 standard and posted to 199 Squadron at Hemswell. /*Charles E. Brown*

its first remotely controlled touchdown on 10 May 1956, the first of three successful such landings that day.

The remote control panels were operated from a van at the far end of the runway from touchdown, and when these landings were first tried, the Lincoln just fell out of the sky as finals were selected, hitting the runway with a bone shattering crunch, with the pilot taking over immediate manual control to initiate an overshoot off the resulting bounce. The disconnect button failed to work on some occasions, always at the most critical moments. The drone Lincoln never flew without a pilot and flight engineer in their places monitoring the controls. As a research vehicle, the Lincoln had distinct advantages over the Meteor for crew observation purposes. Whereas in the Meteor no adjustments to the auto-pilot and servo-motor controls could be made in flight, this could all be done in the relatively roomy fuselage of the Lincoln, thus saving many hours of flight testing.

There were incidents during these trials which caused a mixture of amusement, apprehension and even horror. The throttle and propellor controls had been subcontracted, and the same ultra-enthusiastic engineer who had grounded the Lancaster was in charge of this side of the development. He had wired up a remote control rig at the navigator's table to simulate the ground remote control panel. Unfortunately he had no previous flying experience and on a number of occasions during early flights, caused near heart failure among the rest of the crew by suddenly closing all four throttles together or changing the pitch of the props without warning.

Though there were problems with engine synchronisation, wing flexing, and vibration effect on the cameras, the flight trials conducted by the company continued intensively during 1956 and appear to have been reasonably successful. For some reason, however, towards the end of 1956 the project was suddenly abandoned and at Tarrant Rushton work turned instead to conversion of later marks of Meteors to drones.

After the apparent success of the early trials with RF358, and well after work had started on the modifications to RF395, a specification had been prepared by RAE and issued by MOS on 9 December 1955, only two months before 395 took to the air in its modified form. It seems that on the strength of this specification and in anticipation of an actual contract, Avro's went ahead and did a lot of work on the 20 Lincolns which were already available at Langar, and had been earmarked for the U5 programme. Some of these machines had been flown in specially, others had languished round the dispersals at Langar for some years after withdrawal from squadron service. In the event, no actual contract appears to have been placed, and the cancellation of the project was something of a shock. The U5s had, apparently, been destined for delivery to Woomera.

Most of the Langar Lincolns were later scrapped where they stood, though three gained a temporary reprieve as potential meat freighters, a project described in another chapter. The two prototypes, RF395 and RE366 (which does not appear to have flown at all in the drone trials) were both broken up.

Bombing Trials Unit

The Bombing Trials Unit used Lincolns for over 10 years at West Freugh in remote Wigtownshire. Normal strength was three machines, more-or-less standard but with all turrets and surplus equipment removed to achieve maximum height and payload. *Top:* RF340 'BTU:B' being refuelled at one of West Freugh's grass dispersals, while (*above*) a later 'BTU:B', SX930 visiting Bovingdon on 7 October 1957. Codes (the unit's initials) were yellow and carried for a number of years.

BTU had formed at West Freugh in 1946, Lincolns replacing Lancasters mid-1948. A small but highly specialized outfit, its main function was to offer, on behalf of the Department of Armaments, Research & Development, MoS, facilities for testing airborne weapons, weapons systems and delivery techniques, for which it had the use of the whole of Luce Bay, plus adjoining areas Torrs Warren and Braid Fell. Much of its monitoring gear, theodolites, high speed cameras, etc, were supplied by RAE who actually took over the station and responsibility for BTU in 1957. Much of the VT (proximity) fuse testing took place at BTU; other trials work included lethality, off-set bombs, cluster bombs and a wide variety of 'stores', using both the standard mk XIV and Tachometric bombsights. The stability, reliability and general performance of the Lincoln made it the ideal workhorse until greater height and speed requirements rendered them obsolete. The unit's last three Lincolns were not broken up at West Freugh until 1961./*L. F. Compton; A. Pearcy*

Farnborough

research and experimental weapons. Stability trials were carried out by using skewed bomb racks, which could carry the bomb at an angle to the line of flight and cause oscillations at release. These racks, designed and made by Vickers, were adjustable to various angles. In the case of light bombs, adhesive tapes attached to the fins achieved a similar effect.

The RAE aircraft were also used by A&AEE Boscombe Down on occasions, and RAE sometimes borrowed Lincolns from ETPS (based at Farnborough) for routine and crew-training purposes. Even Porton Down, the Chemical and Biological Research Establishment, had the use of an RAE Lincoln for certain secret germ and biological trials, and soil fertilization experiments.

The Lancasters and Lincolns were the true workhorses of the Royal Aircraft Establishment in the postwar years, the Lincolns until the late 1950s/early 1960s. Their ruggedness and stability was to prove invaluable in the development of not only new weapons, but also of flying aids and techniques.

From 1947 Farnborough acquired a small fleet of three or four Lincolns for general trials work, mainly to do with weapons systems, radar development, and bomb ballistics. They were usually new machines, destined to spend their whole working lives on trials, and were not RAF machines, but transferred to and operated on behalf of the Ministry of Supply. Farnborough had its own nucleus of select pilots and crews, mainly RAF, but some Naval and some civilian.

Much of the work at Farnborough centred round bomb ballistics trials from the earliest days of the Lincoln, and in 1948 and 1949 respectively, RF394 and RF368, using the SABS were involved in dropping trials of a highly secret, rocket assisted bomb, similar to a Tallboy, on the old U-boat pens at Farge (Bremen), to test qualities of penetration on the 30-foot thick concrete roofs. For trial drops of the early nuclear stores from the required altitude, Armament and Guided Weapons Flight acquired RA633 and RF561 from BBU and TFU respectively. These were stripped-down for high-altitude dropping of special 'stores' as the trial bombs were referred to. Both 633 and 561 were fitted with Merlin 114 engines, and reached 42,000ft on some of the trial drops over Cardigan Bay. These and other Lincolns involved in the really top secret ballistics trials were kept in a special compound at Farnborough, guarded day and night, with only certain cleared crew members allowed near them.

Many odd and unusual loads were carried and dropped by the Farnborough Lincolns – Bloodhounds, Thunderbolts, Skylarks. All these rockets were at one time or another dropped to check various operations and to develop parachute recovery systems for

Below: RF533 had a long trials career. Originally delivered to TFU Defford in 1948, she passed to RAE scheduled for weather research, but when the project was cancelled it was adapted for airborne interception (AI) work, and fitted with adapter plates to take all known radomes for testing fighter radars. Due to various unforeseen factors, 533 was not delivered until May 1954, too late to be used, but was instead sent to Farnborough's Armament Department. Here it was used on Black Knight missile nose cone recovery trials and general AI work until transfer in Nov 1955 to Structures and Mechanical Engineering Department for parachute R&D flight trials. From then on it was used mainly for parachute towing trials for approval and testing of brake and anti-spin parachutes, man-carrying parachutes, mine and torpedo parachutes, ejector seat parachutes and the 21ft ring slot extractor parachute for pulling loads from the Beverley. It was also used for research into snatch and breakage trials on parachute towing strops. Banner targets were also towed. Test parachutes were despatched from an aperture in the rear turret and towed on 40 foot long strops fitted with a strain-gauged tension link to enable the load to be displayed and recorded by photographing an oscilloscope. Ciné photography recorded the behaviour of the parachute and other cameras recorded the airspeed, height and temperature. (A temperature of —36°C was once recorded in the rear turret at 25,000ft. The parachute was released by cutting through the strop with a long knife on a pole passed through the aperture in the rear turret.

A total of 1,207 parachutes was tested by this aircraft during its stay at RAE (444 flights lasting 273 hours). Another interesting role was the use made of it for the film *The Guns of Navarone*, in which the sound of the plane taking off and landing was heard. Its final operational sortie at RAE was on 21 April 1961, by when it had flown 950 hours (650 at RAE itself). On 27 June 1961 it was flown to Stanstead for use by the Fire Fighting School. /*Royal Aircraft Establishment*

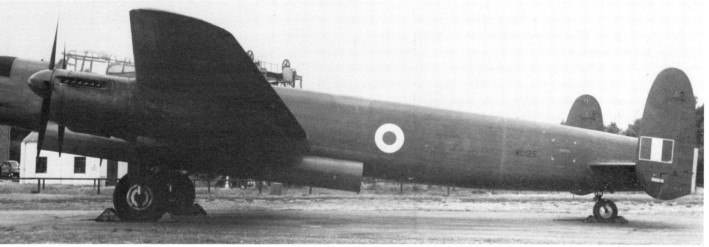

Top: SX974 was employed by RAE on high altitude day and night photography. Specially lightened and streamlined, with cut-away bomb bay, and fitted with Merlin 113s (as in postwar high altitude Mosquitos) heights up to 41,000ft were achieved. To overcome lack of pressurisation crews wore pressure waistcoats. This picture was taken at lower level over southern England with Sqn Ldr Leo De Vigne, DSO, DFC, at the controls. In late 1950, 974 paid a two-week visit to Australia for a series of special missile photographic sorties from Woomera.

Having been with RAE from December 1948, SX974 reverted to standard B2 configuration in March 1954 before allocation to 7 Squadron. Passing to 49 Squadron she was again involved in experimental duties in June 1954 when Flt Lt Jack Higginbottom and crew took a party of scientists from Cambridge to observe and photograph an eclipse of the sun from high altitude. A specially heated box was installed for carrying the cameras./*A. Ashworth*

Above: Seen at Farnborough in July 1955 is the all red WD125, one of two standard Lincolns delivered new in July 1950 to Armament Flight, RAE. As she was involved in dropping highly secret 'loads', a high visibility finish was necessary for identification by other aircraft and ground observers. The red also served as a better background than either black or white for photography on panchromatic film of objects or stores falling from the bomb bay; referred to as 'LMS Red'. Fuselage serial was white./*J. M. G. Gradidge*

Below: An elite unit using Lincolns from July 1946 was the Empire Test Pilots School. Originally formed in 1943 under the aegis of A&AEE at Boscombe Down, the unit was for many years the only institution of its kind in the world. The rapid growth of the A&AEE forced a move to Cranfield in October 1945, a temporary home until space was found at Farnborough in 1947, destined to be its base for over two decades. Pictured is RF538 '17' at Farnborough./*B. Pickering*

Central Bomber Establishment

Left: In addition to its well-known flagships *Crusader* and *Excalibur*, Central Bomber Establishment operated many 'plain Jane' Lincolns such as SX975, with astrodrome in place of mid-upper turret, seen staging through Luqa, Malta, in 1949. CBE, formed at Marham in December 1945 from the wartime Bomber Development Unit, moved to Lindholme in April 1949 and together with the RAF Technical College formed the nucleus of Bomber Command Bombing School formed at Lindholme in October 1952./*P. Clifton*

Centre right: Excalibur and *Crusader* both of Central Bomber Establishment, Marham, were regular globetrotters. Basically standard Lincolns, but always fitted with the most up-to-date bombing and radar equipment, each had three bunks and a divan seat in the fuselage which had observation windows in the starboard side. Astrodomes replaced mid-upper turrets. Their highly polished natural metal finish is evident, and the anti-dazzel panels on the noses were olive drab. Here *Crusader* is seen at Zwartkop, March 1948 during a tour of South African Air Force bases. /*South African Air Force*

Bottom right: Excalibur, RF484 'DF:A'. /*V. E. Della Porta*

Both machines left CBE in late 1949 and served with a number of units. *Excalibur* was used by Waddington's Station Flight for a time before passing to St Athan's Station Flight to be used in the training of flight engineers passing through No 4 S of TT. *Crusader* also went to 'Waddo' in standard B2 guise, serving with both Nos 61 and 100 Squadrons at home and out in Malaya during 1950/51, before finally ending her days at Cosford as a ground instructional machine.

Malaya: War of the Running Dogs

RAF in Malaya

As early as January 1947, with terrorist activity already apparent, the RAF had been called upon to provide a show of strength during Operation Red Lion on which No 7 Squadron had sent its Lancasters to Changi for five weeks. Then in April/May 1948 Red Lion II was mounted, this time No 97 Squadron flying its Lincolns out to Tengah on an operational mobility exercise, and again the opportunity was taken to put on shows of force in various parts of Malaya and Singapore. This was followed by Exercise Centipede in November 1949, involving all the Allied fleets and aircraft operating in the Singapore region, and for which No 210 Squadron flew out its maritime Lancasters from St Eval to Tengah. The Communist terrorists (CTs) were not deterred however, and in the face of increasing guerilla activity, particularly against important commercial interests such as rubber plantations and tin mines, it was decided to add heavy support to the Spitfires, Mosquitos, Brigands, Hornets, Sunderlands and Beaufighters already in action with FEAF in the campaign codenamed Firedog.

In March 1950 the first Lincoln unit was mobilized, No 57 Squadron from Waddington under the command of Sqn Ldr Pete Brothers, DSO, DFC, an ex-Battle of Britain fighter pilot, flying out to Tengah on Operation Musgrave. Tengah is situated at the southern tip of the Malayan Peninsular on Singapore Island. Within only two days of arrival, a maximum effort strike against known guerilla camps was called for and the intense activity continued for several days. By the third day most of the squadron's armourers were laid up with heat exhaustion, having had no time to acclimatize either to the heat and humidity, or to the added effort of handling 500lb and 1,000lb bombs compared to the more usual 10lb and 25lb practice variety in the UK. For the next few days loading up had to be undertaken at a more leisurely pace by the aircrew under the supervision of the few remaining armourers, by then capable of only light duties. The aircrew soon became quite adept at this new task, and were even allowed to fit fusing links.

There were some mistakes, and on two occasions the omission of the all important circuit check prior to loading led to complete 14 x 1,000lb loads dropping off the aircraft as the test plunger was pressed. The bombs fell to the ground with a horrible rumbling noise, with men stepping nimbly aside, then, heads going back, arms pumping, they sprinted for the horizon, with fit, lean young aircrew being overtaken by fat, roly-poly little corporals whose normal morning exercise had consisted of no more than lifting mugs of tea. The word eventually got round that once the bombs had hit the ground, it was safe enough.

The 57 Squadron crews had to devise their own bombing techniques. H2S (at that time the Mk 3G) was of no use over the featureless jungle, and there was no Gee chain to assist; so all bombing, day and night, was visual, 'by use of Mark I eyeballs' as one navigator

Below: First British Lincoln unit in the Far East was No 97 (Straits Settlements) Squadron from Hemswell, here seen winging over Georgetown, Penang, less than an hour's flying time from Singapore their destination. Codenamed Operation Red Lion II, and following in the path of Lancaster-equipped No 7 Squadron two years previously, the detachment left Hemswell 28 April 1948 and stayed at Tengah for six weeks as an exercise in operational mobility and to show the flag at a time when communist terrorist activity was increasing. /F. Cholerton

described it. The one inch to a mile maps needed to be studied very carefully, though even the maps themselves were becoming outdated as cultivation and development of rubber plantations had begun to spread so far, bringing new and unmarked settlements and villages. Roads and rivers were the only reliable features and the method of timed runs from easily identifiable datum points was evolved, and which was used by all the squadrons that were to follow.

The target area was usually 1,000 yards square and bombing had to be accurate. The loads were mostly 14 x 1,000lb but it was found that 18 x 500lb gave a slightly better spread, with the bombs being double-banked down the centre stations of the bomb bay. The bombs were normally dropped in sticks at one second intervals between each bomb, but sometimes in clusters. On one 57 Squadron strike the bomb aimer of one of the Lincolns in the formation of five could not release his bombs in a stick as planned. The target was in the north, near the coast, and had already been shelled by the Navy. It was clearly identifiable, being a deep narrow cleft in a hill protruding from the jungle like a sugar loaf. Through the bottom of the canyon passed a river, and the steep-sided overhanging cliffs were honeycombed with caves, providing a perfect hiding place for CTs. With the one exception the formation had got its bombs away without any particularly spectacular result, but it stayed together while the crew of the 'hang up' Lincoln tried to sort out the fault. After the third unsuccessful run over the target, it was

decided that on the fourth the bomb aimer should use the jettison bar; so the formation ran in again, and the bombs went down in one salvo. It was an absolute dead eye shot, right down into the canyon between the cliffs, resulting in an almighty eruption which sent a huge ring of brown smoke, 50 feet thick, up into the sky, completely encircling the Lincoln formation as it passed upwards, to eventually remain intact at about 15,000ft for several hours.

It was difficult to preserve the element of surprise. Firstly the Army had to find the CT camps, then get clear itself, which took time; and it could take up to a fortnight in those early days to obtain political clearance to bomb, during which the CTs would get wind of the plans, and had often moved out. There could be no dummy run over a target, and anything other than a formation attack gave too much warning. Any wind finding had to be done at least 10 miles away from targets.

Most attacks in these earlier days were by day – as indeed, were to be the majority of the RAF strikes during its Malayan involvement. In the early months also, the strikes were mounted first thing in the morning before the build up of cloud and mist, so the CTs got to know the schedule, and would evacuate their camps just before dawn, knowing that it was safe to move back in by 10am. Only one night strike was attempted during 57's detachment and it was not until later that ground marker flares were introduced.

By the time No 57 handed over to No 100 Squadron (commanded initially by Sqn Ldr Danny G. O'Brien, and latterly by Sqn Ldr Ron A. Jell, DFC, AFC) at the end of June 1950 most of its crews had done 25 or 30 ops in the three months but had seen nothing of the enemy, nor had it learned much about the results of its efforts, a phenomenon which was to persist. In July 1950 No 1 Squadron Royal Australian Air Force also arrived at Tengah to join No 100 Squadron in the fray.

No 57 arrived back at Waddington without incident with the exception of RF517 'DX:X' captained by B Flight Commander Flt Lt W. C. Sinclair, AFC. His crew had already had one nasty experience during the stay in Tengah. On the way to a target the navigator, Flt Lt Bob Peasley, DFC, sensed he was being watched, but a quick glance round at the rest of the crew showed nothing unusual; they were all busy with their own duties. The feeling persisted and on looking round his compartment he saw a king sized rat perched on one of the black boxes, staring straight at him. The rat was chased into the back end of the Lincoln and on landing the local rat-catcher was called in. Several more rats were flushed out of the Lincolns at dispersals, and

suitable precautions had to be taken to prevent them getting aboard again as they had obviously found the covering to electric wiring to their taste. On the homeward journey from Tengah it was on take-off from Castel Benito on 11 July for the last leg that 517 lost its No 3 engine and had to land. Spare engines were in short supply. The outbound 100 Squadron Lincolns had experienced several engine failures along the route, and because of operational commitments, received priority, leaving 517 and its crew stranded for four weeks. On takeoff from Castel Benito again for home following the engine change, the ASI became u/s but by this time the crew had had enough and the pilot decided to press on.

Bill Sinclair was a tough little fellow who, within only three weeks of arrival in Tengah, with little time to acclimatize or train, had won the FEAF all-ranks featherweight boxing title against husky PTI types who had been out there for months. He flew 517 direct to Waddington, nine hours, without autopilot, and with the new No 3 feathered for the last 2¾ hours because of rough running. He was later to return to Tengah as a squadron leader in command of 83 (Lincoln) Squadron, a unit with which he had served as an 'erk' at Scampton in 1938/39.

No 100 Squadron carried on the bombing from Tengah in company with the Australian Lincoln squadron until December 1950 when No 100 was relieved (still under Operation Musgrave), by No 61 Squadron, also from Waddington, and to whom it handed over its aircraft – a new departure. Like No 57 before

Above: When the Japanese advanced on Singapore in 1942, No 100 Squadron, flying Vickers Vildebeest biplanes was all but decimated, so it was a proud moment when the squadron returned to Tengah eight years later to replace No 57 Squadron. RF476 'HW:A' adorned with the squadron's skull and crossbones badge, a name meaning 'Head Hornet' stemming from the unit's motto 'Don't let anyone attack the Hornet's nest', applied for the CO, Sqn Ldr Danny O'Brien, whose pennant she also carries.
/Neville Franklin Collection

it, the Lincolns used by 100 and 61 retained their mid-upper turrets but had no front guns fitted. The turrets were used to the full on the low level strafing runs which always followed the day strikes, sometimes both turrets blazing inwards at the smoking target area as the Lincolns flew round in a wide line – astern circle, while on others a straight run with each turret firing opposite sides. The strafing runs were always carried out under the control of the formation leader.

During this period strikes were still mainly by day, but marking techniques were being evolved. For day strikes, Dakotas and Sunderlands were used to drop smoke flares, a task later taken over by Austers which could fly lower and slower; and for night ops. the Army was experimenting with the placing of ground flares.

No 61 Squadron was to be led on many of its strikes by its CO, Sqn Ldr T. E. (Tiny) Ison, DSO, DFC, a most experienced bomber man who had commanded a wartime Pathfinder Lancaster squadron. He was a sound operator and respected leader. No 61 returned home in April 1951 and with the Australian Lincoln squadron holding the fort it appeared the RAF's heavy bomber involvement in Malaya was over. But it was not to be and a little over two years later No 83 Squadron was called in to supplement the Aussie effort.

Authors' Note
Regrettably space does not allow us to enlarge more fully on the activities of all the Lincoln squadrons which operated in Malaya. In choosing to devote more attention to Nos 7 and 83 Squadrons we took into account that they probably represented the peak of the

RAF heavy bomber involvement in Operation Firedog, though it is acknowledged that the other squadrons played just as important a part in the campaign. Their experiences were basically similar, of course, but it is felt that the additional duties undertaken by the two units highlighted will be of particular interest to readers – sidelines which do not appear to have been published before.

As Operation Bold 83 Squadron (commanded by Sqn Ldr W. C. Sinclair) left its Hemswell base in August 1953, the first Target Marker (Flare Force) unit to become involved in Firedog.

For the outward flight the Lincolns carried in their bomb bays one 400-gallon fuel tank and a spares pack, and in addition to its standard crew of six (now reduced to only one gunner following removal of mid-upper turrets) each Lincoln carried three ground personnel. No 83 had eight aircraft and eight complete crews, plus three reserve aircrew. The squadron was divided into two flights of four, and crews were to stick fairly rigidly to their 'own' aircraft throughout. Added to 83's own strength were two Lincolns provided by Lindholme (RA667 and RF330) flown by crews from 83's sister unit at Hemswell, No 97 Squadron, (Flt Lt J. A. Williams and Flg Off R. W. Lambert). They were to be used on airlift duties to the Cocos Islands in support of the forthcoming England – New Zealand Air Race.

The actual 'exodus' was spread over a 10-day period, the first of the Lincolns leaving Hemswell on 18 August 1953 using the well-proven route via Idris, Habbaniya, Mauripur, Negombo, Tengah, with an overnight stop at each. All arrived on schedule with the excep-

tion of RF539 flown by Flg Off Bulloch and crew, who had an engine failure shortly after take-off from Mauripur, and had to turn back. It was found that all the coolant fluid had been lost because the tank filler cap had been left off. A cylinder had cracked and the engine had to be changed, which took a day. On the next leg to Negombo (Ceylon) one of its spinners cracked, so on arrival all four were removed to balance things up but the backplates were left on. During the final leg to Tengah, the airflow forced one of them back, causing it to foul the cowling diaphram, resulting in the engine having to be feathered for the last 200 miles.

Several of the other Lincolns had experienced the same trouble with cracked spinners on the outward route on reaching tropical climates, and as the spinners were found to be of an earlier, unmodified type, all were removed together with back plates. Some were later replaced with the modified type, but three of the Lincolns continued without them until after their return to Hemswell some months later.

The remainder of the squadron's 92 ground personnel, plus a spare engine, spares and freight were ferried out to Tengah in a BOAC Argonaut and two chartered Yorks, other spare engines, etc, being sent by sea. Facilities at Tengah were good, with adequate offices, hangars, etc, and both air and ground crews accommodated in permanent buildings, comfortable if slightly overcrowded. The airfield itself was busy and congested, the other residents being the Australian Lincoln squadron (No 1), No 45 Squadron (Hornets), 60 Squadron (Vampires) and the Singapore Squadron of the Malayan Auxiliary Air Force, (Harvards and Tiger Moths). The flying side was well established and highly organized under RAF control.

After a few days settling in, collecting tropical kit, attending lectures, and flying practice bombing sorties, familiarisation cross-countries, etc, 83 was soon in action, three of its Lincolns led by Flt Lt Ken Souter, A Flight Commander, joining in an area bombing attack with the Aussie Lincolns in the Sedanak area on 5 September. Nearly all bombing was still of the daylight formation variety, area or pinpoint, all visual, on targets marked by flares from Austers, or by the timed-run method at heights of 5 – 6,000ft. Occasionally low cloud forced the Lincolns to bomb from the minimum safe altitude of only 2,500ft, and always the strikes were followed by the strafing runs from 500ft. It was on one of these runs that Sgt J. O'Keefe, rear gunner to Flt Lt Stones in RA662, thought his last moment had come when the perspex of his rear turret was suddenly shattered. He was convinced that for once the CTs were shooting back, only to discover after recovering from the initial shock that the 'missile' was a large coconut thrown up by the blast from a bomb which for some reason had failed to explode on impact. The turret was wrecked by the blast and had to be replaced. Bomb fragments were an occasional hazard, but there is no known record of a Lincoln being fired upon by the CTs, though some of the Austers were hit by small arms fire.

There were a number of strikes on which all eight squadron Lincolns took part. As usual the bombing called for great accuracy and there were few errors. Responsibility rested heavily on the strike leader – almost invariably a squadron or flight commander, and the strikes were mainly joint affairs with No 1 RAAF Squadron, with responsibility for planning, briefing and leading alternating between the two squadrons. The OC Flying at Tengah (Wg Cdr M. W. B. Knight, DFC) qualified as a Lincoln captain on 83 Squadron's aircraft and led several strikes. Bomb loads were mainly 6 x 1,000lb plus 8 x 500lb, occasionally 14 x 1,000lb, and on three strikes a single 4,000lb 'cookie' was dropped. Only four night strikes were undertaken, plus one other night operation when two aircraft dropped some 4.5in recce flares to help illuminate an area for an Army patrol. For the night sorties the Army provided guidance by means of vertical searchlights. For some of the strikes the Lincolns were deployed to Kuala Lumpur and Butterworth.

On 28 October 1953, Operation Bison was mounted. The two Lincoln squadrons, No 1 operating from Butterworth, and 83 from Tengah, flew more than 30 sorties in the day (some aircraft and crews three times each) to drop 15million propaganda leaflets on 200 different locations, the leaflets exhorting the CTs to surrender and offering rewards to natives for information.

The task of flying supplies to the Cocos Islands soon got under way after arrival in Tengah. A small RAF camp was established, kept supplied as a refuelling stop for RAF aircraft taking part in the race to New Zealand, and then dismantled, some 83 Squadron aircraft and crews helping out the 97 Squadron contingent on occasions. Over a two month period, September/October, 29 return flights were made, all on schedule. The 1,000-mile flight to Cocos often involved flying straight through violent tropical storm clouds which towered well above the Lincolns' operational ceiling. The two Lincolns and their 97 Squadron crews left Tengah for home in late October and mid-November. One (RF330) arrived back at Hemswell on time; but, almost inevitably it seemed, the other (RA667) was delayed due to engine failure en route, spending 14 days at Bahrain awaiting a replacement.

There were other diversions from the operational routine, including in November an intensive ASR search by the Lincolns for a missing Valetta from Changi and of which, tragically, no trace was found. A series of detachments was also sent to Hong Kong (RAF Kai Tak) in November/December 1953 for the purpose of fighter affiliation with 80 Squadron (Hornets) from Kai Tak itself and 28 Squadron (Vampires) based at Sek Kong. It gave the Lincoln gunners chance to simulate counter fire using camera recorders, and served to test the Hong Kong defences generally. Kai Tak airfield had its own brand of difficulties such as close proximity to hostile international borders, hills up to 2,000ft on two sides, close to the circuit, and always covered in cloud; and nearest diversion airfields over 500 miles away. Sqn Ldr Sinclair paid an inspection visit in a Valetta, then took five of his most experienced pilots to Kai Tak in RA672 to check them out personally in the rather unusual local circuit. This was the first time a Lincoln had landed at Hong Kong. Subsequently, four detachments of two aircraft were sent to Hong Kong and on one of these, Flt Sgt Joe Kmiecik, AFM and crew took part in a flying display held on 28 November. The crowd was treated to a show of near-aerobatics and low flying such as had not been seen before with Kmiecik flying his regular Lincoln RE358 like a fighter, springing numerous wing rivets in the process.

From Tengah, aircrews undertook courses in jungle survival with the Army, and a number of air and ground crew took the opportunity to spend a few days with Army units engaged in ground operations. On one of these Corporal Reg Cox was officially credited with shooting a CT while on a night ambush with the 1st Manchester Regiment. It was the nearest the Squadron came to a confirmed kill of a CT.

The Lincoln performed well in Malaya and 83 Squadron achieved an 85 per cent serviceability record, a tribute to the groundcrews working in far from ideal conditions in temperatures often over 100°F. Some minor problems were encountered but generally overcome without too much trouble. In the first few weeks of the detachment there were numerous mag. drops and ignition troubles which were traced to the use of plastic engine covers which did not allow the engines to cool off or dry out fully; then there were further ignition problems which were traced to the adverse effect on plugs of the high lead content in the petrol being used. Fifteen power plant changes were made in the $4\frac{1}{2}$ months in Tengah, the quickest recorded taking only $4\frac{1}{2}$ hours.

The electric wiring also suffered in the heat, especially braided cables as used in the bomb bay, but radio and radar equipment performed well after intercoms and VHFs had been rewired.

The front turrets, too, gave some trouble at first – mainly electrical circuits because the turrets had not been used for some years. The high gun stoppage rate was attributed to link breakages and to the use of Grade B substandard ammo normally restricted to use on the ground. There were two instances of burst gun barrels, one causing damage to the tail of RA672 when bullets were projected sideways into the port elevator and rudder.

Operations continued without pause even over New Year's Eve 1954 when, with a huge party going on in the Mess, Flt Lt Ken Souter and crew found themselves detailed by the CO for a single-aircraft pre-dawn strike at 4am on the morning of 1 January. (It had been the flight commander's privilege to 'volunteer'.) The enforced abstinence did not go down at all well with the crew, and proved just too much for one of the navs, Dean MacKowie, a tough, hard living, hard drinking, rugby playing Highlander, to whom New Year's Eve was an undeniable ritual. He was bundled into the Lincoln by the crew, still wearing his evening dress mess kit. On nearing the target area he was awakened and in full evening dress took his place in the nose, duly letting the bombs go right on the aiming point, a great tribute to his discipline and training. So it was back to Tengah with the dawn broken, and to the party which was still in full swing.

The final operation in which 83 took part was on 13 January 1954, when three of its Lincolns flew on a joint formation strike led by Flt Lt John Blundell, DFC. (B Flight Commander) in RA677. with Flg Off Bulloch (RA662) and Sgt Quinney (RE415). By then the handover to No 7 Squadron had already begun, the first four of the 83 Squadron Lincolns and their crews having left Tengah for home on 7 January, arriving over Hemswell in formation led by Sqn Ldr Sinclair at 1430 hours on 12 January, exactly to the ETA signalled before departure from Tengah.

The remaining four aircraft and crews left Tengah on 24 January, three arriving at Hemswell on time five days later but with the inevitable straggler delayed along the route with engine trouble for two weeks, this time Flt Lt Stones in RA662, again at Bahrain.

So ended 83 Squadron's $4\frac{1}{2}$-month sojourn in Malaya, during which it flew 211 sorties on 72 strikes, in the process dropping 1,820,760lb of bombs (nearly 900 tons) and firing almost

Below: Following Christmas leave 1953 it was No 7 Squadron's turn to pack its bags and fly out to Tengah to carry on the long and arduous fight against the terrorists in the Malayan Jungles – still as part of Operation Bold, and here, one of its Lincoln's thunders away from Tengah bound for a strike up-country. Below the fuselage protrudes the mounting for the radio altimeter aerial. SX982 was to meet a sad end some three years later when returning from duty in Aden with 1426 Flight. */A. Pearcy Collection*

74,000 rounds of ammo. During the whole detachment its flying hours, including transits (833), ops (758), and the Cocos Islands and Kai Tak deployments, totalled 2,444 without a single flying accident. The remainder of the ground personnel flew home in the three Hastings which had brought their 7 Squadron replacements out to Malaya. Before leaving, all items of equipment, spares, etc, were passed on to No 7 Squadron, whose CO was Sqn Ldr D. C. Saunders.

No 7 Squadron's eight crews and aircraft arrived in Malaya in two flights of four over a two week period. For the transit flight the Upwood medicos had been persuaded to authorize the reissue of exhaust shrouds or baffles to prevent crews arriving deaf and remaining so for several days after. By the end of January the Squadron had worked up to full operational standard and taken up where 83 had left off, sharing strikes with No 1 RAAF Squadron, most of the sorties being flown on a joint basis.

During 1953 Flt Lt David H. Tew one of the 7 Squadron Flight Commanders had been involved with other crews in VT (variable time) bomb fuse trials and had flown up from Upwood to the Bombing Trials Unit base at West Freugh for drops on the local range. In December 1953 Flt Lt Tew and his men had also flown to Habbaniya for a few days to conduct tropical trials of the new fuses. He then continued the operational trials during the first detachment in Malaya, during which 113 specially fitted bombs were dropped in the Kulai area of Johore, plus 13 by the RAAF Lincolns. The crews involved just had to hope the fuses did not activate too early, as not all the 1,000lb bombs behaved perfectly, the odd one falling tail first with the fused nose pointing upwards directly at the aircraft. Occasionally the first two bombs to be released would collide, sending one of them into a magnificent, slow, graceful spin, until it would eventually stabilize and slot itself back into the stick or cluster at almost the right spot.

In March 1954, only a month before it was due to return home, No 7 Squadron was called upon to transport two consignments of radioactive material from Australia, Operation Bagpipes. The Americans were to test an H-bomb at Bikini Atoll and had promised British scientists certain samples for research. Canberras were scheduled to fly the 'hot' material back to England, but one by one they became unserviceable. Two of 7 Squadron's Lincolns and crews, including Flt Lt Tew, were detached from Tengah as replacements, positioning first to Changi then to Darwin (10 hours flight), one returning to Changi on 18 March as the test explosion was delayed by adverse weather.

From the UK end, Operation Pony Express was launched. Three Lincolns and crews of 214 Squadron Upwood were called out on 13 March to cover the homeward half of the route, Flt Lt Bill Burden and crew positioning to Mauripur in RE360. The first consignment, a lead-lined pannier containing radioactive isotopes arrived in a 7 Squadron Lincoln flown by Flt Lt Mike Ride, and was immediately transferred to 360's bomb bay, arriving back in the UK on 31 March.

Because of the continued unserviceability of the Canberras, and further delay in completing the H-test, Flt Lt Tew continued his standby at Changi until well after the rest of his 7 Squadron colleagues had returned home from Tengah in April. As further cover for Bagpipes it was decided to use the outgoing 148 Squadron aircraft and crews, due to replace No 7 in Malaya, so phase two of Pony Express commenced, to station Lincolns and crews along the route as reserves for RE362. It was an operation involving a high degree of co-operation and organization, with one of the 148 crews taking RE362 (Tew's Lincoln) on to Darwin to await the radioactive material. There was the almost inevitable crop of engine failures, etc, among the outbound Lincolns, and because of the resulting gaps in the cover, other 148 Squadron crews and aircraft had to be summoned at very short notice.

On 31 March 1954 Flt Sgt Bert Beach and his signaller, Flt Sgt Reg Lucks, had ferried a flight engineer to St Athan in the Upwood station Oxford. As they taxied to the apron to drop their passenger, contemplating a nice spot of afternoon tea, they were ordered by Air Traffic to return to base immediately, setting them wondering what they had done wrong. On arrival back at Upwood, it was to

find their Lincoln (RE357) already fuelled up and ready to go, and the rest of their crew kitted up and briefed, with orders to get to Shallufa non-stop as soon as possible.

At 10.20 that evening they were on the way, with the H2S going on the blink soon after take-off, resulting in the poor signaller working hard throughout the night obtaining more than 100 fixes to assist the navigator as the Lincoln passed down over France and across the Med. Arriving over Shallufa nearly 14 hours later Flt Sgt Beach, by then tired and numb after so long in the air, was faced with landing in a stiff crosswind, not the best of conditions for a Lincoln. A 500-mile diversion was available, but his orders were to get down at Shallufa if at all possible. He overshot off the first approach and on the second attempt got caught in a strong gust just as the mainwheels were about to touch. The Lincoln started to 'weathercock', leaving the runway and making off across country with poor Beach shouting 'I can't hold her' and the flight engineer, M/Eng Paddy Newstead, advising 'let her go Bert'. The starboard wing was very close to the ground as the Lincoln ploughed on and eventually came to a stop in a great cloud of dust, with the crash wagons pulling alongside at the same time, having made a good line of intercept. Apart from badly shaking knees there was no harm done to the crew, but as the dust settled it could be seen that 357 was on the slant, with its starboard undercarriage rather bent.

After two days SX958 arrived as another panic replacement for Beach and crew to take on to Mauripur non-stop, 12½ hours. A week later they brought 958 back to Shallufa and collected their now repaired RE357, which they flew on to Negombo to take up their position as reserve cover for RE362 still standing by at Changi. At Negombo Flt Sgt Beach fell ill with a virus, and was shipped home, his place being taken by Flg Off Dougan who eventually flew 357 and its remaining crew on to Tengah in mid-May to take its place on 148's operational roster.

Meanwhile, back at Changi, Flt Lt Tew's standby crew experienced numerous delays, unpacking and repacking their kit time and again as standbys were brought down from 96 to 48 to 24 hours only to be relaxed once more as the tests were delayed until the weather was right. Then on 8 May RE362 arrived from Darwin with the specially shielded, lead-lined crate stowed in the rear fuselage just inside the door. The 148 Squadron crew climbed out and the 7 Squadron crew climbed in, taking-off as soon as 362 was refuelled.

All seven of the crew had to stay forward of the main spar for the whole flight, which was to take a little over two days. To anyone who knows the layout of a Lincoln, the dis-

comfort can be imagined. The crew comprised two pilots (Flt Lts David Tew and David Emsley), flight engineer (Flg Off Geoff Gallear), two navs. (Flt Lt Chris Webster and Flg Off Colin Palmer) and two signallers. They worked and rested on alternate legs, but for those off duty, trying to sleep on the floor or in the very cold nose was almost impossible.

All services en route had been well briefed on the urgency of the flight, and were kept advised of progress by transmission from the aircraft of the very rare 'Flash' signals. The Lincoln was met at each port of call by the senior officer and MO; fuel and food were immediately ready and at no point did the crew spend more than $2\frac{1}{2}$ hours on the ground, completing the journey from Changi to Wyton via Negombo, Mauripur, Habbaniya, Shallufa and Idris in 43hr 35min out of a total elapsed time of only 54 hours. It must have been something of a record – if not in terms of speed then certainly of human endurance. Neither aircraft nor crew appeared any the worse for wear, and 362 returned to Tengah in July 1954 for a further round of strikes.

Flt Lt David H. Tew, AFC, for his work in Malaya, etc, was Mentioned in Despatches. When No 7 Squadron returned to Malaya in mid-July 1954 to relieve 148 Squadron for another three months he was again A Flight Commander. Unlike 83 Squadron, whose eight Lincolns and crews were divided into two flights of four each, all No 7's aircraft and aircrew belonged to A Flight, with the

ground crew in B Flight. The B Flight Commander was Flt Lt Ian Popay, DFM and Bar, (one of the squadron's pilots as it happens) who had been a wartime wireless operator/air gunner on Hampdens before becoming a pilot.

In mid-October 1954 No 148 Squadron again took over from No 7 at Tengah, again, as in April, the exchange being accomplished by some aircraft being left at Tengah, some being flown home, and others brought out by double headed crews, thus resulting in some of the Lincolns being used by both 7 and 148 Squadrons out in Tengah.

No 148 continued to operate jointly with the Australian squadron, tactics remaining largely unchanged. Then in April 1955 No 148 returned home to Upwood to be replaced at Tengah by No 101 Squadron with Canberras, a sure sign that the Lincoln's days were numbered, though No 1 RAAF Squadron's Lincolns were to continue in Malaya for over another three years. Malaya actually became independent in August 1957 though Firedog did not end officially until October 1960.

During this involvement in Malaya Lincolns completed some 5,576 sorties. In 18,137 hours of flying there was no flying accident of any sort, a most remarkable achievement of airmanship and a great credit to the general standard of RAF training and flying; and to the standard of servicing, not to mention the ruggedness and reliability of the Lincolns themselves.

Below: The tranquil night is broken by the distinctive throb of Merlins as one by one No 148 Squadron's Lincolns prepare for a Guerilla harrying sortie from Tengah in November 1954. Looking like some gigantic moth in the glare of the hangar lights is RE400 as Sgt Don Wimble and crew run through the pre-taxi checks. */D. F. Wimble*

Aussies in Malaya

In July 1950, No 1 Squadron was sent to Tengah (Singapore) to join the RAF in the anti-communist operations in Malaya. Nos 2 and 6 Squadrons remained at Amberley, Queensland, to carry on with home defence, bombing training duties, etc, continuing as part of 82 (Bomber) Wing, while No 1 Squadron became part of No 90 (Composite) Wing, the other component being No 38 Squadron's Dakotas. The squadron strength was to be eight Lincolns throughout its stay at Tengah.

During its early years in Malaya, No 1 Squadron's Lincolns were used mainly on day bombing raids, carrying loads of up to 15,000lb per aircraft plus full ammunition. After dropping the bombs it was standard operational procedure to strafe the bombed area with all six guns firing full-blast, often considered a far more effective deterrent; then to return to base at very low level, flying up to 300 miles directly over villages and towns, and known to the crews as 'the flag wag'. Usually five or seven aircraft would attack the prescribed area in loose formation, trying to raze large tracts of jungle where concentrations of CTs had been reported. Sometimes, single aircraft would be despatched on harassing night exercises, dropping a single 500lb or 1,000lb bomb at regular intervals.

A number of 4,000lb block-buster bombs were also dropped by the Aussie Lincolns, the idea being that one such bomb should clear an area in the jungle large enough for a helicopter to land. Unfortunately the bombs were old wartime stock, rather leaky and with unreliable pressure fuses which tended to explode just above the canopy of foliage, blowing the tops off the trees, but leaving the trunks intact. On return from a formation strike, it was quite a sight to see the Aussie Lincolns running in to base in echelon starboard for a fighter-type break before landing.

The Mk 30s used in the early stages of the Malayan campaign carried only the standard basic navigation equipment; H2S Mk 3, API/GPI, Lucero, and the Marconi TR 1154/1155 radio, with their twin 'dancing ladies' displays in pilot's and nav's positions. By the mid-1950s, improvements included addition of Loran and radio compasses, and the Australians played an important part in developing and improving bombing accuracy and techniques. Several types of target marking were evolved, but the most successful for day ops proved to be smoke flares dropped by low-flying Austers, a highly specialised task carried out by pilots operating under the most difficult conditions. Close co-operation was required between the marker pilots and Lincoln formation leaders to ensure correct timing and target coverage.

Sometimes a target would be bombed solely on a map reference, doing a time and distance run from a datum point which would be either a prominent hill or river bend; or a smoke flare placed near to the target by the Army. Always the enemy remained unseen and rarely were any positive results reported. To overcome small inaccuracies in navigation, marking and bomb aiming, a pattern-

Below: A mixed gaggle of No 7 Squadron RAF and No 1 Squadron RAAF despatch their loads into the jungle on the afternoon of 15 September 1954, dropping on the command of the RAAF bombing leader. The exception is RF347, flown by Flg Off Mike Ride, who's VHF receiver had failed, his bomb aimer releasing visually a few seconds later./*W. E. Youd*

bombing technique was developed, with five aircraft in a 'vic' or 'flat iron', each dropping 14 x 1,000lb bombs at one second intervals or sometimes simultaneously. Also evolved were such techniques as stream take-offs, formation form-ups, weather penetration procedures and a high standard of formation flying for three to four hours on end, by day and night, with an ability to orbit the target area for long periods awaiting clearance of mist and cloud.

On occasions the Mk 30s would bomb in a larger formation with the RAF Lincolns, all the aircraft coming down to treetop level after the bomb drops for the customary strafing runs. The Australian Lincolns were much admired by the RAF men, being beautifully finished and maintained, particularly their pale green interiors which were kept imm-aculately clean and swept by their ground crews. The latter were organised along World War II lines with a flight sergeant crew chief in overall charge, and each aircraft having its own resident ground crew; by contrast those of the RAF apart from having

Above: The steady rumble of 20 Merlins are interrupted by the hesitant squeal and hiss of brakes as No 1 Squadron prepares to set off for their Butterworth advance base. Outboard engines were quite effective for initiating normal turns while taxying but it required a combination of brake and power in order to negotiate short radius turns./*RAAF*

Centre left: Guiding her with the rudders and leading with No 1 throttle to avoid the swing to port, the skipper is about to ease A73-45 off the runway with 95 knots, 3,000rpm and plus 12 boost on the clock. When completely airborne he will brake the wheels gently, retract the undercarriage and pull away with 120 knots and 2,850rpm registering. Flaps will be raised above 300ft and speed built up to 140 knots IAS and, finally, power reduced to plus 9 boost and 2,650rpm, in the climb./*RAAF*

Bottom left: Weather was a constant problem for the Lincolns, which mainly had to bomb visually. Driving rain and swirling mist would often force the formation below the recommended safety height. Here a maximum effort by No 1 Squadron RAAF from approximately 10,000ft, *c*1957. /*K. V. Robertson*

regular engine and airframe fitters were maintained on a more centralised pool basis. To the Aussie ground crews their Lincoln was their tea bar, meeting place, card room – a club house virtually, and the British air and ground crews considered it a great privilege to be invited in for a card school or a cuppa.

The RAAF machines, apart from their different marks of Merlins, also differed from the RAF Lincolns by having electrically operated trailing aerials and in retaining their mid-upper turrets and 2 x 20mm cannon to the end.

In its first year in Malaya, No 1 Squadron dropped 5million pounds of bombs by day and night in 744 sorties and 3,303 hours of flying in all weathers. It was during the squadron's early months in Malaya that its first DFC of the campaign was awarded. On 13 August 1950, A73-36 was engaged in a night strike on a reported CT concentration, with parachute flares being dropped from the bomb bay to illuminate the target area. As one flare was dropped, its parachute opened prematurely and caught on a bomb rack,

swinging the flare back in the slipstream, where it broke through the H2S cupola, lodging in the scanner, burning fiercely. Flt Lt Keith I. Foster, the squadron gunnery leader, quickly extinguished the fire which could have resulted in the loss of the aircraft, claiming modestly that he had to do so in order to reach his parachute stowed on the other side of the fire.

A73-36 was to languish in the open at Tengah for some months, during which it was cannibalised to provide spares for other Lincolns, including three of its engines. Eventually it was decided it should be made airworthy, and flown back to Amberley for major overhaul and repair. A scratch crew was formed of officers due to leave Malaya for home. The crew, captained by Sqn Ldr Doug Harvey, included a flight engineer who supervised the installation of the three engines, the task taking several days as only one fitter could be spared. The test flight went without incident, so the crew eventually set off for Darwin. Towards the end of the 12-hour flight of 1,890 nautical-miles it was

Below: 'Big Stick' was a colloquial term often applied to the Aussie Lincolns during No 1 Squadron's eight year sojourn in Malaya. Noteworthy in this splendid view of A73-21 are the black anti-dazzle panel in front of the cockpit, cabin air intake above starboard wing root, open escape hatch (presumably for ventilation), and uneven exhaust stains across wings and tailplanes. No 1 Squadron's spinners were painted dark blue, though a few aircraft had red spinners – a leftover from service with No 6 Squadron at Amberley back home in Queensland. */Australian War Memorial*

noticed that the No 4's oil pressure was falling slightly, so on landing, the local maintenance crew was asked to have a look at it before the final leg to Amberley. An hour later, a very worried crew chief telephoned through to the mess where the first few beers had already gone down well. The aircrew returned to their Lincoln and were shown the reason for the loss of oil pressure. On each engine were two governor mountings – one each side for either left- or right-hand operation depending on installation position. Whichever of the mountings was not to be used should have been blanked-off by a special metal plate and a gasket firmly screwed down; but this requirement had been overlooked when the three new engines were installed and the only thing holding-in the oil was the small piece of 5-ply held on by thin wire as delivered from the makers. The thoughts of what could have happened on the long flight over the sea had the most sobering effect on the crew.

No 1 Squadron continued its operations in Malaya without a break, its crews being posted in and out on a rotational basis, some for short periods of three months, others for longer spells of up to a year (unaccompanied). Later, however, more permanent postings of up to two years (with families) were adopted. In the early days of the squadron's Malayan operations there was a large proportion of World War II veterans with only a sprinkling of younger men. For the former wartime men who had operated in Lancasters and Halifaxes over Europe, with Master Bombers, Pathfinders, TIs, Oboe, etc., bombing in Malaya provided a total contrast. As the years unwound, however, a new, young postwar generation of air and ground crews appeared, and by the end, dominated the squadron.

With the departure of the last RAF Lincoln squadron in April 1955 (No 148) No 1 was left to carry the main burden of the heavy bombing for another 3 years with medium support from the RAF Canberra detachments. It remained based at Tengah though sometimes operations in northern Malaya would be carried out from Butterworth. In addition to its almost daily bombing duties, the squadron also maintained a regular training routine, and undertook long-range navigation exercises to Australia and Hong Kong, fighter affiliation work and participation in numerous SEATO exercises.

Gradually, tactics changed from the formation day and night strikes, and in the later stages of the campaign the emphasis turned to night bombing, sometimes with three or five Lincolns in formation in ideal half moon conditions, but more usually singly. The Army would search the jungle by day and, having pin-pointed CT positions, would pull out at night leaving the way clear for the Lincolns.

Left: The Malayan anti-terrorist campaign gave the squadrons ample opportunity to adorn their aircraft with bomb symbols, reminiscent of Bomber Command's workhorses during World War II. Some machines of No 1 Squadron RAAF chalked up as many as 200 sorties and this anonymous example, at either Butterworth or Tengah, is typical. Usual symbol colouring was red for night operations, black for daylight./*A. Pearcy Collection*

Below: A No 1 Squadron crew in happy mood on return from a routine strike in the Bertong area./*Sydney Morning Herald*

Above left: During the final push to rid Malaya of the Communist terrorists many night sorties were flown. Operation Tiger, mounted in April 1958, was a particularly busy time for No 1 Squadron and here we see Wg Cdr Ken Robertson, AFC, the CO, running up No 3 engine of A73-32 at Tengah on the night of 16 April 1958, prior to a strike in the Kluang area. No 3 engine, which provided power for the brakes, radiator shutters, supercharger rams, slow-running cut-outs and electric generators, was the first to be started. /*K. V. Robertson*

Left: With throttles almost closed, A73-45 is about to effect a powered landing at Tengah. Normal procedure was to be lined up on finals at 5-600ft with a little flap, reducing power to near zero boost, after commencing the turn onto base leg and maintaining 120-125 knots. Reducing speed and power progressively and putting down full flap, the boundary was crossed at 105 knots, while flapless/glide approaches required an extra 5 knots. /*M. J. Ricketts*

One method evolved in the latter stages of the campaign was to put a Lincoln on to a target every hour or so during all the hours of darkness, sometimes dropping its bombs singly under ground radar control at 5 minute intervals. Of the eight or nine crews on the squadron, seven would be committed every night, working to a roster whereby a crew started the week with an over-target time of an hour before dawn, progressively moving its take-off time back one hour until its day off. With each Lincoln carrying 14 x 1,000lb bombs, it was considered to have the most harrying and morale-sapping effect (on the terrorists that is, not the crews). The constant noise of heavily laden Lincolns getting airborne every hour of the night certainly achieved a degree of unpopularity with the locals at Tengah.

In almost precisely eight years of continuous operations in Malaya No 1 Squadron dropped 33million lb of bombs (almost 15,000 tons – 85 per cent of the total tonnage dropped by all aircraft in Malaya), plus millions of leaflets in 4,000 sorties. In one four-day period the Lincolns created a squadron record by dropping 480,000lb in 40 sorties. The highest total in one day was on 21 February 1956 when seven aircraft, each doing two sorties, delivered 196,000lb of

Ironically the two Lincolns lost by No 1 Squadron during its eight years of Malayan operations were numbered consecutively. Here three views of the first to hit disaster: B30A A73-40. Fifteen minutes after a night take-off from Tengah on 1 February 1957 the Lincoln developed engine trouble. The captain, Sqn Ldr Eric ('Bushy') Goldner, immediately order the bombs to be jettisoned, but even before the bomb doors could be opened the machine clipped the tree-clad peak of the 2,000ft Mount Purelai in the Kulai area. Debris crashed through the windscreen, injuring Goldner and rendering him unconscious. As the Lincoln virtually slithered down the side of the hill through the tree tops the co-pilot, Plt Off Tom Thorpe, managed to regain some semblance of control and, despite the loss of two engines, was able to gain enough height to avoid Pontai Village and ditch 400 yards offshore in the Straits of Johore, all the crew being safely recovered.
/All M. J. Ricketts

Above: A73-40 of No 1 Squadron RAAF, inbound to Tengah, seen over the picturesque waterfront of Singapore Harbour. She was soon to meet a watery end. /K. V. Robertson

bombs. The attacks were against a totally unseen enemy and only twice were the ground forces able to report a positive result to the bomber crews: in February 1956, following a strike by the Lincolns, the bodies of 18 CTs were found, some with notebooks in their hands, the Lincolns having obviously interrupted a planning lecture; then in May 1957, following another attack by the Lincolns, the 7th Battalion, Malay Regiment, found the bodies of four CTs and also picked-up nearby their leader, Negri Sembilian's No 1 terrorist, Teng Fook Loong (known as 'Mr Ten Foot Long'). He died of shock and wounds 10 hours later. There can be no doubts as to the overall effectiveness of the bombing campaign in preventing the takeover of the Malayan Peninsular by the Communists. It deprived the terrorists of food, clothing, supplies of arms and ammunition, and of regular places to settle and become established. Even more important, by its boosting effect on the morale of the local populace, it deprived the terrorists of support and co-operation, without which they could not succeed. Many of the terrorists who were captured or who decided to surrender, confirmed the difficulties of life under the constant air attacks.

By the time of its final withdrawal from Tengah in July 1958, the emergency was virtually over, with the remaining 2,000 or so CT remnants having been banished to the northern jungles, barely finding a living, and mounting very few attacks. The squadron had achieved the most remarkable standards of serviceability and of bombing accuracy, but most remarkable of all was its standard of airmanship and its flight safety record. Apart from the flare hang up incident and the ditching of A73-40 related elsewhere in the book, only one other Lincoln was written off, when A73-39 overshot the runway at Tengah on 30 November 1951 without injury to the crew, a fine record indeed and a tribute to air and ground crews, and to the reliability and durability of the Lincoln.

Before departure from Tengah, No 1 Squadron was presented with its Standard by the C-in-C Far East Air Force, Air Marshal the Earl of Bandon. During its eight-year tour in Malaya, its personnel had won 6 DFCs, 2 Bars and one Second Bar to the DFC, an OBE, a DFM, four BEMs and 15 Mentions in Despatches. On arrival back at Darwin on 6 July 1958 the squadron was welcomed by the Chief of Air Staff, Air Marshal Sir Frederick Sherger. Five of its Lincolns, led by Wg Cdr Robertson then made a 6,000-mile tour of the Australian state capitals, the final landing back at Amberley marking the end of the Lincoln's front-line service as a bomber in the RAAF, No 1 Squadron starting its conversion to Canberras soon afterwards.

A number of the Lincolns were retained in storage for future training needs, but some found their way to civil and military airfields for fire fighting practice, and by mid-1959 most of the B30s had been cut up and sold for scrap.

Warriors Return

A trio of No 61 Squadron's Lincolns at Waddington in April 1951 on return from the Far East on anti-terrorist duty. Personal emblems, none too common on Lincolns, often had obscure origins, an example being (*above right*) *The Mudlark* (RF502 'QR:R'), so named by Flt Lt 'Joe' Waddington, DFC, and crew, following an incident when she became bogged down during a compass swing on the old Japanese runway at Tengah. Operational strikes are represented by palm trees./*T. E. Ison*

Right: Mightymouse ('QR:Y') was the mount of Flg Off 'Mike' Watkin-Jones (the smallest pilot in the squadron) and crew, while (*below*) *Desert Penguin*) was so named after becoming stranded in the Middle East on the outward journey. On return to the UK the emblems were soon removed on orders of higher authority. All three Lincolns carry standard Rebecca (ranging and beam approach aid) aerials under the nose, although *Mightymouse* has two additional aerials under her chin and other visible mods./*Both T. E. Ison*

Left: Lincoln B30, A73-36 surrounded by an admiring crowd at RAAF base Amberley, during an open day after return from duty in Malaya, its nose bearing a bombs tally of 117 strikes with No 1 Squadron. It features elsewhere in this book in both pictures and text. /*B. Suoboda*

There were no fanfares or red carpets awaiting RAF squadrons on return from detachments in sunnier climes. Here we see Nos 7 and 83 Squadrons indulging in some low level work on return from duty in Malaya; (*top left*) RE348 from No 7 Squadron is snapped over Marham, Norfolk, while (*left*) a trio from No 83 Squadron in a neat echelon-starboard formation.
/*Peterborough Citizen & Advertiser; M. J. Cawsey*

Below: Led by the CO, Wg Cdr K. V. Robertson, AFC, No 1 Squadron returns to its homeland following eight years in Malaya, to make a round-Australia tour, encompassing the capital cities of each state. The picture, taken 16 July 1958, shows the five Lincolns over Woolloomooloo during one of two runs over Sydney before landing at Richmond to be met by Air Officer Commanding Home Command, Air Vice Marshal C. D. Candy. Reading from top to bottom the Lincolns are A73-50, A73-41, A73-32, A73-37 and A73-26.
/*Sydney Morning Herald*

The Aussies

B30: Home Service

Plans had been made to set up a Lancaster III production line in Australia, but in 1944 this was changed to the Mk IV as it would be well suited to the more local operations in the Pacific theatre against Japan. Because of delays in the introduction of the new type, the Australian production line was not even under way by the time the Japanese war ended in September 1945. It was nevertheless decided to proceed with a limited production run of 85 machines at the Government Aircraft Factory, Fisherman's Bend, Melbourne, to meet defence contingencies and SEATO commitments.

While the Australian-built Lincolns were allotted the designation XXX to distinguish them from the UK and Canadian-built versions, the first five Australian machines (A73-1 to -5) were assembled from Manchester-made components shipped out from the UK. First flown from Fisherman's Bend

on 12 March 1946, A73-1 was handed over to the RAAF for trials with the Lincoln Development Flight at Laverton on 24 May 1946, and the first all-Australian Lincoln, A73-6, was delivered to the RAAF in November of the same year. A73-1 had a Martin mid-upper turret (2 x 0.5in guns) and a Fraser Nash (2 x 0.5in) rear turret, but both were later replaced by the standard turrets. The five built from British components also had plywood rear doors which caused problems in the hot climate.

In mid-1947 a Lincoln Conversion Unit was set up at East Sale, the first two crews captained by Sqn Ldr J. O'Brien and Flt Lt J. Wilson. On completion of the course both crews flew their aircraft to Amberley, Queensland, to commence the re-equipment of No 82 (Bomber) Wing, with the first production Lincolns planned as replacements for the Liberators serving with Nos 12, 21 and 23 Squadrons. In February 1948 these were renumbered 1, 2 and 6 Squadrons respectively. The work of the three bomber squadrons in the early years was similar to those of the RAF: general bombing, navigation and gunnery training, with detachments away from the home base of Amberley.

The training also included regular air defence/attack exercises and SAR duties. At times the SAR could prove quite onerous, eg, during the four-day Sydney-Hobart yacht races which normally resulted in several getting into difficulties and necessitating some intensive work by the Lincoln crews.

Except for special operations a standard format crew of seven was normal, and included two pilots. It was only when the demands of the Korean War created a shortage of pilots that flight engineers were introduced, but they were the exception rather than rule.

The first serious accident with an RAAF Lincoln occurred on 17 February 1948 at Amberley. Two aircraft had been flown down to Laverton where one was left for trials, and the other brought back its crew, making a total of 16 aboard. On landing back at Amberley the Lincoln, A73-11, bounced, and as the pilot applied full power to overshoot, the cargo of engine blocks and paint which

Below: The date is 18 February 1946, the place Fisherman's Bend near Melbourne, Victoria, and A73-1 emerges from the Government Aircraft factory preparatory to initial engine runs and final fitting out. Built from UK manufactured parts, shipped out in crates, her cockpit instruments and general instructions still read 'Lancaster Mk IV' when handed over to the RAAF 24 May 1946. Clearly defined are walk lines and wing fuel tank positions./*The Age*

had been placed in the fuselage but not tied down, shifted backward, thus affecting the Lincoln's centre of gravity, so that it climbed vertically, out of control, stalled at 300 feet, dropped a wing and crashed, killing all aboard. This accident led to an order limiting the number of persons to be flown in any Lincoln to 11, the same as the number of intercom points and parachute stowages, though in this accident, it is doubtful if the precaution would have served any purpose.

The next fatal accident was on 7 March 1950 when A73-44 dived into the ground from high altitude near Amberley. A co-pilot was being checked out to fly in the left-hand seat, and the aircraft was being put into unusual attitudes. The investigation found that the release box of the pilot's parachute harness (which presumably had been left undone) had slipped down between the front of the seat 'pan' and the foot of the control column where it passed through the floor. This prevented the aircraft being pulled out of the dive, from which it never recovered.

Operation Cumulative took place during the Australian summer, October 1949 – February 1950, lasting a full five months and involving five RAAF and five RAF crews in maximum effort flying to the limits of both men and machines. The crews were based at Amberley and would set off each Thursday at 6pm on a sortie of 11-13 hours duration, terminating in alternate months at Darwin and Kalgoorlie, dropping 4 x 1,000lb bombs on set targets shortly before dawn landings at the destinations. Each trip was the equivalent of flying from England to Moscow and half-way back again. The crews were responsible for all their own bombing up and pre-flighting.

A return sortie was mounted each Sunday evening with another bomb drop before landing back at Amberley in the almost invariably bad pre-dawn weather. The Lincolns always flew at 20,000ft and were routed both ways through the tropical cu nim barriers, upper-air troughs and cold fronts full of frighteningly violent thunderstorms and turbulence. Hail frequently damaged radiators and cracked perspex.

In order to qualify as an operational sortie towards the simulated 'tour', the height, course and airspeed had to be maintained within certain limits, and the pilot's instrument panel was recorded photographically at one minute intervals throughout the flights. The Lincolns carried an eighth crew member in the rear fuselage whose job was to monitor progress and ensure safety of navigation on Lucero, but the crew could only refer to him for a cross-check at certain intervals. Despite some hair raising experiences, all the crews came through safely.

The aircraft carried standard equipment of the period, navigation aids comprising the usual API/GPI, H2S Mk 3, and Lucero. Radio was the wartime-type Marconi TR1154/1155. It was only during the later stages of operations with the B30 that Bendix

Below: Another view of A73-1, seen doing her initial engine runs shortly after being rolled out. When first flown A73-1 had a Fraser-Nash FN82 tail turret and Martin 250 CE mid-upper (both equipped with .5in Brownings) due to late delivery of the intended Boulton-Paul Type D and Bristol B17 respectively. As a true B30, she later served with No 1 Squadron until scrapped following a taxying accident 19 April 1948. */The Age*

Radio Compasses were fitted, and which made life a little easier for the crews.

The Marconi TR1154/1155 radios were not the most reliable or adequate. They would regularly drift off frequency in thunderstorms and at different pressure levels, and retuning could take the w/op a long time, particularly at extreme range. Gradually the sets were improved by fitting a crystal drive unit to the transmitter which helped to stabilise the equipment.

It seems strange the Australians should choose to retain the British radio equipment, because when *Crusader* of CBE, Marham, had visited Australia and New Zealand in October/December 1947, its radios had caused considerable problems, and several times it had lost all contact with ground control for hours on end, something quite common for British aircraft fitted with the standard wartime radio when operating in tropical, humid climates. Frequency drift on both HF and VHF appears to have been the main cause, but the prolonged silences caused a great deal of disruption at times, and led to many unnecessary alerts of emergency services; so much so, that at one stage, the Australia/New Zealand air traffic control authorities were talking quite seriously of banning aircraft fitted with the British radios and insisting upon the far superior US radio equipment. In the event, the Marconi sets, though suitably tropicalized, were never really up to the standard required on long overseas flights. Even so, they survived for many more years, both with the RAF and the RAAF.

The original production batches were fitted with the British-built Merlin 85B engines as in the Lincoln Mk I, but in service these engines proved troublesome due to stretching of cylinder block studs which required modifications. The engines were also in short supply, and with the American-built Merlin 68 unobtainable, it became necessary to seek an alternative. Fortunately, the RAAF had a good many almost new Spitfire LF VIIIs in store, and their Merlin 66 engines (also British-built) were removed and used to supplement the 85Bs. As the Merlin 66 had no provision for shaft drive to engine gear boxes, they were fitted in the outboard positions only, and in service it was not unusual for the Lincoln 30 to fly with Merlin 85Bs inboard, and 66s outboard.

In hot climates this combination resulted in an under-powered situation. There were numerous blow-backs on take-offs which wrecked the superchargers, and there were also carburration problems in the early 1950s which were attributed to a change from Dutch East Indies to Middle East fuel. Generally, those aircraft powered by the Merlin 66 were used by the home-based squadrons with the aircraft used in Malaya being fitted with the 85Bs, though eventually most of these too were repowered with the 102s.

From A73-51, the Commonwealth Aircraft Corporation, Australian-built Merlin 102 was introduced. Some later machines, including Mk 31s, received the 85B for a time, though all the long noses were eventually powered by the 102. As supplies of the CAC 102 permitted, the Mk 30s were also re-engined and the Merlin 102 was generally accepted to be a most reliable power unit.

The Merlin 102 was a universal power plant (ie, it could be fitted in any of the

Below: The Australian Lincoln 'came good' with the fitting of the home-produced Commonwealth Aircraft Corporation Merlin 102 Universal Power Plant. Intensive trials were carried out by ARDU at Laverton over the period August 1949 to March 1950, using Lincoln A73-41, the first Australian-built machine to be cleared to an auw of 82,000lb. This still from a film recorded by a special automatic camera captures A73-41 fairly leaping into the air in the hands of Wg Cdr G. D. Marshall at 120mph, some 5-10mph higher than the normal unstick speed. /*Melbourne Science Museum via G. D. Marshall*

positions on multi-engined aircraft), one of the much-improved postwar 'one hundred' series as developed for the Tudor. The engine included several major design changes which improved power, economy, reliability, and reduced maintenance. The new features included fuel metering by an SU injection pump, strengthened crank case with end-to-end oil feed, better bearings, stronger cylinder blocks and improved supercharger. The same type of propeller was used as on the 85B (DH Hydromatic) and little modification was required for the fitment of the 102 power plant to the Lincoln. The first four available engines were assembled at CAC Lidcombe from British-made components, and after successful bench tests were fitted to Lincoln A73-41 for extensive flight-testing from ARDU Laverton by Wg Cdr G. D. Marshall. The tests, lasting from August 1949 to March 1950, and conducted both from Laverton and Darwin (tropical trials), were highly successful. The Lincoln used was one of the first Australian machines to be stressed for take-offs at 82,000lb instead of the normal maximum of 75,000lb. Even at this increased weight the distance to unstick was only 958 yards. Generally the engine gave a 10 per cent improvement in performance, both in power and economy, and allowed another 2lb of boost (to +20) for take-off, though in service, this was cut back to +18. Apart from troubles with cracked exhaust stubs and some early blowbacks, the 102 proved a most admirable engine, and was quickly pressed into service just as soon as the production line got under way.

The Australian Lincolns were much the same as their British-built counterparts to

fly, of course, though reputed to be slightly lighter on the controls. (Perhaps Australian pilots were stronger!) It is interesting to record the comments of an experienced RAAF Lincoln pilot, Syd Gooding, DFC, who did a tour on Lancs during the war:

'My impressions of the Lincoln are that it was a comfortable aircraft and easy to fly. It was very light on the controls, particularly in minor adjustments of attitude where one only needed forefinger and thumb. However, if one wished to make rapid attitude changes in bank it was a different question; one hand on top and one hand on the bottom of the wheel and wind it around with all the strength one could muster. I found that it helped to reduce power on both motors on the inside of the roll.

'Having always enjoyed aerobatics I used to tip the Lincoln around quite a bit. A favourite manoeuvre was a "peel-off" from a vertical bank which impressed the crew somewhat but not the second pilot, he'd get airsick. At times I rolled past the vertical but the Lincoln pulled through beautifully and always felt as if she would "Barrel Roll" without difficulty. I was more fearful of the consequences of being found out than of the manoeuvre itself and hence never attempted it. When flying at a pageant held at Williamstown, our big fighter base, I mixed it with the fighter boys and did buzz circuits for landing. I'd roll on about 45° of bank and pull round, and found that the old Lincoln coped quite well. To me it was a very satisfying circuit – far more so than the long down-wind, cross-wind and finals of the conventional approach.

'I only witnessed one "beat-up" with a Lincoln; it was at Amberley. A senior pilot put on the show and it demonstrated that the Lincoln was no slouch. This pilot hammered around under 500ft, steep-turning port and starboard at 50-60 degrees bank and hardly got beyond the boundaries of the airfield.'

At the other end of the scale, in complete contrast, Alan Underwood, recently retired air correspondent of the *Courier Mail* (Brisbane) gives his lasting impressions:

'I flew in Lincolns as a RAAF Reserve officer (gunner and wireless operator) during the period they were at Amberley and Townsville. I took part in several exercises with them up at Manus Island (the extreme north of New Guinea), both in the standard Australian-built bombers, and the long-nosed version.

'All I can say is RAAF Lincolns were like all British-designed aircraft, an experiment in what the human airman could possibly endure physically. And with as many little hooks and jagged bits added afterward to make his existence in the beast even more trying. I think our Amberley Lincolns' decibel (db) rating in the cockpit and at the navigator's and w/op tables was about 100, which as you probably know is pain threshold. I may be the only person to have flown in a Lincoln with an umbrella up. This was as a newspaper correspondent in one of the Amberley bomber versions, flying from Amberley to New Guinea, riding in the bomb aimer's nose compartment: there wasn't enough Bostik glueing in the perspex panelling and the rain poured in.'

Both 'home' bomber squadrons were involved in the UK atomic trials carried out in central Australia: No 6 operating from Woomera itself, and No 2 from RAAF Richmond near Sydney, in company with an American contingent. Naturally enough the Australian population was very anxious that the atomic cloud did not drift over the populous SE region of the country, and the explosion was delayed for three weeks before the right conditions prevailed. During this waiting period, the No 2 Squadron contingent lived rather primitively under canvas, the best accommodation having been surrendered to the Yanks, of course.

The first device was detonated on 15 October 1953 and No 6 Squadron carried out the initial tracking of the nuclear cloud. The Americans took over from No 6 on a continuous tracking basis, and on the following day No 2 Squadron took over from the USAF B-29s. Pilot Officer A. Stapleton with Pilot Officer John H. Cooney as co-pilot took A73-25 up to 10,000ft to establish contact with the cloud, which by then had spread into a thick, brownish coloured layer. Their task was to pinpoint the centre of the cloud. An air filter was installed under the starboard wing, and a geiger counter by the signaller's seat.

Headings were flown back and forth through the cloud until readings reached their peaks, thus the centre and pattern of the cloud were established. Auxiliary fuel tanks were carried in the bomb bay, and the Lincoln remained airborne for just over 12 hours, landing back at Richmond very low on fuel and very dirty. The Americans gave the crew a wide berth. It was early days for this sort of business and in their innocence of the effects of exposure to radiation the crew (which included an RAF navigator on exchange posting, Flg Off Richard E. W. Nettley) took their Lincoln back to Amberley, where it was banished to the farthest corner of the airfield. There it was to spend the rest of its days, its fuselage marked with large purple crosses.

The system in its inimitable fashion decided the crew should be blood-checked, and the appropriate signals went forth, but without explanation as the exercise was so highly classified; consequently there was no degree of urgency appreciated. By the time the signals caught up with the crew early in 1954, it had dispersed, and John Cooney, for instance had by then been posted to No 1 Squadron in Malaya. As a fresh faced young pilot officer, he found himself following the path to Changi Hospital, well worn by airmen suspected of carrying another disease!

With the departure of No 1 Squadron to Malaya in July 1950, Nos 2 and 6 Squadrons remained as the nucleus of No 82 (Bomber) Wing at Amberley. The Lincolns of the two home-based bomber squadrons ranged far and wide 'over the country on bombing training, long-range navigation exercises, occasionally search and rescue, displays, and regular defence exercises. The squadrons used Lincolns from the Amberley 'pool' and from the date of No 1's transfer to Tengah, No 6 had the task of training and providing replacement crews, virtually along the lines of an OCU. Both squadrons did good work on flood relief work, mercy flights, medevacs, etc. No 6 also had a commitment to the School of Land/Air Warfare, doing a lot of experimental work on stores and supply dropping. On one of these trial drops a Lincoln's bomb bay was loaded with a huge steel pipe filled with concrete to simulate the weight of a jeep. An Army officer had designed a special quick-release harness which worked a bit too well; as the pipe dropped away from the aircraft it left the parachutes behind in the bomb bay, causing a minor earth tremor as it hit the ground.

No 2 Squadron was to give up its Lincolns first, the last of its Lincoln sorties being on 18 December 1953, the squadron then already converting to the A84 Canberra. On the same date, those crews not converted transferred to No 6 Squadron.

No 6 Squadron was not re-equipped with the Canberra until much later, its last Lincoln flight being on 7 July 1955, and on 11 July, all its remaining Lincolns were transferred to the Lincoln Conversion Flight (still at Amberley) which was then given full squadron status. The unit's main task was to still provide crews for No 1 Squadron.

Aussie Specials

Like the RAF, the Royal Australian Air Force had a number of specialist training and experimental units which made extensive use of the Lincoln which was, after all, the only suitably large, 4-engined military aircraft available in the country following withdrawal of the Liberators.

At East Sale, Victoria, a pool of Lincolns was established for use by the various units based there – the Central Flying School and Schools of Air Navigation, Air Armaments (for bombing and gunnery courses) and Photography. Lincolns appeared at East

Sale soon after the type had completed service-acceptance trials with 1APU, and for some years the pool consisted mainly of the earlier vintage Lincolns with the rather unreliable Merlin 85 engines, prone to connecting-rod failures, plug troubles, etc, and many of the replacements with later marks of engines were aircraft which had seen considerable service with the squadrons.

One of the best known of the East Sale Lincolns was A73-2, used primarily by the School of Air Navigation. It had been delivered new in August 1946 to No 1 Aircraft Performance Unit at Point Cook, Victoria for service acceptance trials, and for early astro navigation and research work, for which it was specially modified early in 1947.

In its modified form, it closely resembled the Aries series of the RAF, with turrets removed, tail fairing and highly polished natural metal finish, giving it 15/18kts more speed. Progressively, it was fitted with all the modern navigation aids as they came along, keeping it well ahead of the standard Lincolns, many of which were later to be equipped with aids proved in service by A73-2 on its long-range navigation and survey flights.

Below: Clearly showing nose-mounted Trimetrogon K17 camera ports is A73-2 during service with 1 Aircraft Performance Unit. Also visible is the mandatory 500lb of ballast in lieu of nose turret. This photo was taken on return from the Point Cook-Macquarie Island flight on 15 March 1947, which established the Lincoln's 4,000-mile-plus capabilities. Protrusions below the nose are an outside air temperature element and repositioned airspeed pitot./*G. D. Marshall*

Above: A73-2 seen at its later home, School of Air Navigation, East Sale, in January 1952 with streamlined tail cone and named *Nyhuan* (carried in black on both sides of nose)./*The Age*

A73-2 was christened *Nyhuan* at RAAF East Sale on 25 August 1947 by Mrs George Jones, wife of the Chief of the Air Staff, the name being a word from the East Gippsland Aboriginal dialect meaning 'scout' or 'pathfinder'. East Sale had another named Lincoln, A73-15, *Brenool*, a word from the same dialect meaning 'traveller'. This, too, was used for long-range navigation training and had its turrets faired over, with additional astrodome and fuselage seats installed. Lincoln A73-8 of the Air Armament School was named *Gundawarra*, Aboriginal for 'weapons thrower', and used for bombing and gunnery training and research in much the same role as the RAF's *Thors* of EAAS. Two other Lincolns, A73-14 and -18 were fitted out as transports, with turrets faired over, and a small passenger compartment in the rear fuselage with eight airline-type seats, side windows, and a galley; they were used on a regular courier service to Japan.

A73-2 had long-range tanks installed in the bomb bay, bringing its fuel capacity up to 3,650 gallons. From an early stage it undertook some very long-range navigation flights, among the most notable being in December 1946, when, captained by Wing Commander Bill Brill, DSO, DFC, it made three flights across Australia at 20,000ft, each track only 12 miles apart, each leg 1,100 miles. The purpose was a photographic survey covering 45,000 square miles, including what was to become the Woomera rocket range.

In mid-March 1947 A73-2 flew a 14½-hour, 2,500-mile round trip from Point Cook to photo-survey Macquarie Island, a tiny pinpoint of land deep in South Antarctica, on which it was proposed to establish a meteorologic research and observation post. The Lincoln was captained by Squadron Leader D. R. Cuming, AFC and Bar, assisted by Squadron Leaders G. D. Marshall and G. H. N. Shiells, DFC, AFC. It was to visit

Macquarie Island again on 31 January 1951 to drop mail, food and urgently needed medical supplies to the men on the island who by then had been cut off for nearly 18 months. Despite very bad weather, complete loss of radio contact soon after take-off from East Sale, and progressive failure during the outward flight of almost every item of navigation equipment, the Lincoln crew eventually picked up the Macquarie beacon only six miles off track after 1,100 miles and some seven hours over the sea entirely on dead-reckoning. In heavy rain, and with a cloud base of only 400ft, the three 'storpedoes' were successfully dropped to the waiting scientists, the only injury being to one of the 10,000 sea elephants on the island.

In the late 1940s/early 1950s, long-range navigation was the 'in' thing, and *Nyhuan* flew numerous single-heading pressure pattern sorties at constant height, speed and heading pre-computed from meteorological data, one such being to RNZAF Wigram, near Christchurch, New Zealand, on 1 December 1951. Soon after take-off from East Sale in very bad weather, the crew was entertained by St Elmo's Fire rattling round the cockpit, this spectacular phenomenon lasting over two hours. The Lincoln was captained on this occasion by the OC Flying of the SAN, Wing Commander C. H. Spurgeon, the aircraft arriving over its planned pinpoint on the west coast of New Zealand exactly on track after 6½ hours over the sea.

'Spud' Spurgeon went on to command No 1 Squadron in Malaya, and like 'Digger' Shiells, 'Gel' Cuming, and Geoff Marshall, was later to achieve Air rank in the RAAF. *Nyhuan* continued in service at East Sale until late 1953, when it was withdrawn and broken up. Part of its fuselage is said to have survived at Woomera until 1962, used as a target storage hut on the rifle range.

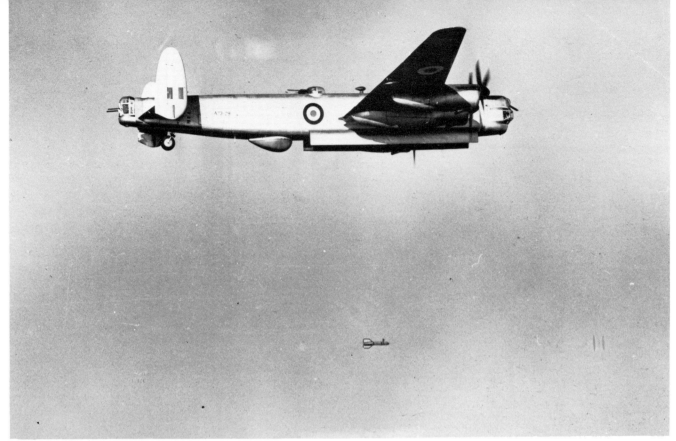

One of the most interesting experiments in which a Lincoln was used was rainmaking. A73-29, an ex-1 Squadron machine, was specially modified and operated by Detachment B of ARDU at Richmond, NSW, on behalf of the Commonwealth Scientific & Industrial Research Organisation (CSIRO) on cloud physics research. The specially formed unit also had two Dakotas and an Auster, and five RAAF crews under the command of a very experienced wartime operational pilot, Sqn Ldr W. N. Nichol.

Basically the purpose was to persuade clouds to produce rain, so most of the flying was in heavy weather, through turbulent, ice-forming cloud, The Dakotas were used to seed the clouds with silver iodide particles from a burner under the port wing, hoping this would produce raindrops from the right sort of cloud. The Lincoln did the same job by electric shock treatment, by putting a half million volt electrostatic charge into the clouds.

A73-29 was extensively modified. It had its rear turret faired over, and its mid-upper turret was replaced by a cockpit canopy from a Vampire fighter to give the observer a better field of view. Its front guns were also removed, and a 9in metal tube protruded from the nose for collection of ice crystals in cloud for on-board analysis by one of the two CSIRO boffins, or 'rain doctors' usually included in the regular crew.

Internally the Lincoln carried a 10hp Ford Prefect engine with its mixture specially adapted for operation at altitude, to drive the electric generator which delivered the charge. In the bomb bay was installed an electrically-operated winch for the high-tension electric supply cables and steel towing wire for 'Betsy', a 4-foot long, 160lb, bomb-shaped drogue which was lowered in flight, through the open bomb doors, to trail 150ft below and slightly astern of the Lincoln. Together with the special X-ray equipment to control the charge, the whole assembly weighed about a ton.

The Lincoln would fly above or into certain types of cloud and deliver its half million volts through 'Betsy'. In the right conditions,

No ordinary Lincoln was A73-29, an ARDU machine fitted out as a flying laboratory for rain making experiments. Among the specialist equipment carried was 'Betsy' a streamlined bomb-shaped weight some 5ft long and weighing 148lb, lowered by winch to trail twin nylon cords through which were passed electric charges of a million volts to 'seed' the clouds. *Left:* View from forward end of A73-29's bomb bay showing 'Betsy' falling away. *Above:* A general view of the Lincoln with 'Betsy' being lowered. At this early stage of the trials, the mid-upper turret is still in place. It was later replaced by a Vampire cockpit canopy.
/CSIRO via W. N. Nichol

such as developing cumulus cloud, the charge caused the hydroscopic nuclei to coalesce to a degree where they became sufficiently large moisture droplets to fall as rain. The work was carried out mainly over the Southern Alps and Blue Mountains of Australia, the aircraft being detached to various bases, wherever conditions looked promising.

The flying was not without its anxious moments. One day, returning from Amberley to Richmond, A73-29 was in and out of heavy cloud when its port-outer engine and propeller 'ran away', developing an oil fire, and refusing to feather. A Sabre jet-fighter heard the Lincoln's 'PAN' call and formated alongside, its pilot confirming the fire. The engine eventually siezed, continuing to pour out smoke as Sqn Ldr Nichol let down through the cloud to Richmond, with the rest of the crew, including the two boffins, prepared to jump for it if the fire spread. Fortunately it did not, and the Lincoln was landed safely. On opening up the cowling, large chunks of metal fell to the ground; a con-rod was found to have broken and caused a virtual disintegration of the moving parts of the engine.

On another occasion, as the high voltage charge was delivered into a cloud, the static build-up in the aircraft itself became too great for the discharge wicks on the trailing edges, and with an alarming bang, a large hole was blown in the top of a wing, exposing an inboard fuel tank. But by far the most serious crisis arose when, on one sortie, the HT and drogue cables touched the fuselage while the Lincoln was flying through very turbulent cu-nim cloud, and blew the master fuse in the nose. On emerging from the cloud, it was to find the drogue riding 30ft above the cockpit instead of 150ft below and behind. The cables had somehow wrapped them-selves round the fuselage, fouling the elevators and rudders. Never has a Lincoln been flown so straight and so level for half an hour as by Sqn Ldr Nichol, as the cables gradually unwound themselves and the drogue returned to its normal position before being very gingerly winched in. Only Sqn Ldr Nichol was permitted to fly the Lincoln, with a regular, specially selected crew, and his previous cloud flying experience during Operation Cumulative was to stand him in good stead on several occasions. No passengers were ever carried on these highly dangerous exercises.

A73-29 and its crew were also involved in measurement of rainfall after seeding by the Dakotas, often below critically low cloud bases, and in measuring turbulence, up draughts, and radiation build up in the most violent of cu nims. Detachment B's small fleet was also frequently called-upon for mercy flights and emergency ASR duties. In December 1956, the Lincoln was used on condensation nuclei sampling flights across the whole breadth of Australia in the wake of micro-meteorite showers, in co-operation with scientists in Florida and South Africa. For these tests, the aircraft was flown at 24,000ft, considerably higher than the usual ceiling with Merlin 85s, and at that height, controls were very sluggish, and props. difficult to synchronize.

The 'rainmaking' trials were considered quite successful, lasting from 1956/59 until the Lincoln was withdrawn, leaving the Dakotas to carry on the work. On leaving Detachment B to take command of No 23 Squadron as it converted to Canberras, Noel Nichol received the Queen's Commendation. Now a retired wing commander, he has turned his attention to community and youth relations.

Below: Spinners apart, the home based RAAF squadrons were devoid of unit markings. When in use spinner colours were yellow for No 2 Squadron; red for No 6 Squadron; pale blue for No 10 Squadron; dark blue for No 1 Squadron; and black for No 11 Squadron. Here A73-31, a B30A of No 6 Squadron Amberley is seen flying over typical Queensland terrain in 1948./*A. B. Boyle*

The Long Nose

So little seems to have appeared in print about the Australian Mk 31 (Long Nose) version of the Lincoln, it might almost be called the ultimate development, that we felt justified in describing at some length the story of the Mk 31 and its crews, in exclusive service with No 10 Squadron, Royal Australian Air Force. We are greatly indebted to Sqn Ldr John Laming, AFC, who did two tours on the Mk 31, firstly as a young sergeant pilot, latterly as a flight lieutenant QFI, and to Sqn Ldr Colin S. 'Dinny' Ryan, a signaller AEO who served on the Mk 31 and also on the Mk 30 for a good number of years, doing two tours in Malaya. Both amassed over 3,000 hours on Lincolns, and we are privileged to have had passed on to us some of their experiences. Modestly, they both described themselves as 'everyday, and typical of life on the Lincolns'. The details and impressions are exactly as related to us. Other contributors to this section to whom we are equally grateful, include Robert Stewart who flew the last RAAF Long Nose.

10 Squadron and the Mk 31

No 10 Squadron reformed at what is now known as Townsville (Queensland) on 1 March 1949. The airfield was, until 8 March 1951, named Garbutt, after the former owners of the land on which it was built. Sqn Ldr Bill Brill, DSO, DFC, a wartime Wellington and Lancaster pilot was the CO, but for the first six months the squadron had only two flyable aircraft, a Wirraway and an Oxford, and the first Lincolns, A73-12 and 22, both Mk 30s, did not arrive from Amberley until 12 September, just in time for the Battle of Britain Day fly past. The aircraft arrived without any tools or handling equipment and it was to be another six months before the squadron had worked up to being capable of meeting its commitments for search and rescue in NE Australia. When the Darwin Flight Information Region was added to its area of responsibilities, it was decided that a detachment of the squadron would have to be positioned at Darwin. The first Lincoln arrived there on 30 June 1950, and throughout the Lincoln era this detachment was a permanent feature. During the initial stages the period of detachment was three months, changed progressively to one month, then one week, and finally settled at a 14-day period. Because of the heavy strain it placed on resources, the squadron establishment was increased to eight Lincolns and one Dakota.

Below: As interim equipment before the advent of the 'Long Nose', No 10 Squadron used the B30 in virtually standard form. Here is A73-36, with full turret armament, and still wearing South East Asia Command markings on its fuselage, though this style had largely disappeared by the time of the Korean conflict. Less than a year later (on 13 August 1950) it was this very machine in which No 10 Squadron's gunnery leader was to win the unit's first award of the Malayan campaign (a DFC). */No 10 Squadron RAAF*

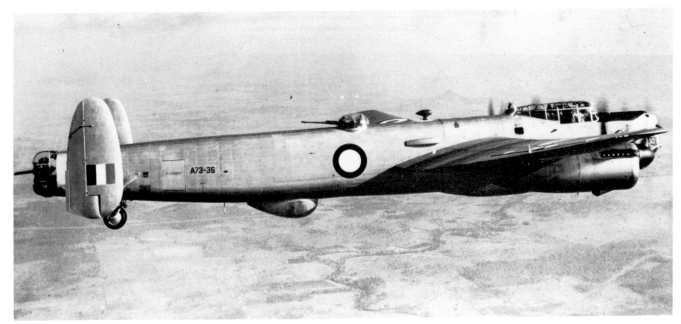

The squadron's role at this stage was that of search and rescue, and general reconnaissance. The Mk 30 'short-nosed' Lincoln with which the squadron was equipped initially was more or less the standard bomber version, with its front and rear turrets fully armed, and much of the time between SAR and GR sorties was spent on bombing and gunnery practice. In July 1952 the Bristol B17 mid-upper turrets were refitted, and fired for the first time in the air against targets towed by Beaufighters. The primary role of the squadron was slowly changed to anti-submarine warfare and on 12 July 1952, the Lincolns took part in their first anti-sub exercises against HM submarine *Tactician* on loan from the RN. The crews were sent on regular courses at the Australian JASS at Naval Air Station Nowra, near Sydney. It soon became obvious that the Mk 30 Lincoln was not an ideal platform for maritime operations and the Mk 31 was evolved. The principle and most obvious difference was the 6ft 6in extension to the nose.

On 21 January 1953 A73-48 the first of the modified Lincolns visited Townsville as a prototype and passed quickly on to evaluation trials at Nowra before going to 10 Squadron on 4 March 1953. Shortly after this, the squadron received three more Mk 31s and for a time both long and short noses operated side by side until the Mk 30 was generally phased out, though one remained with No 10 for training duties until February 1957. The squadron's changing role was officially acknowledged on 20 May 1953 when its title was changed from No 10(GR) to No 10(MR) Squadron; thus it had returned to its wartime role in which it flew the Sunderland.

The Mk 31 conversions were carried out by the Government Aircraft Factory, Fishermans Bend, near Melbourne, the Servicing Dept doing those returned from prior service as B30s, the Main Assembly Workshops those straight off the production line. The new nose sections were referred to as the D1A. A73-48, the prototype, was converted by the GAF Experimental Dept, also at Fishermans Bend. Eight of the Mk 31s were later modified at the GAF plant to the MR31 standard, and two by the RAAF itself, probably at Amberley. (A73-28 and -67). The modified Lincolns were collected by RAAF crews and flown to Laverton for acceptance and test flights. Getting Lincolns out of Fishermans Bend was no easy task, with a short runway of only 1,500 yards, and a river and high-tension cables at the end of it. When the Canberras started to come along the strip proved inadequate and was closed in late 1954 after transfer of the Servicing Dept to Avalon, near Geelong, 30 miles SW of Melbourne, which had a new 5,000-yard runway. Though the factory remains at Fishermans Bend, the former airfield is now a motor racing track.

The newly converted Lincolns were stored at Laverton until required by the squadron. Major servicing was undertaken at Amberley. Usually the squadron crew bringing an aircraft into Amberley for major service would collect the replacement which would have been checked out by the resident test flight crew.

The first batch of long noses were known merely as the 'Mk 31,' being equipped primarily for general reconnaissance, but during 1953 further modifications were made to the next batch to equip the aircraft more specifically for anti-submarine work, and these became known as the MR31. The first four MR31s were delivered to No 10 Sqdn in December 1953. Some of the earlier batch of long noses were converted B30s but most were brand new aircraft.

The first Mk 31s were fitted with the English-made Merlin 85B engine, but in service, the cylinder block studs tended to stretch, and eventually all Mk 31s were fitted with the slightly less powerful (1,650hp) but more reliable Australian-built Merlin 102 engine with fuel injection. Whilst the Mk 30 re-engined with Merlin 102 was redesignated Mk 30A there is no record of the Mk 31 being so. The Merlin 85 had shrouded exhausts, but those of the 102 were 'straight out', making them considerably noisier.

The Mk 31 retained much of the original equipment of the Mk 30 including Loran and Lucero as navigation/homing aids, plus a Bendix radio compass. A Bendix radio altimeter was added, an invaluable aid for long sorties of 12 hours duration in the shadowing role only 50ft above the sea. The H2S was modified to become ASV Mk 7 by fitment of a small prism to the antenna to deflect the impulse for 'snort' searching. Additional AP1/GP1 was installed in the nose for use by the second navigator in the attack or SAR phases, a low level bombsight was fitted, and changes were also made to the weapons-carriage and pyrotechnic systems. Instead of the normal single 400-gallon overload tank, the Mk 31s weapons bay was modified to carry two jettisonable 187-gallon tanks, thus allowing maximum space for carriage of bombs, survival cannisters, directional sono-buoys, torpedoes, etc. Provision was also made for carrying airborne lifeboats.

Inside the rear door was a large chute for dropping flares, smoke markers and non-directional sono-buoys, while the way to the rear turret was blocked by the large ram and motor for the retractable rear facing camera. The rear turret itself was calibrated for drift readings which proved more accurate than the

American B3 gyro-stabilised drift meter mounted behind the bomb aimer's seat.

The standard Lincoln autopilot was not reliable enough at the low levels at which the Mk 31s operated, having been known on occasions to put the aircraft into a sudden roll, so a Smith's electric autopilot was fitted. The maximum auw was increased to 82,000lb following certain strengthening mods to the centre section, wing roots, spar webs and undercarriage bays.

Flying the Mk 31

What was it like to fly such a mighty machine? Apart from the extra-long nose, perhaps not so different to the standard Lincoln, except in crosswinds which had a pronounced effect on the additional large side area of the nose, and at night with virtually no forward vision.

Starting up: An experience in itself, with the pilot handling fuel cocks, pitch levers and throttles while the co-pilot (or flight engineer) operated the three rows of buttons: primers, booster coils and starters, plus ignition switches, rather like a church organist. In the tropics, with engines warm, it was easy to overprime, which caused an alarming conflagration in the exhaust stubs, with 10-foot flames shooting back over the wings only a few feet away from the faces in the cockpit, a particularly frightening spectacle at night. It was a case of keeping the engine turning, to clear the fire by opening the throttle as soon as the engine had caught properly. No 3 was started first to charge the pneumatic and hydraulic systems for brakes, flaps, bomb doors, etc. The bomb doors were always opened before stopping engines, as pumping them open by hand to load stores, etc, could take over an hour. As one Mk 31 was being started up, the No 3 spinner fell off and was caught by one of the turning propeller blades, which hit it horizontally (rather like a flashing cover drive) with a tremendous clang straight through each of the open bomb doors, leaving gaping holes in them, not far below the feet of the startled pilots. All three remaining spinners were found to be insecure, something the crew could not have seen in the pre-flight examination. Until the arrival of Wg Cdr G. A. 'Cy' Greenwood, OBE, AFC, as CO of No 10 Squadron, in June 1959, there was no check list for the Mk 31, the pre-flight checks being done from memory. There was no ground engineering course for crews, it was a question of pilots picking it up as they went along, under the eye of an instructor of course. The co-pilot was responsible for external checks. The Wg Cdr was a very experienced pilot having flown Beaufighters during World War II, and becoming a prisoner of the Japanese after being shot down. He had just finished strapping himself into the left hand seat prior to his first conversion flight in the Lincoln, and the instructor said 'Right, sir, we normally do the cockpit checks from left to right, starting with bomb doors,' but was cut short with the query: 'One moment, Flight Lieutenant, where is the check list?' On being told there was no such thing available, the Wg Cdr said, 'What! No check list for an aircraft this size? Right, out we get, and no-one on this squadron flies until they have a check list'.

Below: A fine study of No 10 Squadron's MR31, A73-66, doing a 'beat up' of sun-baked Manus Island during the combined operation Satex in 1954. The squadron's area of responsibilities eventually encompassed the Indian Ocean, Timor, Arafura and Coral Seas, a large part of the Pacific Ocean, in addition to the states of Western Australia, Northern Territory and Queensland – all in all one tenth of the world's surface./*The Age*

Within a very few hours, the check list had been drawn up by the instructor, and operations returned to normal.

Taxying: Again not without its problems because of the restricted vision and due to a not over efficient braking system. The pneumatic brakes were operated by a single lever on the control wheel and use of rudder provided differential braking on the main wheels. The pressure could soon be exhausted and the brakes tended to fade when hot. To maintain pressure, the ideal rpm caused engine overheating in the tropics. On the other hand, if the aircraft taxied too slowly the engines tended to overheat and the plugs oiled up, so it was a question of compromise. Taxying at night was very difficult because the pilots could never see more than one or two lights ahead, and then only out of the side windows. At Townsville it was decided to replace the older type taxyway lighting (at the side) with centre line lights, and this caused a real problem. The captain had to stand on the rudders and put his head well out of the side window, with a hand on outboard throttles trying to see just one light ahead. It became necessary to have a crew member in the glass nose to call out directions, 'left left steady, right right steady' in best wartime movie tradition.

Take-off: The throttles were set to zero boost until all engines had stabilised on equal power. As the throttles were opened initially towards take-off power, the left one (port outer) needed to be advanced to correct the yaw to the left until there was sufficient speed to make the rudders effective, then all four throttles could be pushed to the first 'gate' to give +12 boost. The start of the take-off run always had to be done by the pilot on the gyro compass indicator until the tail came up to enable him to see forward over the nose. At 3,000rpm overload boost of +18 was available for emergencies, such as short runways, engine failure, etc, but was used only sparingly, except by one old and experienced warrant officer pilot who used +18 for every take-off, his philosophy being that if an engine was going to fail, let it do so as early as possible. On the RAF Mk II Lincolns, with Merlin 68s & 68As a boost cut out lever could provide +21 in exceptional circumstances. At about 100/110kts, depending on auw, the Lincoln could be eased off the ground and would climb away initially fully laden (82,000lb) at 120kts (safety speed), at which rpm could be reduced to 2,850. After retraction of undercarriage and flaps, and build-up of speed to 140/145kts, climbing power of +9 boost and 2,650rpm would give a rate of climb of 4/500ft per min, gradually decreasing with height. The highest noted altitude for a

106

Mk 31 was 28,050ft over Darwin (A73-67 in Dec 1959) taking 1hr 20min to achieve at a climb speed of 119kts. Up to 12,500ft the engines would remain in MS (Medium Supercharger) 'gear' as it was called, but at or about this height would automatically cut into Full or High Supercharger gear (FS). The radiator shutters on the Mk 31 were set permanently open, whereas those on the RAF Lincolns could be switched to operate automatically as required.

Flying: For such a large 4-engined aircraft the Lincoln was relatively light on the controls and could sometimes outmanoeuvre a fighter. One regular exercise was to track the aircraft carrier *Sydney* which carried Sea Furies. The idea was for the Lincoln to remain at a discreet distance from the carrier and home in Canberras from 30,000ft to attack the ship. The Lincoln would try to creep in at low level but the crew would normally spot the carrier visually long before the ASV Mk 7 radar had picked it up. The ship's radar had by then easily spotted the Lincoln and scrambled its Sea Furies to attack. Some violent tail chases often took place, and with skilful handling, a Lincoln could sometimes get behind a Sea Fury, the crew taking great satisfaction in calling 'rat-a-tat' over the R/T.

The Lincolns were regular performers at air displays for Battle of Britain and Anzac Days. Lots of noise and low flying was the simple philosophy. A run in at less than 100ft at VNE (230kts) lightly loaded, a pronounced angle of dihedral, a pull up into a steep climbing turn at +12 and, at 2,000ft, wheel hard over, and the aircraft would gently topple over at the top of the climb,

Above: Lincoln flying, Aussie-style – no pressurisation, no air conditioning – as Flt Lt John Laming of No 10 Squadron swelters at the controls of a 'Long Nose' in temperatures over 100°F on a long-range maritime exercise out of Darwin. The heat made the wearing of flying overalls and Mae Wests almost unbearable – and oh for a lightweight headset! Unlike the RAF Lincolns, the Mk 31 had no distant reading compass in the centre of the coaming. All had dual controls as standard, in this instance providing a convenient clothes-peg./*J. L. Laming*

looking like a stall turn, into a steepish descent, well under control into a low level run with everything down, wheels, flaps, bomb doors, into an all-engine go-around from 50ft with the crowd loving the sight and great sound of the Merlins.

According to Pilots' Notes, 'below 10,000ft the Lincoln should maintain height fully loaded on any three engines.' This may have been so in the UK, or cooler climates, but not in the tropics. On three engines, the aircraft would soon be down to 2,000ft at anything over 74,000lb auw other than by use of take-off power on the three engines, and coolant temperature problems prevented that. On two engines, 'height should be maintained if below 10,000ft at 122/126kts with 2,000 gallons remaining'; but this, too, was not possible in the tropics. Maximum endurance was about 15 hours with little reserve, the average consumption of the Mk 31 being 195/210gph.

The fuel jettison system consisted of pulling a knob in the cockpit, which released two long rubber pipes below the wings, inboard of the inner engines. They resembled an elephant's trunk. If not switched off in time, the last 200 gallons sprayed the fuel all along the fuselage, thus creating a very positive fire hazard.

Two engines: One 'trick' learned by the pilots of the Mk 31 was from an American source. When flying on only two engines it was found that a few vital knots could be gained by dropping down to less than 100ft above the sea or land thus reducing the induced drag. The 8/10kts or so won back enabled the remaining engines to be eased slightly to reduce their overload.

Landing: The real problems in flying the 'long nose' came in landing, particularly at night, and in crosswinds. A good landing in a Lincoln gave great satisfaction but it was a difficult aircraft to land well with any consistency. Few pilots regretted their tours on the Lincoln – one of the best pure flying machines in terms of stability and landing technique. It was possible to do a perfect three-pointer either with or without flap, but it needed skill and not a little luck.

Initial conversion would be carried out at Townsville in the early morning at first light, in conditions of zero wind. Once the sea breeze had got up by 10am, usually 070, 10/15kts across runway 'zero two' it made conditions unsuitable for new pilots, most of whom came straight to the squadron from flying training school, with a mere 200 hours experience.

On a cold, still morning it was something of a thrill even for the most experienced of pilots to achieve a smooth three point flapless landing, literally playing the control column lightly like a Tiger Moth in the hold off until a few inches above the ground; then gradually ease back, changing the attitude to 'grease' the wheels on. An equally satisfying experience was to get lined up on final approach at 500ft on a still, clear day, gradually reducing power and speed to come over the fence at the prescribed 105kts, closing the throttles to idle power, with the Merlins crackling, hold off with the aircraft perfectly stable, relax on the wheel slightly, and touch all three wheels together, with only the slightest squeal from the tyres. A proud moment, and few other aircraft could compare.

It was, however, just as easy to bounce, something the Lincoln always seemed to

Above: Experience tells. Flt Lt John Laming shows how to do a flapless 'three-pointer' at Townsville in A73-57. Because of the poor forward vision with the tail down this was definitely not an exercise for the novice. /*J. L. Laming*

want to do. It would also be keen to swing, especially in a crosswind, and if the tailwheel was touched down first. When this happened, the mainwheels would follow with something of a thump; and if one mainwheel came down before the other, things could happen very quickly if the pilot had failed to anticipate the direction of the ensuing swing. The instructor had no more than two seconds to take over, and these could be heart stopping moments if the pilot was allowed to continue, with swings getting worse as the pilot got out of phase with alternate braking, rudder, and bursts of power on the outboard engines, presenting quite a spectacle to the watchers who invariably turned out at Townsville for introduction of new pilots to crosswind landings.

Instructing was an arduous job, there being only one QFI on the squadron until the later years. Five or six flights per day, with up to 14 hours on duty were common. For the instructor the greatest difficulty was in seeing the runway in a crosswind landing with the huge nose crabbed across to starboard up to 20° into wind. New pilots always tended to touch down with drift on in a crosswind, unable to judge the precise moment to kick straight, so the Lincoln usually bounced up to 10 or 15ft with noisy protests from the tyres. The instructors had to become adept at the 'go around', this being much safer than trying to salvage a bad landing.

The same exercise at night was a hazardous proposition. On one night crosswind conversion trip, Flt Sgt Bill Ankers (later of TAA) was approaching to land in heavy rain on the blackest of nights. As he brought the Lincoln in over the threshold, a sudden blinding squall hit it and sent the one and only wiper right off the windscreen, leaving it standing vertically and uselessly upwards. Neither pilot could see a thing and the instructor, John Laming quickly had to take over and do an all-engines, full-flap overshoot from only about six feet. There was only one artificial horizon in the aircraft – on the pilot's main instrument panel, and the instructor had to accomplish the overshoot with head craned well over to the left to see the flight instruments, while coping with throttles, flaps, rudders and control wheel of a heavy aircraft. It required some skill.

On another occasion, the same instructor was doing a night conversion with Sgt Gurr, and on take-off 'pulled a donk' (throttled-back an engine) to simulate engine failure. The Lincoln climbed away only sluggishly on a dark, hot night, on three engines, with No 4 (starboard outer) throttled back. Before turning base leg, the sergeant asked for $\frac{1}{4}$ flap; the instructor pushed down the selector lever and as the indicator neared the required position pulled the lever back up to neutral only to have the lever come clean away in his hand. The flaps continued to 'fully down', their large area creating a lethal situation.

There was no time to tell Sgt Gurr what was happening, just a quick 'taking over', and never had an idling engine been so quickly brought back to life! All four engines were pushed through the gate to $+18$; the nose reared rapidly $20°$ skywards at 130kts, needing the full strength of both pilots to keep the control wheel pushed fully forward to maintain attitude and avoid the stall. The Lincoln staggered between the hills round on to finals, still on full power. By gradual reduction of power, the aircraft was brought in for a perfectly normal full-flap landing with the bemused trainee pilot still wondering what had happened.

There was a series of flap lever failures over a period of weeks, the cause being metal fatigue of the bottom joint. Fortunately no accidents resulted, though several pilots were glad of their previous zero-flap landing practices. Usually, the flapless landing was avoided at all costs, but better techniques were gradually evolved and most pilots acquired the knack of the longer, more curved approach, thus keeping the runway in view for much longer, then having a crewman in the nose to advise when lined-up on the runway, and keeping the tail higher, touching down on mainwheels at 115kts. It required most of Townsville's 8,000ft main runway to get the tail lowered gradually, and pull up with quite heavy braking and the burning-out of numerous rubber brake bags.

At night, flapless landings were difficult affairs. The landing lamps were poor, and on finals, the pilot started to lose sight of the runway lights at 200ft. At 50ft on round out, nothing was visible over the nose, and the landing became a matter of luck. At the touchdown, the pilot could see, perhaps, two runway lights on the left, none to starboard. After touchdown a tall pilot could just keep two or three lights in view by pressing his face hard against the cockpit window on his left; but the shorter pilot had to stand on his rudder pedals just before touchdown, riding them like a jockey in order to see anything ahead. At the point of touchdown, he then had to release the control wheel, open the side window with a deft flick of the left hand, pulling down his goggles with his right hand, and stick his head out of the side window into the 100kt slipstream, trying to keep the aircraft running straight.

It was an RAF pilot on a two year exchange posting who helped to solve the crosswind landing problems. Flt Lt Lawrie Hampson (now Grp Capt.) was an experienced Shackleton pilot, who had rejoined the RAF after a spell of civil flying on Daks. On his very first crosswind conversion trip on 3 July 1958, in the MR31 Lincoln (A73-28) he demonstrated the now widely-used method of putting one wing down into wind, and applying slight opposite rudder to keep straight. It worked a treat on the 'long nose'.

Near to the end of the downwind leg of Townsville's main runway lay Worth Zoo, which kept a fine selection of monkeys. During one night-flying training session, the tower received a 'phone call from an irate zoo keeper to say the Lincolns had been responsible for the deaths of all his prized monkeys. It appears they slept on high perches and branches by being able to lock finger and toe muscles round them. As the Lincolns selected 2,850rpm overhead the zoo, the noise and harmonics of the unsynchronised propellers in peculiar atmospheric conditions had caused the unfortunate animals to release their holds and fall 30ft or more to their deaths. As a result the zoo not only had to have its stock replaced at considerable cost to the RAAF, but also to be fitted with a red flashing beacon to warn the Lincoln crews. Another regular complainant was the owner of a drive-in cinema which was directly under the base-leg turn. The howl of four Merlins passing overhead at only 1,000ft could be quite uncomfortable for the picture-goers on a warm, still night. A hypnotist lived in the suburb which started just beyond the end of runway O2. He, too, complained but as he was reputed to make illegal use of young ladies in his sessions, he got little sympathy from the crews who, after each complaint, would purposely hold down their fully laden Lincolns a little lower on night take-offs, the noise of four Merlins using $+18$ at 3,000rpm making life very difficult for the hypnotist.

Search and Rescue/Maritime Reconnaissance (SAR/MR): General Duties
Over the years, No 10 Squadron's Lincolns were called upon to perform a variety of roles within its huge area of responsibilities. Frequently light aircraft pilots would fail to report in on arrival at their homestead, usually because of radio malfunction, and such failures could trigger off a long search. A young girl of 13 once wandered away from her remote home station near Cloncurry. A 14-hour search by a 10 Squadron Lincoln failed to locate the child who was later found sheltering under bushes. During the search, carried out at low level with temperatures of $120°$F in the shade, all the food aboard the Lincoln turned bad long before any of the crew had a bite. There were no cooking facilities in the aircraft, and cut rations were issued by the Station Catering Section before each flight, each crew member being allocated one box of rations per three hours flying; chicken portions, rolls, apples, etc. Several cases of bent propellers occurred when food boxes were jettisoned from the nose windows over the sea, but the crews were not certain

whether it was the boxes themselves which did the damage or the rock hard buns which often went out with them. It became standard procedure to feather No 2 before having an in-flight clear-up.

On transit to the Darwin detachments it was usual to carry up from Townsville a couple of panniers in the bomb bay, containing much needed fresh meat, milk, vegetables, etc, always in short supply on such a hot, remote station. The transit flight was usually combined with a low level 12/13-hour 'long way round' training mission which would include some air-to-sea firing, or practice bomb drops in the Gulf of Carpenteria. On one occasion, unfortunately, the food panniers fell away as the bomb doors opened. Fortunately the loss was faithfully recorded by the rear-facing attack camera to prove to the glowering Darwin Catering Officer that the Lincoln crew had not been profiteering.

Much of the time was spent over the Northern Territories searching for missing light aircraft. The Flying Doctor's Beech Staggerwing once ran out of oil and landed on crocodile-infested mudflats, being found by a Lincoln after a whole day's search.

During the night of 4/5 February 1956 another Flying Doctor aircraft went missing, Anson VH-MMG operated by MacRobertson Airlines. It had picked up a nursing sister and sick baby from Broome in NW Australia, on the Indian Ocean, 450 miles north of the Tropic of Capricorn. It was a wild night in the middle of the wet season, a cyclone having passed through only a few hours before. The Lincoln on standby at Darwin, A73-55, was called out and Flt Lt W. N. (Nick) Nichol and crew arrived over the search area at first light, 4am, to find it completely covered by water. They landed at Broome after 11 hours and for the next four days the crew searched for 11/12 hours. Their aircraft went 'out of hours' ie beyond its scheduled major inspection time, on the second day; but there was no replacement available so it was a question of just pressing on. By the sixth day a replacement arrived but went u[s, so its crew took over the time-expired Lincoln to give Flt Lt Nichol and crew a day's rest. By the time the search ended, the Lincoln had done 120 hours beyond its time, but had performed perfectly, with one exception: the autopilot had become u/s from the start of the detachment which meant that Nichol and his co-pilot had to do all the flying manually, low level in very hot, bumpy, tropical conditions. It was physically demanding and each pilot flew for only one hour at a time, spending the 'rest' hour (sic!) asleep on the catwalk under the second pilot's seat. There was no such thing as a rest bed. A73-55 was believed to be the first 4-engined land-plane ever to land at Broome, which was more

accustomed to handling seaplanes. The only refueling facility was a truck carrying 44-gallon drums. As each search virtually emptied the Lincoln's tanks, the crew was also faced after each flight with man-handling over 3,000 gallons of fuel which then had to be hand-pumped into the tanks.

The remains of the Anson were not discovered until three months later when the flood waters receded.

The civil aircraft on the northern routes could call out for S & R at any time, but from June 1958, the RAAF was relieved of the responsibility for the civil side except in the Darwin FIR.

Other calls included, in 1953, an intensive (and successful) search for Japanese pearl fishermen who were known to be illicitly fishing the beds off Darwin; searches for missing boats, etc, were commonplace. Some of these flights were not without their dangerous moments. Townsville could be a hot spot, being well in the tropics, but detachments at Darwin, only 12° south of the Equator were particularly demanding for ground crew, all of whom were held in the highest esteem by the air crews. With temperatures usually well into the hundreds, no air-conditioning, open hangars, and no cover out on the flightline, a Lincoln would often be called out on some urgent mission, only to have to taxi back to dispersal with a rough-running engine caused by bad plugs. The ground crews, such men as Sgt Cec Twist, Cpl Mal Winson, LAC 'Paddles' Hawkins, would pile on to the engine immediately, trying to change red-hot plugs in order to get the aircraft away again on its vital sortie. The ground crewmen were always given as many trips as possible and appreciated the chance to try their hand at flying. The engine fitters (with vested interests) were always taken up after an engine change.

During the Darwin detachments the crew were allowed 10 hours of 'fill-in' flying per week, and this would be used for pilot and crew continuation training, practice bombing, etc.

Some of the buildings at Townsville were in need or repair and it was decided to send a Lincoln to a disused US airfield at Manus Island north of New Guinea, to collect some roofing tiles which had been spotted going to waste on a previous trip to the area. On 21 March 1958 Lincoln A73-65, flown by John Laming with C crew, duly landed and had its bomb bay panniers loaded to capacity with the tiles. The weight was obviously tremendous, and on take-off, it was just a question of holding the Lincoln down on its mainwheels until the sea came up and the land fell away at the very end of the runway and hope that it flew on. The $9\frac{1}{4}$-hour journey back to Townsville was used as a low level MR exercise, as rebel Indonesian boats and aircraft had been reported operating round New Guinea.

At 1,500ft a warship was spotted through binoculars at 10 miles range. As usual, the ASV7 radar was checked to confirm the contact (ie *after* the visual sighting), and it was decided to carry out a mock torpedo attack on what was thought to be an Australian Navy frigate. With bomb doors open, the Lincoln, obviously looking most menacing, swept in at 400ft towards the ship which immediately started to weave and churn out a black smoke screen. The Lincoln roared over the ship at only 100ft. Not a soul was to be seen on deck, but every gun aboard followed the aircraft round. There was no sign of a flag either. As the Lincoln pulled up, the crew spotted the US flag being run up. It was with some relief that on the second run, sailors could be seen waving. On the HF link with Area Guard, the Lincoln crew got a message back from the Captain of the USS Bowbell. 'Be more careful next time. Thought you were Indonesian rebel bomber. About to order open fire'. In return, the Lincoln pilot replied to the effect that had the ship fired, it would have been bombed with 22,000lb of roofing tiles. The USN Captain came back on the radio to ask for clarification of 'roofing tiles – repeat roofing tiles. Is it code name for new weapon?' He was left to wonder.

Anti-Sub Role
A patrol or exercise normally lasted 12 to 15 hours and each crew would average two such trips per month. Townsville was 1,400 miles from the nearest submarine base, and there were only two submarines available in any case. The training consisted mainly of dropping patterns of active and passive sono-buoys which sank to a depth of 50ft and transmitted to the Lincoln any sounds from submarines. The difficulty was to find the submarine in the first place, especially at night, because the ASV7 radar was so poor. It had an effective range of only 30 miles or so, and would not pick up a periscope. It would reflect a snorkel at 14 miles, and a submarine on the surface at 40 miles. Once found at night a submarine could be seen at quite a depth if it kept its navigation lights on. The aircraft had a VHF radio link with the submarines.

On one major exercise in the Timor Sea area, seven Lincolns were operating out of Darwin with RN and RAN destroyers shadowing and protecting an imaginary fleet. Two RN subs were acting as the enemy which the Lincolns had to find. At night there was no means of illuminating a sub on the surface, the aircraft carrying parachute flares but no Leigh light. At 2am one Lincoln navigator called 'action stations – contact ahead – 12 miles', some 25 miles off the coast. There was no bell to ring for effect but the crew prepared itself thinking it had caught one of the British subs attacking the phantom fleet. The destroyers were 100 miles away investigating another contact, so the Lincoln crew decided to simulate an attack, sweeping in at low level from about eight miles towards what was obviously a real live sub. At five miles, bomb doors were opened to prepare for the sono-buoy drop and at three miles the captain called for 'landing lights on'. Unfortunately at 220kts, the lamps were ripped clean out of the wing and disappeared backwards and into the sea with a huge flash. There was only one means of illumination left – the Aldis lamp. The bomb aimer was ordered to switch it on for the second run and aim at the sub. Now the Aldis is a very powerful light, and on a pitch black night, only 300ft above the sea, its effect inside the aircraft nose was nearly catastrophic, with blinding reflections from the optical glasses in the nose temporarily blinding everyone, including the two pilots. The huge flashes of light plus the roar of four Merlins at plus 12 boost must have frightened the submarine into a crash dive, as the contact was lost. However, the sono-buoys picked up the unmistakable 'chuff chuff' of engines and the Lincoln crew tracked it for half an hour travelling north-east towards the fleet. The RN ships were called up and 'one sugar sugar' (submerged sub) was reported – only to be told in reply by the RN that they had both subs with them on the surface. It took the ships four hours to reach the area, by which time the Lincoln had returned to base low on fuel. The ships failed to find the reported sub, and at debriefing, the RN discounted the Lincoln crew's belief that it had discovered a Russian sub following the fleet exercise. The RAN put the 'chuff chuff' down to 'copulating whales', which was most upsetting for the airmen. Some 12 hours later another Lincoln picked up a contact on the same track, 100 miles on, indicating 8kts underwater; so obviously the squadron had found a real foreigner after all, but it was not followed up by the naval types.

On the anti-submarine exercises from Nowra, the Lincolns would fly the creeping line-ahead type of search. The aircraft would drop down to 50ft initially to stay below the subs' radar cover, and observers in the rear turret would often complain of spray being thrown up by the propellers. In the anti-submarine and anti-shipping role, the Lincolns would sometimes act as low level hunters and then call down Canberras, homing them in from high level to deliver the attack.

One night anti-sub exercise nearly brought disaster. Two aircraft were detailed, one to act as hunter operating at 3,000ft, the other as killer, at 800ft, the target being a T class submarine near the Timor coast. Strict radio silence was to be observed, and no navigation lights were to be shown, on what was a pitch black night. Flt Lt Rick Tate and crew were flying the 'killer' at the lower level, and after a few hours' flying came the time to change tanks. In accordance with normal operational practice, the pilot climbed to 2,000ft before doing so, and as he levelled out, all four engines died. Unknown to the crew, the auxiliary tank gauges reading 'full' were faulty and the bomb bay tanks had actually been empty from the start, operation of the fuel transfer pumps having caused a huge air lock in the supply lines to the engines.

The signaller, Ray Parkin, distinctly saw the exhaust flames die one by one and immediately transmitted a Mayday. The pilot could not reach the fuel transfer switches, but fortunately, the co-pilot, big Jim Chataway, who had been sent aft to check the fuel cocks, realised what was wrong and immediately leapt into action, hurdling the navigator and radar op to reach the booster pump switches in the nick of time. The all

Above: Blue-spinnered 'Long Noses' of No 10 Squadron on the apron at Townsville, Queensland. Though A73-60 is shown, top right, with dorsal turret, all had been removed by October 1957. This also applied to the tail guns but nose guns remained in operation until October 1959 when the .5in Brownings were declared obsolete. Three ports evident in a raised panel on top of the rear fuselages were for housing illuminating rockets or flares, rarely, if ever, used, but the holes were left for added ventilation. Centre is A73-67, with A73-62 beyond. /No 10 Squadron RAAF

Left: A fine action-shot of a No 10 Squadron RAAF MR31 releasing a load of 'storepedoes'. Squadron crews had to be versatile and dropped such varied essentials as medical supplies, mail, fresh food and life saving equipment. Sets of 'Lindholme' flotation survival packs were frequently dropped. The Lincolns also had provision for carrying airborne lifeboats, use of which was abandoned at an early stage. Trials were also carried out with airborne torpedoes./J. Pickwell

112

silent Lincoln lost 1,700 of its 2,000 feet of precious height within seconds before the engines picked up again, and it was a very shaken crew who returned to Darwin. The only casualty was the radar-operator, quite unaware of the situation, working away under his blackout curtain. His nose was badly squashed against the screen by Chataway's size 13 boot in the co-pilot's dive for the switches.

Another serious incident involving a Mk 31 occurred during a supply drop on Willis Island, a tiny piece of coral and sand, barely 300 yards long, 500 miles north-east of Townsville on which stands a weather station, its purpose being to report cyclones. The dropping of mail, newspapers and supplies to the three lonely men who manned the isolated station was a regular, three-monthly task for the Lincolns of No 10 Squadron, using cannisters with small parachutes, and known as 'Storpedoes'. The island was always covered with sea-birds and gulls and a dummy run over it was inadvisable because it roused the thousands of birds into the air like a huge cloud.

On 31 August 1954, A73-64, captained by Flt Lt K. K. Wilson (a former wartime Halifax pilot) had found it necessary to make a trial run because of very strong winds. The Lincoln was being flown at the time by the co-pilot, Sgt Arthur Barnes (now a wing commander) from the left-hand seat, and on the actual dropping run, ran into a huge flock of terns which rose from the island as the aircraft approached again. One of the birds

Above: Cyclone Agnes leaves its mark at Townsville in March 1956. By the time its predicted course had changed there was no time to fly out No 10 Squadron's aircraft, and winds of up to 89mph flattened a hangar and virtually destroyed the two Lincolns inside. The picture shows the two stricken aircraft surrounded by the remnants of the hangar; on the left, A73-43, a Mk 30 used on the squadron for some years for training and general duties; on the right, Mk 31 A73-70. Both were 'converted to components'. Note rear-facing camera housing behind tail wheel of the Mk 31.
/No 10 Squadron RAAF

shattered the front left-hand windscreen, entering the cockpit like a bullet, hitting the pilot's head in a flash of blood and feathers and glass, before hitting the bare chest of the wireless operator standing behind the two pilots (Dinny Ryan) and finishing up down his unzipped flying-overall.

Arthur Barnes was knocked unconscious by the blow, with a gaping wound over his eye. He was lifted into the rear fuselage by his crewmates as the captain took over control and flew the aircraft back to Townsville, landing it from the right-hand seat. The story had a happy ending for Arthur Barnes, who was flying again within a month; he eventually married the nurse who attended him in hospital. There was to be no such happy ending, however, for A73-64 as the following year it was lost in the most tragic of circumstances.

At 10pm on Easter Saturday night, 9 April 1955, No 10 was requested to do a Medevac flight from Townsville to Brisbane. A two day old baby had a severe breathing problem with which the small local hospital was unable to cope. With most of his crews on leave or stand down, the Squadron CO, Wg Cdr P. J. Costello decided to undertake the trip himself, and as his crew, took the station engineering officer as flight engineer/co-pilot, plus the squadron navigation and signals leaders. The baby girl and her nurse were installed in the nose with an oxygen supply, and the Lincoln (A73-64) took off late that night for its 1000-mile flight south. Some four hours later, around 4.15am, the Lincoln flew into 4,500ft high Mount Superbus, seven miles NW of Woodenbong, New South Wales, when letting down out of cloud, instantly killing all aboard.

The wreckage was sighted soon after dawn by a Lincoln sent up from Amberley.

The subsequent investigation suggested either that the radio compass was tuned to another beacon with a similar frequency to Brisbane, or that the magnetic variation had not been allowed for. No 10 Squadron decided to arrange the burial of the baby and nurse at Townsville with full military honours, and a Lincoln was despatched the day before the funeral to collect the bodies from Brisbane airport, a sad task indeed. On starting up for the return journey, the Lincoln's engines flooded as the booster pumps were switched on, thus preventing start up. The problem could not be traced and it was several hours, with time running short, before the crew got the engines going and prepared to taxy out: this time, the G3 compass spun madly and would not stabilize or synchronize. With bad weather forecast en route, flying on the magnetic compass only at night was out of the question. Nearby Amberley was unable to supply a replacement, so the crew of the Lincoln arranged for the bodies to be transferred to the TAA DC3 due to leave on its northward newspaper/mail run at midnight. On doing engine checks before take-off, it, too, came under the jinx and suffered a 'dead cut'. Finally, in the early hours of the actual day of the funeral, the bodies were again transferred, this time to an Ansett DC3 which duly arrived at Townsville with two hours to spare, but only after suffering complete HF/VHF radio failure en route. That morning, the Lincoln crew decided to have another try at returning to base, and this time the Lincoln performed perfectly with no sign of the previous night's problems. Seven silent and subdued crewmen flew safely back, convinced that certain souls were determined never again to fly in a Lincoln.

The Mount Superbus crash was to be the Squadron's only fatal accident in 12 years of Lincoln flying, a most remarkable safety record. As it happens, the tail section of A73-64 was recovered from the original mountain crash site on 2 February 1977 by a RAAF Iroquois helicopter from Amberley, and has been flown to RAAF Point Cook to be put on display. Regrettably, the commemorative plaque erected at the site shortly after the crash by the RAAF has been stolen.

There were other interesting incidents involving 10 Squadron's aircraft. Two machines were destroyed when one of Townsville's hangars collapsed during Cyclone Agnes in March 1956. One was a Mk 31, A73-70; the other, strangely enough, a B30, A73-43 listed as belonging to 10 Squadron at the time. After the storm had passed, all the squadron's Lincolns were grounded for thorough inspections for damage, so badly had they been battered.

An unusual incident at Darwin resulted in A73-59, a Mk 31, being written off on 22 July 1954 when landing at Darwin. After a perfect three-pointer the throttles were closed, but due to a missing split pin in the injection system linkage, the port outer suddenly roared up to full power. Flt Lt Wally Wearne and crew could do little to control the Lincoln as it careered off the runway, hit a ditch which ripped off the undercarriage, and finished in a crumpled heap. The crew got out without a scratch.

One of the squadron instructors, Flt Lt Syd Gooding, DFC, also had a lucky escape on 12 March 1953 in the first Mk 31 crash at Townsville. He was doing an asymmetric crosswind touch-and-go with No 1 feathered when, on applying full power on the roll, an uncontrollable swing developed. At a height of 10ft, power had to be taken off again, but it was too late to stop the Lincoln hurtling across the airfield towards a firing range where other aircrew were undergoing their annual small arms check. Before reaching them, the aircraft hit a telegraph pole which

Above: Plt Off Robert Stewart and crew of 10 Squadron prepare to board A73-65 at Townsville on 14 June 1961 for the final flight by an Australian Lincoln – delivery to Darwin for use there by the airport fire section. From left to right: Plt Off R. D. Stewart, pilot; Plt Off John Gazley, navigator; Sgt Vince Crowle, signaller; Flt Sgt Kev Kersnovske, signaller; Plt Off Graeme Perske, navigator; Flg Off Terry Neill, second pilot; Flt Sgt Bev Davey Senior, signaller.
/No 10 Squadron RAAF via R. D. Stewart

Left: Complete with wing-mounted rocket rails is No 10 Squadron's A73-65 photographed shortly before she made the final Australian Lincoln sortie on 14 June 1961. Crews found the MR31 an excellent aircraft for visual search even if comfort was somewhat lacking when compared to the Lockheed Neptune replacement. The nose compartment was the coolest and most comfortable part of the aircraft, with padded seats, and deep enough to allow crewmen to walk upright.
/R. D. Stewart

115

swung it round before it hit the ground and burst into flames. Fortunately all the crew escaped, the only casualty being an AEO with a slight injury. The tailwheel was virtually all that remained of the Lincoln. After getting clear of the burning aircraft the crew had to restrain Syd Gooding from going back in to rescue his wallet. Having been paid earlier in the day he was very concerned about what his wife would say if he went home without the housekeeping money.

This accident was one of the factors which prompted the RAAF to decide that asymmetric touch-and-go's should be discontinued. Certainly on the Mk 31 with an outboard engine feathered or throttled back, there was little chance of going round again as there was insufficient rudder control to keep the aircraft straight, particularly in a crosswind.

Though there were other incidents involving the 'Long Noses' and their crews, they were relatively minor in relation to the thousands of sorties undertaken by these exemplary workhorses. In the first 10 years of Lincoln operations, No 10 Squadron's aircraft amassed 25,281 flying hours, with only the one fatal accident, a fine record.

The Lincoln was never intended to be more than an interim MR/anti-sub aircraft, and in October 1959, the decision was taken to replace them with the Lockheed P2V-7 Neptune. No 11 Squadron, which had reformed at about the same time as No 10,

had operated Lincolns for a few months from Pearce and Richmond, but had soon been re-equipped with a Neptune of an earlier mark.

In June 1961, serious corrosion was discovered in the main spars of No 10 Squadron's Lincolns, which by then were the last remaining in service with the RAAF. As a result, they were immediately grounded, A73-65 having flown the last sortie on 4 June 1961. On 14 June, the same aircraft became the very last RAAF Lincoln to fly when Pilot Officer Robert Stewart and his crew flew her, rather sadly, to Darwin to be used for firefighting training.

Several of the others were put to the same use at various RAAF bases and civil airfields, but the rest were bought by a local scrap dealer and broken up in a field adjoining their former home base at Townsville. Unfortunately, none were saved for preservation. This sudden end left No 10 Squadron without aircraft until the replacement Neptunes arrived early in 1962. A total of 20 'Long Noses' was produced: A73-48 (the prototype); A73-28; A73-55/57 and 59/73. Only 10 were fully equipped for the MR/anti-sub role: A73-28, 55, 57, 60/62 and 65/68. The last Lincoln, A73-73 was delivered from GAF, Fisherman's Bend on 23 September 1953. Lincolns logged some 93,000 flying hours in RAAF service, most of the Mk 31s doing about 2,000 hours each, slightly above the normal average.

Below: The old and the new side by side at Townsville 30 July 1962, the day the breakers moved in to tow away No 10 Squadron's long serving MR31s. Despite the advantages of tricycle undercarriages and jet assisted power (not to mention ash trays!) on the new P2V-7 Neptunes, crews mourned the passing of their Lincolns. This crowded scene shows A73-62 being towed past a line of the Neptunes, with a visiting RAF Valiant in the background.
/Townsville Daily Bulletin

Kenya:
Hot and High

In 1953 a wave of terrorism in Kenya was reaching serious proportions. Bands of Kikuyu tribesmen were laying claim to certain areas in the country and were terrorising the local populace. The terrorists practised a form of worship, witchcraft or black magic which was used to influence or coerce other natives to join or assist them. This was known as Mau Mau, and the terrorists themselves came to be known as 'the Mau Mau' by Europeans. When the Lincolns were called in, the acts of terrorism, some of them beyond description in their horror, were moving uncomfortably close to Nairobi itself.

The hope was that heavy bombing might not only act as a destroyer of morale, but also help to flush out the gangs from the areas prohibited to them, enabling the ground forces to round them up more easily. The basic aims were, therefore, similar to those of the Malayan campaign against the CTs, on which considerable experience with the Lincoln had already been acquired by the RAF. Perhaps it was in the spirit of its execution that the campaign against the Mau Mau differed, and seemed to become a slightly second-rate event for the Lincoln crews, many of whom wondered if their efforts were worthwhile, or were ever even appreciated.

There were other distinct comparisons between the two campaigns. At Eastleigh the squadrons lacked the highly organised, well established operational set up which existed at Tengah, an airfield with fine runways, ideally suited to heavy aircraft. In contrast, Eastleigh was hot and high with only one runway, metalled at each end, but red, dusty soil in the middle. There were few of the normal service facilities, and a shortage of equipment and vehicles, even of bombs, with everything being a little makeshift. There was a certain air of unreality about doing two early ops after breakfast, each taking less than an hour, and by mid-morning being back at Eastleigh enjoying a cup of coffee in the civil air terminal with the BOAC and other airways crews. It may have been a combination of these and other factors which led to a number of flying accidents which marred the record – in sharp contrast to Malaya, where, between 1950 and 1955 the Lincolns operated without a single mishap.

Morale was also undoubtedly affected by the fact that the Lincolns were known to be nearing the end of their days, and the squadrons which operated in Kenya felt left behind in the jet conversion stakes. In Kenya, the Lincoln men felt they lacked the normal degree of moral support to which they were accustomed. Whereas in Malaya the bombing was against sinister, universally disliked, largely impersonal Communist terrorists, in Kenya it was an indigenous people who were involved, native tribesmen fighting for a degree of recognition of rights with which there were sympathies. Kenya was closer both geographically and emotionally to British hearts, and to its politicians, many of whom voiced loud protests about the bombing. In Parliament, there were some wild and unfounded claims about the indiscriminate nature of the attacks by the bombers. This did not endear the politicians to the bomber crews who took the greatest care at all times to ensure accuracy. There were visits by some quite high-powered parliamentarians of cabinet level which may or may not have affected morale.

Perhaps the 'wind of change' was already beginning to blow at that time in East Africa, but whatever the side issues involved, the Lincoln and its crews had been set a task which they undertook with as much determination as they could reasonably muster. The squadrons were deployed to Eastleigh as follows: 49, 11/53-1/54; 100, 1/54-3/54; 61, 3/54-6/54; 214, 6/54-12/54; 49, 12/54-6/55.

No 49 Squadron was the first Lincoln unit to be called to Kenya. In November 1953 its Lincolns were on a month's 'Sunray' at Shallufa and had been there only a few days when its CO, Sqn Ldr Alan E. Newitt, DFC, received a personal visit from the SASO Middle East. He was told that General Sir George Erskine, C-in-C East Africa, was complaining about the inadequacy of the RAF in Kenya where Mau Mau terrorist activities were in full swing, with the ground forces having their hands full, and the action moving uncomfortably close to the cities, particularly

All the fours. Two views of white-spinnered RF444 at Eastleigh being prepared for a strike in November 1953, soon after No 49 Squadron's arrival. Improvisation was the order of the day during much of No 49's first detachment, as shown by the wooden 'sleepers' used for holding the bombs and rolling them under the aircraft from the lorry. In evidence is the distinct lack of ground clearance under the Mk 4A radar, and the surprise reappearance of the downward observation blister on the pilot's side window, very rare on Lincoln's and normally only fitted on the starboard side. Immediately aft of the H2S radome can be seen the flare chute, complete with deflector which lowered automatically when the bomb doors were opened./*Both A. E. Newitt*

Nairobi, the capital. The small 25lb bombs being dropped by the Harvards were proving no deterrent, and the general was pressing strongly for bigger aircraft capable of dropping much bigger bombs, mindful, no doubt, of their success in Malaya.

It was suggested to the squadron leader that three Lincolns should be loaded up with 1,000 pounders and flown to Kenya to report for duty to General Erskine on a purely temporary basis. It appeared that all the general wanted at that juncture was one big bang with which to warn the terrorists. The CO was told that on no account were the bombs to be dropped all together, but that he was to spread the load over a two week period, then return to Shallufa, hoping this would satisfy the general. Sqn Ldr Newitt duly left Shallufa for Eastleigh in SX979 on 10 November accompanied by two more Lincolns, routing via Khartoum. The first bomb drop took place on 18 November and the Lincolns had been at Eastleigh only a few days when, much to the surprise of the CO and his other crews, a number of Lincolns suddenly appeared over the airfield, joined the circuit, and landed. From their large serial numbers they were immediately identifiable as the rest of No 49 Squadron's detachment from Shallufa. As each aircraft shut down on the apron, their opened bomb doors revealed full loads of 1,000 pounders. Each Lincoln was also full of ground crew, and crammed with everything imaginable in the way of spares and supplies.

Whilst Sqn Ldr Newitt was only too pleased to be able to welcome his men, it was nevertheless with a strong feeling that not only would they not be going back to Shallufa, but neither would they be returning home to Wittering for some time. The news given to the CO was that the squadron could return home as soon as a replacement was found, and spare Lincoln squadrons were by then rather rare as everyone knew only too well.

The squadron started from scratch on operations and was left very much to its own devices. Early ops centred round pin-point bombing of known or suspected Mau Mau hides in the thick jungle, the targets being marked by smoke bombs or grenades dropped by Piper Pacers of the Kenya Police Air Wing, or the Harvards of 1340 Flight, RAF, whose CO was Sqn Ldr C. G. St. David-Jeffries, DFC. Sometimes a single Lincoln would bomb; on other occasions, four or five would make an area attack or bomb in line astern on a marked spot in the jungle. It was nearly all visual day attacks, often hampered by cloud over the forest. Just as in Malaya, H2S proved largely ineffective because of the confused returns on the CRT, and it was only used on time and distance bombing runs when a positive datum point could be established. The targets were in the region of the Aberdare mountains, round the slopes of Mount Kenya, and in the forests north of Nairobi. The most distant targets involved a round trip of little more than an hour, while some took only 35-45min from take-off to touchdown.

The Lincoln proved an ideal aircraft for the task, requiring little modification other than tropical sand filters for engine air intakes, slightly weakened coolant, and a different oil for continuous high temperature operation. It could fly high enough without loss of power for bombing targets sometimes nearly 10,000ft above sea level, and was manoeuvrable enough, too, for dodging down valleys or round hilltops. Eastleigh Airport was itself 5,500ft above sea level and Mount Kenya, well in the target area, stood 17,000ft high. When using 1,000lb bombs, 2,500ft above ground was considered a reasonable safety height, but sometimes when using 500 pounders this was reduced to only 1,000ft or so. As it was, occasionally after 'bombs away' matchwood and debris could be seen flying past the cockpit. The maps in use in the early stages of the bombing were old and inaccurate and pinpoint heights had to be gauged from known mountain and hilltops.

At first, target information was supplied by the ground security forces, but it was a slow method and the intelligence could be out of date by the time it reached the Lincoln crews. Target spotting from the air, both visually and by means of stereo-pair photography proved a great improvement and enabled the Lincolns to be brought on target within hours instead of days. The hides could often be spotted from the air by the tell-tale

fires lit by the gangs for their evening brew up, and the photography would show up fresh tracks and other signs of activity.

As it was, the climate was far from ideal for low level bombing operations. The moisture from the forests generated banks of cloud and mist at low and medium level, which at times built up into great thunderstorms with cu-nims rising well above the Lincolns' normal operating ceiling of 20,000ft or so. Most visual bombing sorties had to be carried out in the early morning, with some take-offs at 0600 hours in order to get the strikes in before the inevitable build up of cloud.

An occasional night strike was also attempted during a clear full moon period. One night at Eastleigh in mid-December 1953, RF349 swung on take-off with a bomb load, its undercarriage collapsed, and it finished in a crumpled heap at the end of the runway. Fortunately the crew got out virtually unhurt but the Lincoln was completely destroyed by the ensuing fire. It was not the last time this was to happen. In the hot climate on take-off from a high runway, it was a temptation to put on too much power too soon, causing an uncontrollable swing.

Several of 49's aircrew (and those of the Lincoln squadrons later involved) took the opportunity to fly with both the Harvards and Pacers to see what was involved and to observe the bombing from the sharper end. Sqn Ldr Newitt's sortie in a Pacer was, for him, an experience he was not likely to forget, as described in his own words:
'My trip in a Pacer was most exciting. I had an invitation from the Kings African Rifles to visit a Forward Post on the edge of the

Above: The cluttered interior of the Lincoln's main cabin is well illustrated in this view taken from the nav/plotter's seat in RF335 of No 100 Squadron as the crew prepare to start up for a strike on 20 January 1954. Flg Off Jim Michie, the nav/radar (foreground), will be waiting to switch on and test his equipment once the engines are running, though there wil be little work for his H2S set over the featureless forests, and his main task will probably be to operate the front turret. Once the engines are running, he will certainly need his close-fitting flying helmet, as without it, nothing can be heard above the sound of the Merlins with which he is directly in line. The flight engineer on his tip-up seat with fold-out backrest leans out to check that all is clear for starting No 3, no ground crew near the props, and chocks in position, while the pilot, Sergeant George Scripps does the same his side and gives the controls a preliminary check for full and free movement.
/D. Botting

forest. There, on a small landing strip, I met a Major Bearcroft, who very kindly offered to take me on a trip. He was an unusual pilot to say the least in so far as he had only one hand. Where his right hand had been was a hook with interchangeable attachments. He flew the aircraft with a clip on the stick, leaving his good hand free to operate the throttle, etc. He not only dropped the smoke markers but also added his own contribution to the war by dropping hand grenades. His method was to fish a grenade out of a grip he carried with him, which not only held the grenades, but also his sandwiches and other private belongings. He would pull out the hand grenade with his left hand, put it to his mouth and pull out the pin with his teeth. Holding the grenade with the catch down with his good hand, he would then fumble about with the latch on the cockpit window and in quite a hairy operation, managed to slide back the window, still with the grenade in his hand, do a steep turn over the area and lob the grenade out. This was somewhat disconcerting, I must say, as he had not given me any warning. When I realised what he was doing I kept a close eye on the proceedings. I had visions that if he dropped the grenade, we would be groping about trying to find the wretched thing with limited time at our disposal. Great memories I must say.'

These KPAW Pacers were flown on a reserve spare time basis by pilots of great courage, several of whom became virtual legends. Some also lost their lives in crashes in the thick forests, Lincolns being involved in several searches for missing Pacers, regrettably without success. The Lincoln crews had the greatest admiration and respect for the low level boys.

No 49 Squadron's unexpected tour ended in January 1954, when it returned to Wittering, though it was to return to Eastleigh later. A sister unit from Wittering flew out as replacement, No 100 Squadron, commanded by Sqn Ldr R. I. Alexander, DFC.

Eastleigh was a civil airport with a small RAF establishment under the command of a group captain, originally based there for staging purposes only, under the control of GHQ East Africa. It was decided to put the bomber operations on a proper basis and, coinciding with the arrival of 100 Squadron, an operations staff was established, consisting of Wg Cdr Charles E. Newman and Sqn Ldr Freddie Proctor, experienced Tactical Air Force officers, whose job it would be to assess targets and initiate bombing sorties. A practice was established whereby two Lincolns were kept permanently bombed up with two crews and an ops officer on stand by at all times. The bomb load rarely varied at that stage from 5 x 500lb plus 5 x 1,000lb, a

principle factor in enabling the squadron to guarantee that at least two Lincolns could be airborne within $1\frac{1}{2}$ hours of a target coming through. 1340 Flight's Harvards were used for the more urgent target attacks. Bombs were a mixture of instantaneous and long-delay fuses. They were old and unreliable and frequently leaked. One of 100 Squadron's greatest difficulties was a shortage of bombs, a situation which was to persist throughout the campaign. Frequent runs had to be made by the Lincolns to Khormaksar (Aden) to collect supplies of bombs pending the arrival of supplies by sea.

Bombing tactics continued more or less unchanged: visual attacks, followed by low level strafing runs, using both front and rear guns whenever cloud permitted. Most of 100's targets were in the foothills of the Aberdares. The squadron took all its eight Lincolns to Kenya and one was written off when on 20 January 1954 RF335 crashed on taking off from Eastleigh for Aden, its fuselage breaking off aft of the main spar. Again there was no loss of life but the front part of the aircraft was burnt out. It was another case of power applied too rapidly.

No 100 Squadron returned to Wittering in mid-March 1954, disbanding soon afterwards, its Lincolns being passed to the Reserve Holding Unit. Its relief in Kenya was another

Above: Lined up at Eastleigh on 20 January 1954, No 100 Squadron's Lincolns are prepared for the second strike of the morning. In the foreground is RF335 to be flown by Sgt George Scripps and crew, some of whom gather under the nose for a cup of coffee, each wearing a revolver and jungle knife. This was not to be their lucky day. On their first strike of the morning they failed to rendezvous with the KPAW Pacer spotter plane which, unknown to them, had diverted to search for a missing Pacer, and so were unable to bomb. On the second sortie several bombs failed to release and had to be brought back. On the approach to base the undercarriage refused to lower, and was only jerked down and locked after some fairly rough manoeuvres. Late that night, the aircraft swung on take-off for Aden and crashed, fortunately without loss of life. Somehow, all the omens had been apparent – not unusual in flying accidents./D. Botting

Wittering squadron, No 61, commanded by Sqn Ldr A. P. Huchala, DFC, a Canadian on exchange posting from the RCAF. It was the second time 61 had been sent overseas to take over from 100, the previous occasion being in Malaya. This time, however, there was no handover of aircraft.

No 61 Squadron's outward flight was fairly routine, only one of its aircraft, RE360 flown by Flt Lt Mike Waight, being delayed for a day by engine failure on take-off, perhaps an omen for this particular crew. The navigators' briefing for the flight via Idris and Khartoum is interesting in its simplicity: 'From Idris fly eastwards until hitting the Nile; then turn south, and when you come to a river junction, that should be Khartoum'. It was, and all the aircraft made it safely to Eastleigh. One, flown by Flt Lt Ken Lang, one of the Flight Commanders, had a somewhat eventful arrival. After the long flight from Idris the crew was greeted on final approach by a red Verey cartridge fired from the Control Tower (apparently at the behest of the squadron commander for a reason never disclosed or discovered). As the pilot opened up again to overshoot the flare landed in dry grass at the side of the runway and within minutes the whole airfield was ablaze. Poor Lang and his crew had to orbit for some time before being able to land, fortunately with enough fuel in reserve to do so – as if it

Above: All the fives. Pushing through the cloud tops, the towering magnificence of Mount Kenya forms an imposing backdrop to RF555 cruising sedately aloft during No 61 Squadron's tour in Africa, March to June 1954. Displaying coloured spinners (believed grey), enlarged serials and a grey/black finish, coupled with lack of mid-upper turret, she is representative of the breed in the final phase of Bomber Command service.
/Ministry of Defence

Left: As Mau Mau activities spread through Kenya, a vast country still largely untouched by the white man's civilisation, so the need arose on occasions to utilise advance landing grounds in remote areas. This is SX979 'up country' and the centre of attraction at Nakuru, the first large aircraft ever to land there. On this occasion, April 1954, Flt Lt Ken Lang and his No 61 Squadron crew did not require assistance, but often the Lincolns became bogged down on the grass strip and the local natives would be rallied to manhandle the aircraft.
/K. R. Lang

was not hot enough already at Eastleigh with temperatures of 80°F meeting the crews, who were thankful for the open bashas in which they were housed!

The squadron got down to business immediately and the day after arrival its crews started flying on familiarisation sorties with the outgoing 100 Squadron crews on their final strikes. The squadron commander was keen to introduce round the clock bombing and the first two night sorties were carried out less than a week after arrival, by Flt Lt Lang and Flt Sgt Alan Myers against targets in the Aberdares. It was obvious, however, that this type of attack was unreliable as there was then no means of pinpointing without the assistance of the Pacers for marking.

On 22 March 1954 a night bombing sortie was laid on. The duty pilot became ill with heat exhaustion and Flt Lt Waight was detailed to take his place. Now Waight and his crew's arrival had been delayed by engine trouble and they had landed at Eastleigh less than 48 hours previously. The pilot had had no time to do any local familiarisation flying and expressed his apprehensions about being called upon so soon to operate at night. He even asked to be taken off the detail, but was refused. The duty crew had been stood down because of the pilot's illness. Waight tried to get them together again, but found himself short of a signaller and rear gunner. He telephoned round his own crew who were officially off duty anyway, including the signaller, Sgt Alan Clarke, who had already enjoyed a couple of pre-dinner drinks, or who would otherwise have readily volunteered to go with his skipper. Flt Lt Waight decided to fly without a signaller, as there was little for them to do anyway, and managed to recruit a gunner from a Lincoln about to set off on some night circuits.

Again, just before setting off, Waight expressed his misgivings about the whole thing. It was quite out of character for him, but his request to cancel was refused, so off he and his scratch crew went into the dark night in RE297. The pilot's doubts were soon to be realised. The Tower lost contact with him after receiving a brief message that he was turning for base after bombing, and the subsequent repeated failure to communicate began to have a sinister meaning.

At daybreak on 23 March, two Lincolns, flown by Flt Lt Lang and Flt Sgt Myers took off and searched for four hours without success over the vast area of jungle. Later in the day, Mike Bearcroft of the KPAW, flying a Pacer, located the wreckage of RE297 in the thickly forested Ruathia Ridge area, 300ft below the summit of Mount Kinangop. There were no survivors. Such is fate. A few days later, after a brief ceremony on the apron at Eastleigh, SX974 with Flt

Sgt Alan Myers at the controls and with Sgt Alan Clarke as signaller, flew over the site to drop wreaths.

As a replacement for 297, No 61 Squadron received SX944, only recently returned home with 100 Squadron.

The regular flights to Aden to collect bombs continued, and at least they provided a shopping break for the crews. Other 'duty cross-country navex diversions' were also made to Mombassa, a popular and attractive resort for crews on 48-hour rest leaves. It added to the slight unreality of the situation of bombing targets only 20 miles or so up the road from Nairobi, a crew sometimes doing two or even three strikes in a morning when cloud permitted, the quickest recorded op taking only 35min. In an effort to overcome the cloud problems, the squadron attempted bombing by use of the Eastleigh Beacon, but this was totally unsuccessful and inaccurate, though 214 Squadron were later persuaded that the trials were worth continuing.

For the strafing runs which would normally follow each strike, one of the navs would man the nose turret, often clad only in shorts. The guns would frequently jam soon after they had first fired. They then had to be hoisted to the central position to get at the breeches which, even after a few rounds, got very hot, burning arms and elbows and covering the gunner with oil and grease as he struggled and sweated to find and overcome the foul up, the Lincoln being banked steeply round the 'race course' pattern adopted for strafing. The skipper would be shouting politely over the intercom for the guns to be got going again as it was not done to return to base with any rounds left. The rear turrets

Above: In order to achieve close liaison it was essential the security forces and the Royal Air Force understood each other's problems. For the Lincoln men it was a welcome opportunity to accompany jungle patrols. Here we see Sqn Ldr Ken Bowhill, CO of No 214 (Federated Malay States) Squadron, suitably attired in jungle green, flanked by Major Rawlins (on his left) and an NCO of the King's African Rifles, engaged on a routine patrol./*K. R. Bowhill*

Right: On an unusually fine day No 214 Squadron's yellow-spinnered RE299 drones among the cloud tops near Mount Kenya, while (*below*) Flt Lt Steve Nunns, DFC, and crew perform a 'baraza' exercise in the Thika reservoir area on 1 August 1954 flying the same machine. Such shows of strength were mounted at regular intervals for the benefit of the security forces, who rounded up reluctant tribesmen and villagers for the occasion.
/*C. Trotter; East African Standard*

worked well enough with few stoppages, quite the opposite of general experience in Malaya.

In mid-June 1954 No 61 returned home after its three month tour and almost immediately disbanded, rather ingloriously. It was relieved by 214 Squadron from Upwood whose first three Lincolns, led by the CO, Sqn Ldr Kenneth R. Bowhill, arrived at Eastleigh on 12 June. There was a week's handover during which 214's pilots and navs flew on familiarisation strikes with 61 Squadron and also took early opportunities to fly with the 1340 Flight Harvards. The ground crews were flown out by civil airline, the eventual total complement being 6 aircraft, 38 aircrew and 52 ground crew. Within less than a week, the incoming squadron was well into the swing of operations, initially with four Lincolns, sometimes managing six strikes a day, morning and afternoon, with the now standard load of 14 x 500lb bombs, which was the maximum permitted in the 'hot, high' conditions, but which gave optimum target coverage and blast effect. There were also the daily PR details of target evaluation and bombing results.

It was during 214's stay in Kenya that certain new techniques were evolved, which were to set a standard for the rest of the campaign. They also served to bring the bombing effort to a peak, and we have, therefore, felt justified in expanding on this phase of the war, aided by some excellent diaries which were fortunately made available to us.

The greatest enemy remained the weather, strikes sometimes being thwarted by low cloud for days on end, including the now regular

Above: After each bombing sortie, the Lincolns would drop to tree-top height, weather permitting, for a strafing run, firing both front and rear turrets. Here, RF335 of No 100 Squadron banks low over the Aberdare Forest with rear turret firing shaking the aircraft from stem to stern, the smoking stream of point fives visible down the angle of the tailplane. Slightly above and behind is the smoke from the attack by the front turret on the suspected terrorist positions. The Lincolns would remain at extreme low level for the return flight to Eastleigh, rarely more than 100ft above the ground, scattering frightened villagers, their animals and chickens in all directions./*D. Botting*

night details which had been introduced by 61 Squadron (rather more on a nuisance basis than an exercise in bombing accuracy). First light in the morning was the only really reliable time to bomb and strafe. Strangely the Lincoln crews received no special training in jungle survival, it being considered they either knew enough already or perhaps that survival would be virtually impossible in the event of a forced landing. Sqn Ldr Bowhill and one or two ground crew volunteers took part in ground patrols with the security forces. It was not for nothing that the CO was affectionately known as 'Hunk'.

On 1 July, the remaining two Lincolns and crews of 214 arrived to complete the full establishment of six (two less than the normal Lincoln squadron strength). There was a minor rotation of crews and aircraft to and from the UK on promotion, courses, leaves, etc.

The continued frustration of visual bombing by adverse weather prompted trials using M/F and portable Eureka ground beacons in mid-June, but without success. Further 'loop-bombing' trials followed, using the Eastleigh NDB flying a radial using the aircraft D/F loop and the old L/R indicator in the cockpit for time and distance runs towards a target, but this was even less accurate and was abandoned. On one particularly good day in late July, six successful strikes were flown on which 39,500lb of bombs were dropped, and for the first time, double ammunition loads were carried and expended, with guns being rearmed in the air. Against this success,

however, came a set-back on the ground, the defeat of 214's star soccer team by the Harvard boys of 1340 Flight – 6-2.

On 14 August 1954, tragedy again struck at a Lincoln Squadron in Kenya. It was a Saturday, fine for once, with cloudless skies, and getting off to a good start with three successful strikes and a PR sortie in the morning. The crews had been stood down and were relaxing after lunch when a report came through that the Army had run across a large concentration of Mau Mau (known to the crews as Mickey Mices) in the Nyeri region. A maximum-effort op was required immediately, and an on the spot meeting showed that three crews could be mustered by getting some out of bed, etc. The op was laid on so quickly that some of the crews had no time to change back into uniform, merely donning flying overalls over their civvy clothes. Fortunately three Lincolns were already fuelled and bombed up, so within less than an hour of first receipt of the request they were airborne, led by Flt Lt Steve Nunns and crew who had already done a strike that morning. The other two Lincolns orbited Nyeri Hill while Nunns in RE332 dropped down low to inspect the reported target, finding the cloud base to be only 900ft. Nunns bombed first from just below the cloud. Not knowing whether fuses were delayed or instantaneous, and conscious of being below safety height he slipped behind a hill for shelter as Flt Lt Roy Matthews flying RE299 followed him in to bomb; then came Flg Off Stan Crockford in SX976, his bombs being released at minimum interval, going down in a close, almost continuous stream.

As the first bomb exploded on impact with the trees, so its shock wave exploded the following bomb while still well above ground; the second did the same to the third, the string of sympathetic explosions passing right upwards, bomb by bomb, the final one bursting just below the open bomb bay of the Lincoln. Two large pieces of shrapnel passed vertically up through the bomb bay with tremendous velocity, one at the rear end, causing little damage. The other piece, however, came up through the cockpit floor, hitting the engine control pedestal and seriously injuring the flight engineer before passing out through the canopy roof. It knocked the two starboard propellers into fully coarse pitch, jamming the control levers and setting up a severe vibration which caused the pilot to think that both starboard engines had themselves been hit. The nav/radar, Flg Off 'Jeff' Jeffery, leapt forward to tend the stricken engineer, and help feather the starboard engines. He and the other nav, Flg Off Doug Malpas, did their best to lift the engineer out of his seat and into the nose, severely hampered

Left: Portrait of a fated crew. Flt Lt Stan Crockford and crew pose for a picture before departing from Upwood for Eastleigh in Lincoln RA709. Left to right, back row: Doug Malpas, nav plotter; Stan Crockford, pilot; unknown ground crew; Pete Elliott, signaller; John Groom, rear gunner. Left to right, front row: Lon Pinn, flight engineer; Dave Jeffery, nav radar. */D. S. Jeffery*

by the aircraft having dual controls. The cockpit was a frightful mess. Crockford had broadcast that he was in trouble, and inadvertently the R/T was left on in the heat of the moment so that the crews in the other two Lincolns heard the terrible agonies of Crockford's men as they escorted 976 back to base. By a skilled piece of flying, Stan Crockford somehow nursed his Lincoln back on two engines, along valleys, round hills, before setting her down perfectly at Eastleigh with no margin for error. Tragically, the flight engineer, Lou Pinn, died on arrival at sick quarters. It is equally sad to record that a few years later Doug Malpas also lost his life in a flying accident in a Varsity at Manston.

On 18 August the last PR sortie by a Lincoln was flown and the duty was taken over by PR Meteors of 208 and 18 Squadrons posted in from the Canal Zone. From early August strikes were stepped up to put greater pressure on the Mau Mau and round the clock tactics were reintroduced with every possible method being tried to overcome the weather and cloud problems which persisted. A slight improvement in the weather on 25 August enabled a record 12 strikes to be flown from 0600 to 1600. Of course, this happened to be the day when the electric bomb winch decided to go u/s, leaving 200 bombs to be hand loaded by the sweating ground crews, most of whom worked for 15 hours virtually non-stop, a magnificent effort. A minimum of eight strikes daily was being aimed for, day and night, and in the three weeks of Phase I of the area bombing effort

on the southern Aberdares, 112,000lb of bombs were dropped. In August 1,000 x 500lb of bombs were dropped and 25,000 rounds of ammunition fired. The bombs remained unreliable and one crew observed that 11 out of its 14 bombs failed to explode on impact. On 1 September the Squadron dropped its 1,000,000th pound of bombs in the campaign.

Occasionally passengers were taken on strikes, such as a party of NCOs of the King's African Rifles on 1 September. They were highly delighted to see it all happening from the air, and the two or three of them in each of the Lincolns broke into excited Swahili as the bombs exploded on the targets. It was gratifying to the crews to carry such enthusiasts, because rarely did they hear of any results of their efforts. Nothing positive could ever be seen from the air and it was only on odd occasions that a message of thanks and congratulations might come back to the crews through the Black Watch or Royal Inniskillings after a specially requested strike. There was never any great find of terrorists killed by the bombing, the highest reported number in any one instance being 13 at a camp in the Nyamberi Forest. This aspect was to remain a frustratingly sore point with the bomber crews.

The only encouraging signs at this juncture were an increasing number of terrorist surrenders and also that the targets were moving further north, to the Mount Kenya area, suggesting that the terrorists were being pushed away from Nairobi and district. During September the intensity of effort increased still further, both day and night, and a new crew (Flt Lt John Meckiff) arriving at Eastleigh in their Lincoln from the UK were told, 'Don't shut down you're on a strike'. The very next day they were too!

As a blind bombing aid, trials were carried out in late August using a mobile radar control post (MRCP). This consisted of an anti-aircraft No 3, Mark VII radar mounted in a vehicle placed at Mweiga, one of 1340 Flight's advance airfields on Mount Alsop, to the north of the Aberdare range. It provided the necessary breakthrough for bad weather and night bombing, the latter being aided also by a searchlight on the summit of Mount Alsop as a marker point, and the use of green Aldis lamps by ground forces to mark the bombing runs. The MRCP enabled the Lincolns to bomb from their more usual operating height of 20,000ft. Under the control of an RAF officer in the van, they would run along a line from his overhead position and drop on his countdown, either in total darkness, or through cloud. By this method, two Lincolns would operate most nights, usually dropping a 500lb bomb every 18 minutes in order to keep the Mau Mau on the move; but on other occasions, full night strikes would be carried out by single or paired aircraft in response to sudden calls from ground security forces.

Night ops, particularly the harrassing one bomb at a time type, were long, cold affairs at 20,000ft. The climb itself was hard work and boredom soon set in. The crew welcomed the calm, confident guiding voice of the ground controller, Flt Lt Bill Gray, over the R/T. Occasionally he would ask them 'How is it up there Able? (or Baker or Charlie)'. 'Cold Bill' would come the answer. 'Well it's perishing down here too'.

On one night op, SX976 which had been repaired and returned to the fray in late August, had more troubles. Its bombing circuits had become progressively troublesome and it was down to being able to carry only 10 bombs. Just before the bomb run started, its circuit became fully live, the panel looking like Blackpool Illuminations (the bomb aimer's description). A 500lb bomb fell on to the closed bomb doors and, as they were opened, the whole load fell off, fortunately over the forest, with the bomb release tit still in its housing. The six shaken crew resolved there and then to lead good clean lives in future. At least it was better than practice bombing at Wainfleet, which was about all many of the crews could say of the campaign.

With the help of the new blind bombing aids, the effort in September 1954 was stepped up appreciably, to such a degree, in fact, that in the month, 179 sorties were flown and 998,500lb of bombs dropped (1,997 x 500lb), almost as much as in the previous 2½ months combined. It also left the squadron short of bombs, at one stage down to only two days' supply. Even on the duty diversionary navex to Aden and Mombasa, a strike would be carried out en route. Visual bombing and strafing continued whenever possible.

On 12 November the squadron was visited by the Bishop of Croydon who told the crews he was no stranger to flying, having first taken to the air in 1915. He was asked by one of the aircrew 'Was that in a Lincoln Sir?'. The ops continued with such intensity in this peak period that in their five month tour, one crew achieved 99 operational strikes.

On 30 November the first relief contingent of 49 Squadron arrived, again commanded by Sqn Ldr Newitt, who had brought out the first detachment of Lincolns to Kenya. The last three of 214's aircraft and crews left for Upwood (rather thankfully it would appear) on 10 December after a week's 'screening' of their 49 Squadron successors who were to carry on with the new techniques and tactics developed for round the clock, all weather bombing.

No 49's second tour in Kenya was not to be wholly without incident or tragedy. On 19 February 1955, SX984, returning from a strike, was doing a low 'flagwag' run over a police post when its tail struck a radio aerial, wrenching off the rear end of the aircraft. The Lincoln climbed steeply, stalled at some 300ft, and fell to the ground killing all on board instantly. The rear turret had hit the ground with the rest of the tail section with the rear gunner still in it, but he, too, was to die of his injuries a few hours later.

Gradually the combined effects of bombing, strafing, and the work of the ground forces overcame the resistance and resolve of all but the remaining few hardcore bands of terrorists, who had been pushed well up into the forests of the northern areas. The pressure was steadily eased, and operational strikes began to tail off, with the emergency obviously nearing its end. Then, one day, Sqn Ldr Newitt received a signal to say his squadron could return home in one week's time, and it flew its last sortie against the Mau Mau on 16 July 1955. Again unheralded and unsung, 49 Squadron returned to the UK, its Lincolns finally departing from Kenya on 28 July, leaving the KPAW and 1340 Flight to assist the ground forces with any further troubles. Almost immediately following its return home, 49 gave up its Lincolns and by May 1956 had converted to Valiants. On 11 October 1956 it had the distinction of dropping the first British Atom bomb, followed on 15 May 1957 by the first H-bomb, quite an advance over its role of less than two years previously.

Test Beds

Above: Air Service Training Ltd adapted SX971 to take a Rolls-Royce Derwent for use by the National Turbine Establishment, Pyestock, an adjunct of RAE; delivered to NGTE Flight, Bitteswell, May 1951; moved with the flight to Farnborough in August 1952; retired to 10 MU Hullavington mid-1956; sold to International Alloys for scrap August 1957. Seen on visit to Hucknall, April 1951./*Rolls-Royce*

Above right: The first Bristol turbojet ready for flight testing was the Phoebus, installation in RA643 was by Napiers at Luton. After only 23½ hours' flying, the tests were abandoned, 643 returning to the RAF. /*Bristol Aeroplane Company*

Right: The neat, accessible Theseus installation in RE339. The Theseus was first flown in Lincoln RA716 'G', 17 February 1947. The next two conversions, RE339 and RE418, were operated by the Theseus Lincoln Flight of RAF Transport Command based at Lyneham. Over a four year period from May 1948 over 1,000hr were amassed on a regular service to the Canal Zone. 339 and 418 were later to serve with ARDU in Australia, 339 fitted with Pythons outboard. /*Bristol Aeroplane Company*

Right: The Proteus turbo-prop, weighing 2,900lb and originally fitted to RF368 for initial tests, proved a highly successful engine. Lincoln SX972 was loaned to Bristol's in November 1948 and ultimately completed 958 hours of development flying following the initial flight on 12 December 1950. Returned to the RAF, she was scrapped at 49 MU Colerne in July 1953. /*Flight International*

Top right: Operating with the Armstrong-Siddeley test bed 'fleet' from Bitteswell, (an airfield shared with the associate company Sir W. G. Armstrong Whitworth Aircraft Ltd), was RF403, fitted outboard with axial-flow Pythons, each weighing 3,150lb. The first Python test bed was Lancaster TW911, followed by Lincoln RE339 'G' (first flown 10 July 1951), the latter later to join RF403 on high altitude ballistics trials in Australia. The Armstrong-Siddeley Division later became part of the Bristol-Siddeley Engine Group./*Hawker Siddeley*

Centre left: D. Napier & Son of Luton were early starters in the design of gas turbines and installed their Naiad in the nose of RF530 in 1948 but the project was abandoned when the Blackburn YB1 design was dropped in favour of the Fairey Gannet. However, the company already had another string to its bow – icing research – and by 1948 was ready to begin flight trials on a mock-up Naiad fitted in the nose of newly-acquired RF402, thus beginning a long line of research by the company's Icing Research Unit. RF530 was later to pass to Rolls-Royce for use as a Tyne testbed. /*Air Britain Collection*

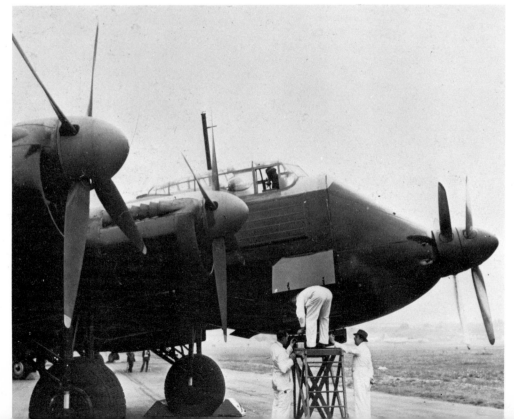

Bottom left: Napiers used SX973 (seen here at the 1952 SBAC Show at Farnborough) to test the huge, two-ton Nomad, a compound diesel/gas turbine which proved unsuccessful. /*International News*

Centre left: Photos of the highly-secret operations from Martlesham Heath are very rare and this gem shows the Python Lincoln RF403 and Avon Lincoln RA716 together when in use by the Ballistics Trials Flight of the Armament & Instrument Experimental Unit. Both were capable of over 40,000ft and had a vastly superior rate of climb. For service with ARDU at Woomera from February 1954 RF403 was painted all-white. She was eventually dumped at Tocumwal, NSW, 1958./*A. E. Johnston*

Below: Avon Lincoln RA716 cruising off the English coast. Originally the Bristol Theseus test bed prototype, she went to Air Service Training at Hamble in May 1951 for the change of engines, the pure-jet Avons at only one ton each being much lighter than the Theseus – no propellers. Consequently she was capable of heights up to 43,000ft with a 10,000lb bomb load, though the ceiling was usually restricted to 35,000ft due to lack of heating and pressurisation. RA716 was to remain in the UK and also operated with the Bombing Trials Unit, West Freugh until sold to International Alloys for scrap, November 1957. /*Ministry of Defence*

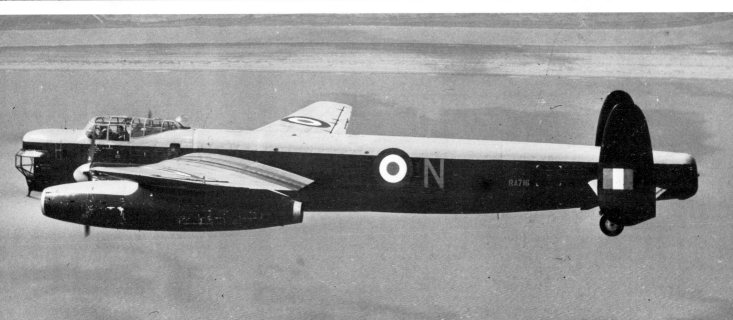

Left: After use by Napiers RF530 arrived at Hucknall 27 August 1954 for installation of the Tyne, and, re-registered G-37-1, first flew 28 June 1956. The Tyne fitted was an early development engine with a 14ft 6in DH propeller as scheduled for the Vanguard. Later models for the Transall and CL44 had larger props so a high-winged Ambassador took over. Photo shows the ice deflector fitted to the nose from June 1959; also the three F24 recording cameras, and top right (as viewed), mirror for use of crew. Underside of rear fuselage specially ribbed for ballast load and to deflect jet efflux. The Tyne Lincoln was retired in June 1962.
/*Rolls-Royce*

Centre left: At over 30,000 feet is high-flying RE242 'B' which, in July 1948 joined RA633 'A' at Bomb Ballistics Unit, Martlesham Heath. Born in 1946, BBU shared the airfield with the Blind Landing Experimental Unit until the two were merged as the Armament and Instrument Experimental Unit. With higher ratio superchargers, 242 and 633 could reach nearly 40,000ft., but pushing the Lincoln beyond its design ceiling produced problems such as engine failures and loose aileron chains caused by wing shrinkage in the intense cold. The crews, too, had their problems despite electrically heated clothing and petrol-burning Janitrol heaters.
/*A. W. F. Burge*

The Lincoln, available in quantity, proved an ideal stable platform on which the boffins could install their new equipment. Notable among the highly secret radar trials machines were RF561 (*right*) and RF342 (*below right*) operating from TFU, Defford, the flying element of the Telecommunications Research Establishment at Malvern (later renamed Royal Radar Establishment). After use by Telecommunications Flying Unit, both Lincolns were to continue in other research fields, 561 with RAE, 342 on icing trials, the latter surviving as a museum exhibit. RF561 ended her days at the Proof and Experimental Establishment range at Shoeburyness in March 1956 for use as a ground target.
/*Both Royal Radar Establishment*

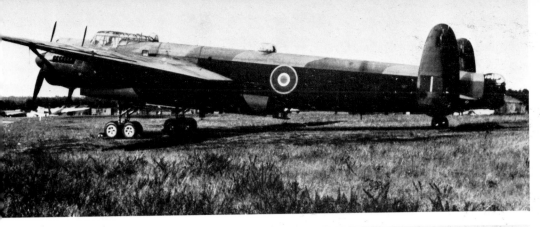

Top left: The Bristol Brabazon airliner, weighing-in at 129 tons, posed many problems for its designers and the Lincoln was called upon to test the Messier bogie undercarriage, albeit in scaled-down form. The Bristol Aeroplane Company was loaned RE284, a BI taken from storage, and began taxying trials 21 February 1947, followed by the first air test on 7 March. RE284 seen at Farnborough's SBAC Show, 10 September 1949. Note observation position aft of bomb bay./*A. Pearcy Collection*

After completion of Naiad icing trials RF402 was used in the development of combustion heaters on behalf of the Ministry of Supply. Then in 1956 Napiers fitted their new Spraymat system consisting of a multi-nozzle 'washboard' spraying water from two 60-gallon bomb bay tanks onto aerofoil test sections mounted atop the rear fuselage. Provision was made for automatic filming and droplet measurement of the section under test.

Centre left : This photograph shows heater intake protruding from top of rear fuselage, and camera fairings at side. Early in 1957 RF402 was allotted civil registration G-APRP but in the event was cannibalised to keep G-APRJ/RF342 flying. /*J. M. G. Gradidge*

Left: Flying with Caravelle wing section. Each type tested was recorded on the nose of the aircraft. /*Charles E. Brown*

Right: With PA474 running out of engine hours it became a more economic proposition to use the Lincoln when the College's programme of laminar flow research was extended; so RF342 was granted a new lease of life, certain equipment, including closed-circuit TV being transferred from the Lancaster. A camera port is visible in the starboard wing in this view as the Lincoln is prepared for a test flight, March 1965./*D. Hunter*

131

Around the Globe

Aries

Aries II RE364, the first 'Lincolnian', was delivered from Langar to the Empire Air Navigation School at Shawbury on 20 February 1947 to replace its worthy predecessor, *Aries I*, a converted Lancaster. In the Lincoln's bomb bay were installed 3 x 500 gallon Lancastrian-type fuel tanks, another 250-gallon tank in the faired nose bringing total fuel capacity up to 4,600 gallons which weighed approx 15 tons. The fuselage was partly soundproofed, and in the rear section were Lancastrian rest bunks and seats, with some small windows. Additional up to date radio and navigation equipment was also installed, including twin radio-compasses, ILS, etc.

Aries II was also fitted with the newly introduced Merlin 68A engines in place of the 68s. The suffix A identified engines of both 68 and 85 marks having automatic charge temperature control incorporated, and which maintained the charge temperature in the induction manifold above 45°C, below which lead deposits tended to foul the sparking plugs. It enabled lower rpm to be used for economy cruise settings in low temperatures, and improved efficiency and overall reliability quite dramatically. *Aries II* was christened at a special ceremony on 24 February 1947 by Lady Coningham, wife of the C-in-C Training Command, Sir Arthur Coningham. Only two months later it was off on a tour of South Africa for liaison visits to South African Air Force bases. On the way out it was decided to attempt the London-Cape Town official record. Captained by Wg Cdr G. F. Rodney, DFC, AFC, a Canadian, with Wg Cdr Black, a South African, as co-pilot, *Aries II* left Manston on 30 April 1947. Soon after passing overhead London Airport to start the record attempt, the autopilot became u/s. Bad weather persisted for much of the way, thus preventing much astro-work by the navigators, and a lot of the time was spent in cloud. There was also loss of radio contact for some hours after the last firm fix on the North African coast, and it was dead reckoning all the way down to Kano, the first stop, and which appeared under the port wing one hour after the ETA calculated by the three very highly qualified navs. Flight time to Kano was 12hr 36min, and after a refuelling stop of only 54min *Aries* was on her way again, arriving over Brooklyn Airport (Cape Town) in 13hr 27min, a total record-attempt time of only 26hr 57min, which is perhaps worth comparing with the present day timing of almost exactly one-half by Boeing 747s flying a 6,000-mile great circle route non-stop in 13 hours, almost effortlessly, and in perfect peace and quiet for the passengers and crews.

By a most extraordinary coincidence, and without any apparent collusion, Transport Command had also decided to attempt the

Undoubtedly the most famous Lincolns were RE364 *Aries II* and RE367 *Aries III*, successors to *Aries I*, Lancaster PD328.

Below: Aries II in the snow at EANS Shawbury during the hard winter of early 1947, still factory fresh, and with blanked-off cockpit side windows and 'high speed' natural metal finish./*Avro*

same record on the same day, using a Mosquito on delivery to the South African Air Force. It, too, left from Manston three hours behind the Lincoln, and, flying via the Middle East, with four refuelling stops, reached Cape Town in 21hr 35 min, some two hours ahead of *Aries*, and over five hours faster, thus depriving the Lincoln of the record. The Mosquito was piloted by Sqn Ldr H. B. 'Micky' Martin, DSO, DFC, of wartime Dambuster fame, his navigator being another very experienced wartime man, Sqn Ldr Teddy Sismore, DSO, DFC. (The Mossy was said to be carrying more DSOs and DFCs than any other aircraft had ever done!)

The arrival of *Aries II* in Cape Town was almost a disaster. Brooklyn airfield lay to the north of Table Mountain and with the certainty of a Katabatic wind in an evening, it was obvious the landing direction would be to the south, 200 degrees. The tower correctly passed the runway heading as 'two-zero', but perhaps due to tiredness at the end of a long flight, this was misinterpreted by the two pilots, who lined up in the opposite direction of 020 degrees, something which, from personal experience, is easily done on these two particular reciprocal headings. The warnings of the navigation team for some reason went unheeded and *Aries* arrived over the southern threshold at 50ft, heading north with a strong following wind. Halfway along the short runway and still floating, the captain gave the order to cut all engines, and the aircraft thumped down 'deadstick', brakes locked hard on, squealing to a halt in only a couple of hundred yards, right at the perimeter, and all this in front of the Mayor, Civic dignitaries, the entire Press of Cape Town, a large crowd, and the Mosquito crew.

The headlines next morning read: '*Aries* makes spectacular arrival'. The rest of the tour was (relatively) uneventful apart from one take-off incident. On 3 May, the Lincoln had taken part as a static exhibit in a display at Baragwanath. Taking off afterwards in front of a large crowd, on a short grass runway, the Lincoln ground-looped (ie swung through 180°, still on the ground due to sudden application of full power). It just got off at the second attempt, its wheels brushing through some trees on the airfield boundary, leaving the crew rather silent and shaken.

After its return to the UK *Aries II* was used in general and advanced training and research by the various instructional and specialist navigation courses held at Shawbury, making numerous long range overseas flights, but after only 10 months in service, it was to meet its unfortunate end in a hangar fire at Shawbury in January 1948, in which it was extensively damaged. The fire was caused by failure to use a bonding wire to connect the refuelling pipe nozzle to the aircraft to eliminate sparking due to static electricity absorbed by aircraft during flight. As refuelling started, an explosion took place, and the fire rapidly took hold, only prompt action by the fire and ground crews preventing a complete write off. As it was, the centre section and mainplanes were burnt out, and for some months, it looked like the end of the Aries series. However, the powers that be decided eventually to order a replacement aircraft to meet specialist training needs, and to undertake a series of liaison tours originally planned for *Aries II*. The remains of RE364 were dismantled, and the salvaged nose section and part of the fuselage were transported to Langar by road, with the most urgent of requests to Avro's for another Lincoln to be adapted along similar lines. Perhaps it was the pending reorganisation of the senior staff training courses which prompted the special order, but whatever it was, a high priority conversion job was completed in record time. RE367 was specially flown in from Woodford to Langar, its fuel tanks were drained, and work started on it the same day.

By this time there were no Lancastrian nose or tail fairings left, the last available ones hav-

Below: Aries III staging through Luqa, Malta soon after delivery and still in standard bomber camouflage which was carried for a time after the rushed conversion./*R. J. Hobbs*

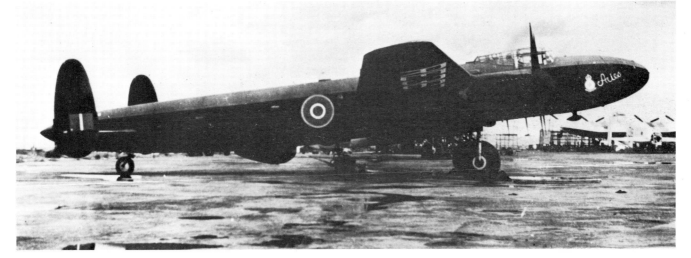

Above: This picture was taken after 11pm by the light of the midnight sun at Keflavik, Iceland, on 25 July 1951, catching *Aries III* about to embark on a 3,553-mile flight over the North Pole to Alaska. In the background is one of the four other Lincolns from Manby which at the same time completed trips well into the Arctic Circle./*BIPPA*

ing been used on the Argentine Lincolnian, B-003; so the nose of RE364 was removed and fitted to RE367, but a new streamlined tail section had to be built from scratch, all parts being hand made at Langar. Time would not allow for the aircraft to be stripped of paint to obtain the same silver finish as Aries II so it was decided to leave 367 in its bomber colours. In one night shift it was completely resprayed – an enormous task on so large an aeroplane. What would normally have taken many months to achieve had been accomplished in only a few weeks, a great tribute to the spirit and expertise which prevailed at Langar in those days. Named *Aries III*, RE367 was handed over to the RAF collecting crew on 1 October 1948 for delivery to the Empire Air Navigation School, Shawbury.

Aries III was shared on occasions with the Empire Flying School at Hullavington, an establishment specialising in the latest flying and instructional techniques. To even qualify for the course, pilots needed a minimum 3,000 hours, and an 'above average' or 'exceptional' rating, the latter the highest flying rating awarded by the RAF. Most would finish the course with a Master Green Instrument Rating Examiner's Certificate. One of the tasks set to the EFS students, flying Lancasters and sometimes Aries III (and its predecessors) was the nightly 'milk run' from Hullavington round the Master Diversion airfields, Manston – Waddington – Valley – St Eval, to test the efficiency and

accuracy of landing aids and Air Traffic Controllers, doing a roller landing at each. The flights took place whatever the weather, often in thick fog, and with cloud bases below 100ft, when all other aircraft were grounded. In April 1949, *Aries III*, flown by EFS crews, was specially called-out in zero weather conditions which had stopped all airline flying to test the newly installed Calvert crossbar approach lighting at Heathrow. Apart from one inadvertent landing on the grass side of the runway lights, the tests were highly successful.

EFS was one of the Empire units absorbed into the Royal Air Force Flying College at Manby in July 1949, along with EANS and EAAS. *Aries III* operated from both Shawbury and Manby for a time for the benefit of the expiring final courses at EANS and the new RAFFC course, its official date of transfer to Manby being 7 June 1950.

Manby: Royal Air Force Flying College
The course at Manby was for officers of squadron leader or wing commander rank who were destined for higher responsibilities. Many were, in fact, to reach Air rank. The course lasted almost a year, and towards the end of each one, staff and students would be sent off in a 'flock' of up to seven aircraft, which usually included *Aries*. Following the formation of the RAFFC, Manby was supplied with a small fleet of five or six Lincolns, some taken from storage at MUs others

delivered brand new, all fitted with extra fuel tanks to give a 4,000-gallon capacity. The Lincolns formed No 1 (Heavy) Squadron, and together with the College's two Hastings, were to take part in a number of worldwide liaison and training tours lasting 3-4 weeks.

One such exercise took place in Oct/Nov 1950 towards the end of the inaugural course, with RF362, RF380 and RF405 visiting USAF and USN experimental establishments, and RF358 the US bases in the Arctic Circle. RF405 was a last-minute substitute for RF523, *Thor II*, which had gone u/s at the last minute. At the same time, *Aries III* embarked upon a 28-day, round the world flight of 25,000 miles, captained by Sqn Ldr J. C. T. Downey DFC, who was later to return to Manby as Commandant (with the rank of Air Commodore) of the College of Air Warfare as it was later to become.

Before the actual world tour, however, it was decided to do a 'shake-down' training flight, non-stop, Manby – Khartoum, partly to ensure that the hurriedly prepared *Aries III* was properly run in. It was also decided to attempt the London – Khartoum record. *Aries* was positioned to Strubby (Manby's satellite which had a longer runway for heavy take-offs), and left there on 20 October 1950, carrying a crew of 11, and 4,600 gallons of fuel. It passed overhead Heathrow for official timing by the Royal Aero Club officials, and flew the 3,064 statute miles to overhead

Khartoum in 14hr 23min, averaging 213 statute mph, and achieving the record. This was to be short lived, as it was broken soon afterwards by John Cunningham in the Comet I, in only about half the Lincoln's time. Aries returned from Khartoum non-stop, and shortly afterwards set out on its round the world flight, via Khartoum (again non-stop) – Mauritius – Perth, this last leg of 3,200 miles thought to have been the first non-stop West to East crossing of the Indian Ocean by a landplane. It set an unofficial London-Perth record of 62 elapsed hours (approx 2½ days) of which 49 were spent in the air. Then followed a tour of RAAF bases before continuing its east-about route via Fiji, Hawaii, San Francisco and Bermuda back to Manby. By using various range flying techniques, an average of one nautical air mile per gallon was achieved.

The next notable long-range efforts by the College Lincolns were in July/August 1951 when *Aries III* and four of the other Lincolns positioned to Keflavik in Iceland for a series of arctic navigation exercises. *Aries*, captained by Wg Cdr R. T. Frogley, OBE, DFC, made two flights over the North Pole, on 24 July, flying Keflavik – Point Barrow – Eielson Field (Alaska), 3,090nm, in 18hr 5min, returning 10 days later via the North Pole – overhead Thule – Manby, 3,590nm in 19hr 35min, a tremendous feat of endurance by aircraft and crew for those days. The other four Lincolns flew well up into the Arctic

Above: Aries III at Manby, 17 November 1950, on return from a 25,000-mile circuit of the world. The codes (which read FG-AW on the port side) were removed in late 1951. */Flight International*

135

Left: Aptly named *Thor*, RF523, flagship of the Empire Air Armament School, Manby, was delivered in July 1946 to replace similarly-named Lancaster I PB873. The first tour by *Thor II* was to Canada and the USA in November/ December 1946. She was a more-or-less standard BII with addition of passenger seats, rest bed and windows in the rear fuselage. Taken over by the RAF College in June 1950, she remained in service at Manby until early 1953, bing finally scrapped by Enfield Rolling Mills in August 1957. The natural metal finish will be noted, and unusual positioning of serials. /*Flight International*

Circle itself on long-range 'to the limit' sorties.

In September 1951 by way of complete contrast, *Aries III* flew to Ascension, a tiny volcanic island in the South Atlantic off West Africa 500 miles south of the Equator. It flew Strubby – Accra in $15\frac{1}{2}$ hours non-stop, using astro nav, D/R, and primary radar only. On reaching Ascension, *Aries* was greeted on landing at the former wartime American staging strip by the whole of the island's population, 30 Europeans working for Cable and Wireless, and 130 St Helenamen, there being no indigenous natives.

In Jan/Feb 1952, with the second course nearing its conclusion the Lincolns were again sent out on worldwide liaison flights, crewed by both staff and students. By then, the College was taking delivery of some brand new Lincolns from the MUs, of which SX953, flown by Sqn Ldr R. S. Radley, DFC, flew a 22,500-mile round trip to Australia, and WD143, captained by Wg Cdr R. I. K. Edwards, DFC, AFC, visited New Zealand on a tour of training and experimental bases. (WD143 was later to become the last Lincoln to serve with Bomber Command.) At the same time, *Aries III*, captained by Sqn Ldr R. G. W. Oakley, DSO, DFC, AFC, DFM, visited Japan, and once again carrying its maximum fuel load of 4,600 gallons, made UK – Singapore in two legs of $18\frac{1}{2}$ hours each, with a refuelling stop of $4\frac{1}{2}$ hours only at Bahrain. To anyone who has not flown in a heavy, 4-piston-engined aircraft, such as a Lancaster, Lincoln, Shackleton or Hastings, the physical and mental endurance required by the crews on such long flights is difficult to imagine. Apart from the normal mental stresses of long-range overseas flying with all

its attendant worries and intense concentration, the noise alone is particularly wearing, and though *Aries* had a little more to offer in the way of crew comforts than the standard Lincoln, the crew must, nevertheless, have arrived very tired indeed; no doubt slightly unsteady on legs affected by continual vibration and the slight 'Dutch roll' movement of the aircraft, not unlike seamen setting foot on land after a long voyage. The slight, but continuous movement of the aircraft also affects the sense of balance, so that for a while after landing, the brain is making correcting trim changes. The noise and vibration take several days to clear from the head and senses completely, and for a night or two after a long flight, the Merlins could still be heard when the ears were placed on a pillow.

Aries landed at Haneda (Tokyo) and while in Japan, the crew visited a USAF bomber unit in action in Korea, two of its navigators actually flying on a B-29 mission. *Aries*

Above: The Debden-based Empire Radio School also had its own 'executive classroom' – RE414, *Mercury II*, which had replaced *Mercury I* (Halifax VI RG815) in April 1947, and the following month began a series of overseas liaison/ goodwill tours which took it to Canada, the USA, New Zealand, etc. Disbanded in October 1949, ERS became part of the RAF College at Manby. RE414 ended her useful life as a ground demonstration aircraft until finally scrapped at 15 MU Wroughton in April 1950. /*W. A. McNeil*

returned home via Singapore – Negombo and Habbaniya. To complete this particular series, two Hastings from the College had visited the United States and Canada. These mass exodus long-range exercises were, however, gradually cut down on account of costs.

In early 1953, *Aries IV* appeared on the scene, a Canberra B2, and though *Aries III* did not leave Manby for 20 MU until September 1953, the end of the Lincoln era seemed imminent. But it was not to be, and transfer of the Specialist Navigation Course from Shawbury to Manby in May 1952 gave the Lincoln a new lease of life at the Flying College. The Spec N Course, as it is always colloquially known, was for middle-rank officers of flight lieutenant to squadron leader status, lasting 11 months, and teaching the most advanced navigation techniques. From October 1952, a replacement batch of six new Lincolns all in the SX series was delivered, and all were fitted at Langar with 3 x 400 gallon extra fuel tanks in the bomb bay, being referred to there as 'Long-Range Lincolns'. They were used extensively not only by the Spec N Courses on long-range and polar navigation flights, operating alongside the Canberras, but also by the Flying College staff courses, on which they were used during the nine week attack phase of the syllabus, and also for general handling, maritime exercises, navexs, and visual and H2S bombing training. Gradually, however, both courses made increasing use of Canberras, Meteors, and Valettas.

Polar navigation and use of pure grid navigation techniques at high latitudes had long been an RAF training speciality at Shawbury, and was continued at Manby

until late into the Lincoln era. Each year in June/July (when polar navigation is at its most difficult) the Manby Lincolns were detached to Norway for a series of polar navexs using Bodo, a Norwegian Air Force airfield inside the Arctic Circle as a forward base. In June 1956, four of the College Lincolns, including SX938, 946, and 955, made the trip to Bodo ($13\frac{1}{2}$ hours) for the annual exercise, crewed by staff and students of No 14 Spec N Course, all wearing the special clothing developed by RAE. Each Lincoln was crammed full with spares packs, and two tons of survival equipment – parachutes for use as tents, shotguns, ammunition, snow shoes, skis, cooking stoves, etc. A mobile Eureka beacon and its supporting equipment was also carried, and was set up by the groundcrews on arrival at Bodo to facilitate approaches and landings in the bad weather which so often prevailed there. The detachment was commanded by Grp Capt

For the Polar flights the Lincoln crews were supplied with special clothing, largely developed by Farnborough, owing much to the Eskimos and consisting of: string vests, woollen shirts with sweat rags round the necks, sweaters, silk gloves and mittens, fur trapper caps, leather knee boots, mukluks, outer parkas with fur hoods, and snow glasses. *Above:* Preparations at Manby, each aircraft being loaded with over two tons of survival gear./*D. B. Fitzpatrick*

Top: A view of the bleakness of Bodo, Norway, used as a forward base, 67 15′N, 14 25′E, inside the Arctic Circle; SX938 taxying out for take-off, 7 June 1956./*D. B. Fitzpatrick*

J. R. A. Embling, CBE, DSO, Chief Instructor at the Flying College.

7 June was the big day, when two of the Lincolns, SX938 and SX946 set out to overfly the North Pole, getting as far as 87° 35′ north, only 140 miles short of the North Pole itself (90°N) but at the very limits of their range if Bodo was to be reached with sufficient fuel reserves, bearing in mind all the time the unreliable weather and almost total lack of diversionary airfields. At such latitudes the magnetic compasses were unusable and navigation was by grid steering on the G4B gyro instrument which needed to be frequently checked and reset by reference to basic aids, such as sextant readings of the sun and moon (both permanently visible in the 24-hour Arctic daylight), drift meters, and occasionally, H2S from the few known identifiable landmarks. The constantly changing geography of the icecap, and the 'reversed returns' effect of the ice and snow on the H2S rendered it rather helpless for most of the time. It was pure dead reckoning grid navigation at 9,000ft (the optimum height for the Merlins' range) in outside temperatures of minus 60°C. There were few radio stations from which to obtain 'fixes' and complete loss of all radio contact for several hours at a time was not uncommon. The two Lincolns landed back at Bodo after a round trip of nearly 2,500 miles in 14½ hours.

On the same day, SX955, captained by the Wing Commander (Flying) at Manby, Wg Cdr D. B. Fitzpatrick, set off from Bodo for a grid-steering navex to the north-east of Greenland and Spitsbergen. It encountered very heavy icing and suffered an engine failure when nearly 'at limit', returning over the Arctic wastes to land safely back at Bodo, not the healthiest part of the world over which to spend seven hours on three engines!

This was the last occasion on which Bodo was to be used, because of economic and logistic problems, and the following year, Kinloss, in the north of Scotland was used as the forward base for the Arctic flights which took place in July 1957. The Lincolns could still reach 70° 75′ north which was considered sufficient to meet the needs of the Spec N Course. Wg Cdr Fitzpatrick was again involved, flying SX953 up to North Greenland, a round trip of 12¾ hours. This was to be the last series of polar flights in which the Lincolns participated in any numbers, as their withdrawal commenced the following year, the Spec N work being taken over largely by the Canberras, Meteors and Valettas.

When Scandinavian Airlines System introduced its 'First over the Pole' DC6 Viking service to America, a most handsome tribute was paid in the inaugural souvenir brochure to the research work of the RAF and RAFFC in polar navigation. Wing Commander Fitzpatrick (now a retired Air Commodore, CB, OBE, AFC, AFRAeS, MBIM) tells us:

'It should be remembered that polar navigation was not the only research technique investigated and practised by the Spec N course in Lincolns at Manby. We literally went from cold to hot and very hot. It was necessary to train specialist navigators, for obvious reasons at that time, in navigation at high and low level over "relatively uninhabited and fairly unmapped territory". We used the ubiquitous Lincoln once again and flew detachments to Gibraltar, from which base, by arrangement with the French authorities, we did long flights by day and by night deep into the Sahara Desert.

'On 3 December 1956 we were in Gibraltar with four Lincolns, and made flights along the Mediterranean coast, turning south into the interior at Oran and then flying down to such out of the way places as El Goumria and El Golea, reaching a latitude of about 25°N before turning back for Gibraltar. I made several of these flights in Lincoln 946, and my log book reminds me of one eventful sortie on 6 December 1956, when, approaching El Golea, deep in the Sahara, at low level (around 500ft) we "lost" No 4 engine, followed shortly afterwards by No 3! We turned immediately for Oran in the north, and by dint of careful coaxing Lincoln 946 made it on two engines to the coast, and as the fuel load reduced, we even climbed a little to get over the coastal hills and made it to Gibraltar. However, it was not the kindest type of terrain over which to lose two engines at low level, but the Lincoln was a tough old lady. Neither is the Rock of Gibraltar, with its mountainous north face near the eastern end of the runway, the easiest place on which to make an approach on two engines with the infamous "Levanter" east wind blowing causing tremendous turbulence. Somehow one always felt confident and safe in the Lincoln even in the most adverse conditions.'

Two of the Lincolns remained in service at Manby until early 1960, used spasmodically for general handling practice, enabling senior officers to maintain their 4-engined ratings, etc. They were also called out occasionally as support aircraft for long-range Canberra flights.

SX938 remained until March 1960, as did WD144, both being flown to 23 MU Aldergrove where they were put into storage. WD144 had not appeared at Manby until April 1959, resplendent in arctic markings. On 22 March 1961 it was written off at Aldergrove after an unauthorised flight which ended with a rather untidy belly-landing, not a happy ending for the last of Manby's Lincolns. It had always been something of an odd job aeroplane, and in early 1956 had served for a few months with 236 OCU at Kinloss during the conversion phase from Neptunes to Shackletons in Coastal Command.

Shawbury: Central Navigation and Control School

Following the establishment of the Flying College at Manby, the resulting absorption of the Empire Schools, and the taking over of the Spec N Course, Shawbury was left as the Central Navigation School from 1949, and from 1950, became Central Navigation and Control School, one of its tasks by then being the training of air traffic controllers. On the navigation side, it took graduate navigators beyond the normal skills acquired in service training and routine operational tours, and fitted them for specialist instructional, staff, research and liaison duties. The staff crews at Shawbury included some of the most experienced and highly qualified flying men in the RAF, typified, perhaps by its Wing Commander (Flying), from November 1952

to August 1955, Wg Cdr I. C. K. Swales, DSO, DFC, DFM, who had commanded a Lancaster squadron during the war.

In 1951 the School was still using Wellingtons and Lancasters, but gradually these were replaced by Varsities, Valettas, and Lincolns, the first Lincoln squadron being established by early 1952 under the command of another famous wartime bomber name, Sqn Ldr J. S. Sherwood, DSO, DFC, who had taken part in the Augsburg raid in 1942.

The school had the task of flying the navigators on the advanced courses on various exercises designed to fit them for any future role in the RAF: bomber, coastal, or transport, low or high level. It was exacting work for the crews who were required to fly to the most precise limits to ensure the success of the exercises, which included polar and astro sorties, and usually a final overseas flight to Gibraltar or Idris using gyro steering and grid navigation techniques, with 1,000-mile single-heading legs from the south coast of England to Cape Burgaroon (N Africa). Astro, polar, and coastal exercises lasted four

Below: The Central Navigation and Control School, Shawbury operated Lincolns for some years on specialist navigation duties and instruction techniques. Here, one of the CNCS fleet is lined up for inspection at a Royal Observer Corps Open Day, Hooton Park, Cheshire, May 1954, wearing yellow 'Training' band as introduced circa April 1953. RF399 is named *Vega./M. P. Marsh*

Left: With bomb doors open, and 15 degrees of flap, Manby's last Lincoln, WD144 shows its slender lines at a Royal Observer Corps open day, Coltishall, June 1959, the red-painted arctic markings visible on rudders, tailplanes and outer wing sections. */Neville Franklin*

139

hours, and the astro sortie involved flying above cloud which, in midwinter, could mean a long hard climb to altitudes of 18,000ft, beset by heavy icing and intense cold. On some occasions, coffee has been known to freeze in the cup lodged on the throttle pedestal, so ineffective was the Lincoln's heating. Recovery through cloud would be by means of Gee let downs, limited QGH, or Eureka/BABS with which some of the navigators were not too familiar, the experienced staff w/ops sometimes having to come to the rescue.

Coastal exercises were very long affairs of 7-8 hours over the North Sea or Bay of Biscay at such low level that the autopilot could not be used. It involved finding a suitably sized 'target' ship, estimating its size and course, then flying off out of sight, carrying out various patterns, to return some hours later to find the same vessel (if the nav was lucky!).

Far more interesting for the Lincoln pilots were the simulated Transport Command jaunts which offered them the opportunity to get any low-flying ambitions out of their systems, with official blessing, thundering across the countryside at extreme low level, over Northern Ireland, East Anglia, etc, doing an hour at 150-300ft before climbing to 800ft just before the planned DZ for a simulated supply drop. Many complaints were received, the most common type being from Norfolk turkey farmers claiming that the low flying Lincolns caused the birds to huddle into one corner of their cages, resulting in many of them suffocating.

The overseas flights to Gib/Idris were usually approached with mixed feelings. They were scheduled to leave Shawbury at midnight, proceed to a point on the coast near Southampton and then fly a 1,000-mile single-heading pressure pattern course to North Africa at about 18,000ft. A day off, then back to the UK via Cape Trafalgar on a coastal exercise lasting up to 15½ hours.

One of the main concerns of the crews was the take-off from Shawbury's relatively short runways, particularly on a warm night with no wind. Heavily laden with full tanks, (main and overload), several ground crew, servicing equipment, etc, the Lincolns had difficulty getting airborne and the 'tit' frequently had to be pulled for the extra boost. Sometimes four Lincolns would take-off for Gibraltar in one night. Icing was an ever present danger and on one exercise, Wg Cdr Wardell (Wg Cdr Flying) was so badly iced up, that despite continuous use of hot air he eventually had to feather two engines on one side, but made a successful landing at Lisbon Airport, requiring a great deal of skill.

The Lincolns continued in use at Shawbury until 1 Oct 1955 when they were withdrawn in line with the general phase out of the type. There had been some interchanges of machines between Manby and Shawbury following major overhauls etc, their special long-range fuel systems being basically similar, examples being RF399 and SX943. The navigation training was gradually dispersed from Shawbury, the work of the Lincolns passing to the more commodious types such as the Varsity and Valetta.

Below: Most of the CNCS Lincolns were named, using the star theme, and here WD133, *Fomalhaut* is seen on the apron at North Front, Gibraltar, 1953, during one of the regular long distance navigation exercises frequently undertaken by students and staff./*I. C.K. Swales*

Aden: 1426 Flight – Whose Baby?

This flight of six Lincolns was formed at Khormaksar in January 1956 to perform the traditional 'colonial policing' duties of patrol, reconnaissance, proscription and, very occasionally, bombing and strafing. Increasing rebel activity and incursions from the Yemen made the up-country border towns of Dhala, Beihan and Mukheiras particularly vulnerable and there was a need for aircraft capable of long-range patrols along the borders between the Aden Protectorate and Yemen and Saudi Arabia, and of long duration patrol over other specific areas.

When No 7 Squadron disbanded at Upwood on 2 January 1956 a number of its crews already on detachment in Aden remained out there to become 1426 Flight, control passing from Bomber Command to Headquarters British Forces, Aden Protectorate (known to the crews as HQBF). The ex-No 7 Squadron men found themselves in something of a vacuum, working for a set up which had little knowledge of Lincoln operations, and missing the well ordered routine of Bomber Command's easy chain of organisation and standardised methods. There seemed to be no-one to turn to for guidance, orders, or even supplies and maintenance, and there arose the feeling among the crews that they did not quite belong, so much so that a unit badge was designed, its centrepiece being a stork flying with a baby slung from its beak and underneath the single word motto, 'Whose?'. It was never painted on the aircraft but it symbolised the attitude of the men.

The patrols, etc, continued on a rather haphazardly organised basis until, towards the end of January, it was decided to put 1426 Flight on a more formal basis, by the appointment of a flight commander, Flt Lt Peter Davison. He had just finished a tour with Nos 83 and Antler Squadrons on Lincolns at Hemswell and was to take charge of 1426 Flight's six Lincolns and five crews, arriving 10 February 1956.

There was no handover period, the 7 Squadron personnel being only too glad to stand down immediately the new contingent arrived, and to depart as soon as possible for home. What little 'showing round' took place

was by 8 Squadron Venom pilots who flew with the new Lincoln flight commander when the first recces were made to remote forts and abandoned drilling rigs in the middle of open desert. Later the role was to be reversed with the Lincoln crews taking 8 Squadron's new pilots for up-country tours before they went off alone in their single-seat Venoms. The two Squadrons were to operate together on occasions with the Lincolns acting as airborne ops centres and communications links with HQ.

During the early weeks lack of qualified pilots and serviceable aeroplanes caused some difficulty; of the four Lincolns inherited from 7 Squadron (RA664, RE345, SX982 and RE322) only one was fit to operate. Gradually, things improved, first with the arrival from Hemswell of two 'current' Lincoln pilots, Flg Offs Cedric Hughes and John Wolfe with their crews, plus more ground crew men; and a CO was appointed, Sqn Ldr David Smyth, a navigator with little previous experience on Lincolns, but a good humoured, first class

Left: In the early days of the flight, the unit was receiving orders from everyone and anyone, which prompted the unofficial plaque. The Lincoln detachment had been run on a three-month basis by various squadrons sent out from the UK, and when Bomber Command retreated it seemed the flight was 'up for grabs'./*D. P. Davison*

141

administrator, who was immediately able to take over the day to day running of the flight, leaving Flt Lt Davison to concentrate on the flying side, an arrangement which was to work extremely well. In mid-March two 'new' Lincolns arrived from the UK, RF340 and RF558. A set of dual controls was obtained and fitted to RE345 and by mid-April the full complement of five crews had achieved operational status. Demands on the aircrew were heavy, flying daily low level patrols in extreme heat over hostile, barren territory using, in some parts, only primitive sketch maps.

The routine operations comprised low and medium level patrols to combat violations of the border and gun-running activities to serve dissident tribesmen within the Protectorate. Apart from any feelings of dis-enchantment felt by some tribesmen towards their rulers and the colonial power, the opportunity to possess the prime symbol of manhood – a rifle – persuaded otherwise contented individuals to play the dissident game and fire off the arbitrary number of rounds at any available targets in order to qualify for the issue of a rifle and ammunition from Yemeni sources. Any suspicious sightings were reported to base and, where possible, to the Intelligence Officers (RAF IOs), one of whom was located at, or near, each of the border garrison towns. Contact with the latter was sometimes difficult to establish because their small portable VHF sets were rather inadequate in the mountainous terrain. These RAF IOs were a remarkable group of Arab-speaking officers who served up-country for long periods, living rough and establishing their own network of informers among goat-herds, etc, who tended their flocks in the border areas, and, who it must be said, quite often worked for both sides.

The non-routine sorties took the form of air support for ground forces, or sometimes even for individuals such as an RAF IO or Government Guard Officer who might find himself under attack from rebels or Yemeni irregulars. There were also long-duration patrols to deny the use of certain areas, eg cultivated and grazing lands used by dissidents or law-breaking tribesmen. The tribesmen would be warned in advance that any people or animals using the area would be fired on, and the mere presence of the Lincoln overhead was usually sufficient to deter them. It was learned that the tribesmen had christened the Lincoln 'the pregnant camel' as they believed it had the capability to give birth indefinitely to bombs.

Local knowledge was sometimes more important than a knowledge of the art of navigation, and on one occasion Sqn Ldr Smyth had the mortifying experience of having to take on board a local tribesman to

direct the aircraft to a village over which leaflets had to be dropped and which did not appear on any of the maps. So to 1426 Flight fell the task of trying to map the whole of the Protectorate. Unfortunately, the Lincolns' F24 cameras were of the wrong focal length for accurate mosaics and the great differences in height of the mountains and wadis caused distortion. Several weeks were spent flying at medium and high level trying to devise a suitable system. For the extremely hot, low level flying, the sealing round the front turret had been removed to provide more through ventilation. When operating up to 25,000ft, however, the cold and draught were so intense, the crews had to take to wearing full protective clothing. There was no transport available to them at Khormaksar and carrying full flying kit across from hangars to dispersals was exhausting in itself; but wearing full high level flying kit for taxying and take-off was even worse. Eventually, after several weeks of trying, the photographic mapping was abandoned. A small detachment of PR Meteors was called out from the UK and completed the whole job in one day with their special cameras.

The regular patrols along the border and of the British forts and outposts continued. It was hot, bumpy and exacting work, some of the sorties lasting up to six hours. Camel trains were hard to spot, and once seen, the inspection runs had to be low enough to determine whether the camels were loaded with normal stores such as blankets, etc, or

Above: Showing who's boss. In front of gathered villagers and tribesmen Flt Lt Peter Davison and crew strafe the lower reaches of a hill in the Nisab area, 29 May 1956, in order to show the devastating fire power brought to bear by the turrets of RE322. This vivid demonstration – one of several mounted by 1426 Flight during its Aden commitment – followed the disappearance of a grain lorry./*D. P. Davison*

Less than 12 months after returning from Malaya No 7 Squadron was policing a number of Middle East trouble spots, notably along the Yemeni Border. Among the crews involved was that captained by Flt Lt John Stephens, operating Lincoln RE345 out of Buraimi Oasis near Bahrain from July 1955 on a special single crew detachment called Operation Bonaparte. They were still there when the Squadron disbanded at Upwood and actually reported to the newly formed 1426 Flight at Khormaksar on 9 February 1956 – 38 days after the squadron officially ceased to exist! They are seen flying RE345 over forbidding territory near Bahrain.
/Both *J. B. Stevens*

with guns. The Lincolns carried the (by then) standard crew of six with each operating together as a unit whenever possible; pilot, flight engineer, signaller, radar and plotter navigators (either of whom could fire the front guns if needed) and rear gunner. Sqn Ldr Smyth flew as a navigator whenever possible and he pays this tribute:

'In speaking of the aircrews I would make special mention of our air gunners who were probably the last of their breed to be employed in their proper role; if they were, their farewell performance was a notable one. The ability to use one's eyes was a vital asset and the air gunners in particular displayed a marked talent for detecting those objects on the ground in which we were interested, ranging from camels bearing "suspicious" burdens to armed dissidents lurking in the hills and mountains in the sensitive areas'.

There were the occasional periods of light relief, such as two weeks leave during which most took the opportunity of a quick visit

Below: Flt Lt Peter Davison and crew of 1426 Flight sweep low over an RAF supply convoy near Thumeir, after helping to see it safely to its destination through rebel territory, 14 October 1956. /D. Smyth

home, usually by lift-thumbing a Hastings; also the odd break in routine such as the demonstration of a Lincoln on the visit of Emperor Haile Selassie of Ethiopia on 10 August 1956 when the Flt Cdr put RE345 through its paces with a short take off, steep turns keeping within the airfield boundary at only 400 feet and single engined flypasts.

On 6 November 1956 the whole flight flew to Bahrain at only 24-hours notice following the Suez invasion, each aircraft carrying a full load of supplies in bomb bay panniers and all fully armed. In addition to the six crew, each carried 10 passengers, some of them HQ staff, this being the only occasion on which lorries were provided for the long trek to dispersals. It was a maximum effort affair, and every available Lincoln had to go, including RA664 which had a ruptured fuel tank. Flt Lt Davison and crew took it with only two tanks full. At Bahrain fuel was strictly rationed, so the next day they brought '664 back to base with only 1,600gal aboard. Unforecast strong headwinds resulted in arrival back at Khormaksar with only 70 gallons remaining, though the Lincoln was supposed to have a minimum dead fuel limit of only 100 gallons. It was returned to Bahrain a few days later, still with the tank unusable, for the remainder of the $2\frac{1}{2}$-week standby during which several patrols were flown. The whole flight returned to Aden on 22 November.

RA664 was to remain something of a rogue aeroplane. It had been flown back to the UK by a ferry crew in March 1956 for a major overhaul, rejoining 1426 Flight in early September. Its fuel tank problems were to bring about its end. There were also c of g problems making it difficult to trim and often reluctant to land. Another rogue aircraft (and every squadron had one) was SX982, also inherited from 7 Squadron, and pictured elsewhere in this book operating with its former owners in Malaya. It was often in trouble, and spent long periods out of service for various reasons, doing little flying on the unit until mid-1956. It, too, was to meet a somewhat ignominious end.

Maintenance of the aircraft was a major problem, and here we must again quote Sqn Ldr Smyth:

'One must again salute the ground crews who had to work in conditions as unpleasant as it is possible to imagine. The aircraft were parked in the open and in the prevailing conditions of temperature and humidity it was little short of miraculous that the airmen were able to cope as they did under the control of an excellent senior NCO, Flt Sgt Brown, who had also serviced the Lincolns at CNCS Shawbury'.

The Lincolns were to stand outside the whole time, even during sandstorms, and for servicing, rectification, repairs, etc which had to be carried out by the sweating ground crews in murderous heat at dispersals which themselves were outside the actual western boundary of the airfield, far away from stores, equipment and hangars. Whilst cockpits, wheels, and other vital parts were kept covered whenever possible, there were times when the ground crew were unable to work on the aircraft, particularly inside the fuselages which became like ovens, with outside temperatures up to 130°F in the shade. Only for heavy repairs or engine changes could a Lincoln be booked in to a hangar, with much of the work then having to be done by the flight's own men, so hard pressed were the Tech Wing.

So the patrols and escort duties continued, but the days of 1426 Flight were numbered. Early in January 1957 the first of the replacement Shackleton 2s of 37 Squadron arrived, to operate this time strictly under the control of Coastal Command, and several of the Lincoln men flew with them in the brief handover period to show the new crews 'up-country' and along the borders. The Shackleton was rather better equipped with navigation aids than the Lincoln, and had a little more in the way of crew comforts.

The final Lincoln sortie was undertaken by Flt Lt Davison and crew in RE322 on 16 January 1957, when air cover was provided for an Army convoy bound for Dhala. The convoy was attacked and pinned down for several hours by rebels firing down from both sides of the steep valley. They were clearly spotted from the air and clearance was obtained by radio to open fire on them (one of the few occasions a live attack was permitted) and it was reported by the Army to be one of the most successful sorties yet flown. It cleared the path for the convoy which proceeded safely to its destination. Before disappearing, however, the rebels had fired back at the Lincoln with heavy automatic weapons, scoring two direct hits and denting the bomb rack immediately below the signaller's seat. Bomb racks were not normally carried, and on this occasion it saved the sig's life. The other bullet hit and bent the No 3 engine bearer, only narrowly missing the most vulnerable

Below: Twenty years ago we had still largely to rely on rather stilted black and white news reels shown in cinemas, and thus little film is available showing Lincolns in action over Malaya, Kenya or Aden. Shown is a candid view of a cameraman 'shooting' RF558 from a Valetta over Aden in June 1956. This Lincoln, a late arrival on 1426 Flight, had come straight from storage and still bears interim-size fuselage serials, in addition to primer-finish bomb doors. /D. P. Davison

part of the Lincoln, the starboard side fuel collector box. So ended 1426 Flight's involvement in Aden, or so they thought!

By the time this last op was flown, some of the crews had already left Aden, flying their Lincolns back to the UK and eventually there were three Lincolns and two crews remaining.

On 9 January, Flg Off Cedric Hughes and crew had relievedly departed from Khormaksar in SX982 which had not always been the best behaved of aeroplanes. But the jinx which had seemed to dog 1426 Flight struck again on 982's homeward journey, as graphically described by its engineer, Bryan Bardon.

'Our crew were flying SX982, our regular aircraft, and another Lincoln piloted by Brian Corley was on the same route. We took off at 3am from Idris with a low cloud scudding in from the sea and a fine drizzle. It was the last leg on our flight to the UK where the aircraft were to be broken up, but we subsequently saved them the trouble. The route had been Khormaksar, Entebbe, Kano, Idris, the long way round because of the Suez trouble. After getting airborne we climbed to about 10,000ft and headed over the Med via North Point, for home. After about an hour the skipper, Ced Hughes, felt a bit weary (Old Marco's 'John Collins' were very good in those days), and handing over to me, went into the nose for a kip. We flew along quite happily for about $2\frac{1}{2}$ hours, 1,000ft above $\frac{5}{8}$ strato-cu with the moonlight making the cockpit quite bright.

'We were all chuffed to be going home, some of us for the warm, flat English beer (though we didn't remember it that way) and the skipper to his bride of some three months, whom he had not seen for 10 weeks or so. Ian McNaughton, the nav, gave me a course change, 5° left, and as I commenced turning, the No 1 engine cut, swinging us sharply to port, with Mac bleating that he had said 5° not 15°. I was telling him to shut up while I controlled the beast, and the rest of the crew were gently snoring. I got it trimmed out and back on course, then had a 'shufti' to see what was wrong. No 1 was showing about minus 10lb boost and the throttle lever was unusually free to move. Subsequently I found that the auxiliary gear box drive had sheered at the rear end and had then lashed around on its flexible drive, breaking the throttle cable. Ced had returned to the cockpit in response to my frantic messages via the nav and blearily surveyed the scene. After fiddling about for a while (not knowing of the threshing drive shaft) we feathered No 1 and sat morosely looking at the resultant 130kts air speed. Ced commented that at this rate we would soon be going backwards. How right he was.

'The dawn was just revealing a grey, washed-out looking morning, when Mac piped up that he had just found a wind, and that it was 100kts on the nose. With various hoots and cries of derision the entire crew told him to get his finger out and get the proper wind sorted out. He came back 10 minutes later with a correction, 110kts! By this time it was light enough to see the ocean, and the state of it, even from 10,000ft led us to think that Mac was probably right. A simple five minutes with the computer showed us that with 130kts airspeed and a headwind of 110kts, we could expect to get to the UK about $4\frac{1}{2}$ days behind ETA, so we did the only sensible thing. We unfeathered No 1 to try and get it going to win more airspeed. It unfeathered okay, and we fiddled with it for about 2min to no avail, the extra drag from the windmilling prop bringing us down to 118kts. So it was feathered again and we decided to carry on to Istres (Marseilles) to get it fixed. But the flailing drive had now completed its job and had severed all the controls including the feathering to No 1 engine. With a speed of barely 120kts less an almost equivalent headwind, we decided to put out a 'pan' call to Istres. After telling an

Below: A pal holds the ladder steady for a 1426 Flight engine fitter out at dispersal at Khormaksar. Tempertures of 130°F were quite common, rendering any metal parts virtually untouchable.
/*D. P. Davison*

indignant Brian Corley to shut up on Istres VHF frequency we got through to Istres and told them of our plight. Corley's engineer later told me that as our sorry tale unfolded over the air, the other crew, about 10 miles behind us, went into hysterics; they always did have a strange sense of humour.

'Istres told us that we could not land there as the airfield was closed, with 90kt winds gusting to 110. I had never heard of the Mistral until then. Just at that moment, No 3 engine did its party trick. We knew from previous experience of this aircraft that No 3 used to vibrate heavily after prolonged use of full power, and now we found out why. The top inner engine bearer snapped and I thought the thing was going to shake itself out of the wing. I reduced power to bring the vibration down to just a teeth-rattling level and this further reduced our speed to 110kts, but the vibration made the instruments difficult to read. Ced told Istres we were coming, ready or not, and we started our descent, the speed perking up a bit. Crossing the coast with the airfield in sight, we had it made, or so we thought. Undercarriage down, ½ flap at 700 feet and about a mile and a half to the runway. Then we hit it. At 500ft the turbulence took us and shook us like a pea in a whistle.

'I don't know exactly what our movements were, and neither did Ced, but at one time I was falling into the cockpit roof. We came onto an even keel, 180° from our runway heading at 200ft; woods were ahead and the turbulence was the worst I had ever encountered. We opened up to full power on 2, 3 and 4 engines with the turbulence just about masking the shaking from No 3; but we could not climb and the ASI was jerking between 100 and 110kts. With the under carriage coming up I saw a flat field ahead to our right and screamed to Ced, "over there". It was very flat and big and just beyond a small pinewood. We selected undercarriage down and with Ced absolutely fighting to keep up the wings, scraped over the wood, through the last few tree-tops, and the undercarriage locked down two seconds before we hit. We stopped immediately, somehow having landed into wind on Istres' emergency strip a few miles north of the main runway. We taxied off with great difficulty, actually being blown backwards at one stage. I cut the engines and we became aware of the tower at Istres calling us. "Are you down?" they asked, and when Ced confirmed that we were, they followed up with "Can you taxy?", the answer being a definite "No". We were at a very funny angle, due, I found out later to a buckled right undercarriage cross tie. It was 7 o'clock in the morning and I felt we had already had a very full day.

'Half an hour later a crash Land Rover arrived and we were taken back to the airfield. They decided we should carry on by Beverley which was due in the next day, but after a long liquid breakfast we decided we were never going to fly again and asked for rail and boat tickets. By mid-afternoon we had made such an uproar, staggering around in the gale without, bottles of lunch under our arms, that the RAF CO feared a diplomatic incident and at 7pm we departed Marseilles by train. Poor SX982 was sold to a French scrap merchant. She and Ced did well to get us down safely'.

In the event it was to prove the last time that Bryan Bardon ever flew, but his pilot went on to complete a further tour on Lincolns at BCBS, and subsequently flew Vulcans.

Even this was not the end of the saga. The last two pilots, Flt Lt Davison and Flg Off John Wolfe, were left with three aircraft and two scratch crews, several of the aircrew having elected to stay on in Aden to complete a full overseas tour, including Sqn Ldr Smyth who became Senior Operations Officer. Departure of the final contingent was planned for 21 January with Flt Lt Davison to fly RA664 and Wolfe RE322, leaving the third Lincoln to be brought back later by a ferry crew. RA664, its ruptured fuel tank long since repaired, was fuelled up and made ready for the journey home the next day, with take-off scheduled for early morning. At first light, however, the fire tenders were called out to her dispersal where she stood in a huge pool of 100 octane petrol. During the night, her fuel tanks had given up the ghost and every drop of fuel had run out. The decision was taken to abandon poor old 664 in Aden and she was eventually scraped where she stood.

The Davison crew therefore switched to RF558, and in company with Wolfe and crew in RE322 did a formation fly past and peel off over Khormaksar airfield as a farewell gesture before setting course for the UK via Entebbe, Kano and Idris. Flt Lt Davison made it to Lyneham without incident on 29 January and, after clearing customs, took 558 straight on to Hullavington for scrapping, with only a little over 300 flying hours on its airframe. Wolfe was not so lucky and in his case the '1426 jinx' persisted. Halfway from Aden to Entebbe, one of 322's engines started vibrating violently and popping and banging. It was feathered and the Lincoln turned back and landed at Khormaksar. When the engine was stripped down a camshaft was found to have broken, not surprisingly, due to the discovery of a large screwdriver in the rocker box. Aircraft and crew finally made it to the UK a week later after an engine change.

So ended 1426 Flight, on almost the same unhappy sort of note on which it had been born. So, too, ended the Lincoln's days in front line operational use with the RAF.

On Parade

Above: With wartime restrictions largely lifted the RAF could once again show its wares to the public at open days such as the annual Battle of Britain displays. Here, three of Coningsby's contingent practice for the September 1946 event, with a No 97 (Straits Settlements) Squadron machine flanked by two from No 83 Squadron. All are virtually new aircraft following the squadrons' recent conversion from Lancasters, and some variations in camouflage patterns are evident./*D. G. Roberts*

Below: The Coronation of Queen Elizabeth II gave the Royal Air Force a chance to assemble a varied assortment of front and second line aircraft, including this line up of eight Lincolns at Odiham, July 1953 with three National Servicemen applying plenty of 'elbow grease' prior to the Royal Review. Nearest machine, RF448, came from ? OCU. Scampton while RE411, next in line, was from No 100 Squadron Waddington. Note that only one Lincoln still retains its mid-upper turret./*Fox Photos*

Top left: Hemswell provided nine Lincolns for the Royal Review flypast on Wednesday 15 July 1953, led by Sqn Ldr Bill Sinclair, AFC, and crew of No 83 Squadron. This was the largest ever public showing of the Royal Air Force, involving a fly past of 641 aircraft spread over a period of 28 minutes. The Lincolns, 45 in all, were required to fly at alternating heights of 700 and 1,200ft, speed 166mph, with Hemswell's group bringing up the rear. Surprisingly RA668 still bears her original red fuselage serial. */R. C. H. Poynton*

Centre left: One can almost hear the deafening 'music' of Merlins in this beautifully composed picture of the Hemswell formation making its way across England en route to Odiham, Hants, on 15 July 1953. Coloured spinners – introduced from July 1951 and originally grey for No 83 Squadron (later blue), and red for No 97 (Straits Settlements) Squadron – had to some extent lost their meaning by now and much cross-usage of aircraft took place./*R. C. H. Poynton*

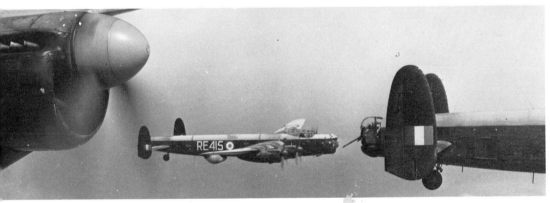

Below: A striking contrast to the sleek, streamlined Hawker Hunters of No 92 Squadron's Blue Diamonds aerobatic team, RF505 'K' from the Central Signals Establishment Watton warms up before her turn to entertain the crowd. The picture was taken at Biggin Hill in September 1962, the event being the last Battle of Britain display in which Lincons participated. The small chin radome housed special detection/jamming gear and tended to affect ASI readings in crosswinds. */P.K. Petchal*

149

More Owners than one

The Argentine: Foreign Affair

During World War II the Argentinians had been unable to acquire replacements for their ageing twin-engined tactical bombers, but, like other South American republics, wished to establish a strategic bomber force with which to maintain a certain aura of strength to guarantee independence and security. Interest was expressed in the Lincoln soon after it became established in RAF service, and in 1947 a group of Argentine Air Force officers and Government officials visited Binbrook for an on-the-spot assessment of the Lincoln in squadron use. An order for 30 machines was placed soon afterwards.

They were supplied in two batches, the first 12 being Avro-built (at Chadderton) aircraft which had been delivered new to Langar in October/November 1945 where they had been stored in the open as surplus to immediate needs; so they were sold back to Avro's by the Ministry of Supply in June 1947 for resale to the Argentine. They were prepared at Langar, where certain RAF equipment was removed, such as the H2S

radar, Rebecca, Gee, etc; otherwise they were standard Mk II Lincolns with full turret armament, and in usual RAF bomber finish, though none had seen any service with the RAF.

A party of Avro's technicians preceded the Lincolns to Argentina as a product support team to advise on ground operations and training, and to set up maintenance schedules, spares back-up, etc. A party of Argentinian pilots, flight engineers and ground crew spent some weeks at Langar under training. They were all dark, handsome young men, most with Clark Gable-style moustaches which were obviously considered part of the uniform image of a flying man. Their knowledge of English was not extensive, and this, plus a certain lack of experience in handling large 4-engined aircraft, caused the resident test pilot at Langar, Peter Field-Richards, some heart stopping moments as he supervised their conversion. Fortunately, all 12 of the Langar machines were fitted with dual controls. The Lincoln on which most of the crew training was carried out, B-005, was also

Below: Shown here is a standard Lincoln in Fuerza Aerea Argentina colours, B-005, pictured at Avro's Langar factory prior to delivery. Note serial on wing leading edge./*C. S. Waterfall*

Top left: Several Lincolns were adapted for use by the *Fuerza Aerea de Tareas Antarticas*, the support element supplying the Argentine's Antarctic Research groups. B-003, the first conversion, is seen here at Langar on 12 June 1948 prior to delivery. Fitted out as a transport, she could carry 12 passengers in addition to freight in the nose and tail cones. At one time given the civil registration LV-ZEI and named *Cruz Del Sur* (meaning Southern Cross), she ultimately crashed in July 1961. /R. Sturtivant

Centre left : LV-ZEI at London Heathrow in May 1953./R. Nicholls

Left, and below: Two views of B-022 before and after conversion for FATA service. One of the 18 machines built specifically for the *Fuerza Aerea Argentina* by Armstrong Whitworth, B-022 was modified in the Argentine. /Pilot Press; Aviation Photo News

151

used for development trials of the Merlin 621s (transport engine) with which it was fitted in place of 68As in February 1948, shortly before delivery. With the exception of B-003 (earmarked for special conversion) deliveries from Langar were from September 1947 to February 1948, serials being as follows: B-001, ex-RE343; -002, 349; -003, 350; -004, 351; -005, 352; -006, 353; -007, 354; -008, 355; -009, 356; -010, 408; -011, 409; -012, 410.

The first, B-001, arrived at Moron (near Buenos Aires) in October 1947. Some were ferried out by Silver City Airways aircrew who normally flew Lancastrians. They acquired various Argentinian 'airfares' supernumeraries on the outward journey, complete with an amazing collection of contraband, items unobtainable in Argentina for local consumption. The customs, such as it was, lived in fear of the armed services, so the Lincolns were unloaded of personal imports at the miltary base before being taxied to the civil end of the airfield for customs clearance.

The second batch of 18 Lincolns, which followed from August-November 1948, were built as new by Armstrong Whitworth at Baginton (Coventry), being allocated to the Argentine contract straight off the production line. The senior Argentinian technical representative who attended the factory had to ensure that everything was more than perfect before he signed the acceptances. Not a scratch, nor a loose screw, for the simple reason that anything short of perfection could virtually cost him his life! The Baginton-built machines, known at the plant as the 'Lincoln As' were never, as far as is known, allocated RAF serials and from new received Argentine serials B-013 to 030. It is not possible to actually identify them from the gaps in production serial numbers, but they were built and delivered at the same time as the 'SX' batches. Exclusive of spares or service back up, they appear to have cost the Argentine about £50,000 per machine, of which the airframe accounted for approximately one half, and engines the rest.

The Lincolns equipped *Grupo 1 de Bombardeo* of the *V Brigada Aérea, Fuerza Aérea Argentine*, which had worked up to operational status by April 1948. They were to remain the sole heavy bomber in the country for many years, supplemented to a limited degree by a number of ex-RAF Lancasters delivered later. The Lincolns were used in normal defence exercises and roles, but one of their main tasks was to patrol the many thousands of miles of remote borders of Argentina, a vast country; in particular, those with Bolivia and Chile, keeping watch for drug smugglers and cattle rustlers. The Lincolns operated from a number of widespread bases including Moron, Cordoba, San Luis, Villa Reynolds, Rio Quarto, Villa Mercedes, etc. They undertook the occasional show of force when uprisings or coups were reported to be imminent, and were quite active during the Peron era revolutions and counter-revolutions of 1955/6, again as a show of force rather than by dropping bombs in anger. Like their RAF counterparts, much of the time was spent in flying-, bombing-, and gunnery-training when serviceability permitted.

Over the years, however, the number of available Lincolns gradually diminished due to crashes and flying accidents, mainly caused no doubt through inexperience in the operation of heavy bombers. At least 19 out of the 30 are reported to have crashed, or been written off; one (B-023) having been destroyed in the air by its own bombs.

A few received radar apparently similar to H2S Mk 3G, or possibly the Mk 2C (eg B-017 and B-022). B-024 received what appears to have been a retractable ASV 'dustbin' type ventral radar scanner in the H2S position. It retained its turrets but had guns removed and was probably used in the MR role. It may have been one of the two Lincolns involved in the fruitless search for an unidentified submarine in the Golfo Nuevo in January/February 1960. The report of a contact by three Argentine Navy frigates set off a 25-day, round the clock search involving just about every ship and aircraft the Argentine could muster, Neptunes, Catalinas, Corsairs, Harvards, etc. Even the USAF was called in to help with C-124 Globemasters carrying sonar equipment and depth charges. When serviceable, the Lincolns patrolled the Gulf continuously, and one actually carried out some sort of attack on a reported enemy position, but without result, and the submarine, if there ever was one, disappeared without further trace.

During the mid-1950s Avro's had actually drawn up a specification for an MR version of the Lincoln for the Argentine Air Force. It was to have a retractable scanner housing Ekco ASV 19b 3cm radar, and carry a crew of nine to include two beam window observers and two sonar/radar operators in the fuselage. The bomb bay would be modified to carry directional sonarbuoys of both British and American design, plus depth charges, etc. Internally carried pyrotechnics were to include smoke and flame markers and floats, but there was no provision for night marking or illumination, all the reconnaissance flying to be done strictly by day. Strangely, both the mid-upper and rear turrets (ideal observation points) were to be faired over. One Lincoln was to be flown back from the Argentine to the UK for trial modification, and, if successful, 11 more were to be modified in Argentine Air Force workshops from parts

supplied by Avro's; but in the event, the project was cancelled and second-hand Neptunes were bought instead.

The Lincolns achieved their greatest distinction, perhaps, as long-range transport/support aircraft, a role for which two were specially adapted. The first was B-003 which was fitted out as a special long-range transport and navigational training aircraft, with long-range tanks, etc, virtually to the same standards as *Aries II*. The modifications were carried out at Langar and it first flew in its modified form in July 1948 and was delivered in February 1949. The same aircraft returned to Avro's at Langar for overhaul, this time civil registered as LV-ZE1 in April/May 1953. As a long-range transport aircraft, it is also reported to have become T-101, and was usually referred to (like the *Aries'*) as a Lincolnian. It crashed at Salta in the Andes in July 1961 when still in use as a support aircraft for Antarctic South Polar research teams.

Another Lincoln, B-022, was also used in this role, fitted with long-range tanks from F-86s in the bomb bay; also as a fuel transport for the Fuerza's Sabre fighters on long-range operational detachments. For the Antarctic support work the Lincolnians were operated by FATA (*Fuerza Aérea de Tareas. Antarticas,* or Antarctic Air Task Force). B-022 was still reported to be going strong in 1965 when it flew from Rio Gallegos to an army base on the Filchner ice barrier near the South Pole to deliver spares for a stranded C-47, a distance of 4,176 miles non-stop in 20hr 37min. [This information is taken from a letter which appeared in the June 1966 issue of Flying Review International. The same letter, from what appeared to be an authoritative source, also reported that FATA still had a Lancastrian and three Lancasters in service!]

By the mid-1960s the Lincolns would undoubtedly have been showing their age, and spares always had been in short supply, this factor having grounded most of the Argentine Lancasters by then. The last Lincolns recorded still in service as bombers were in 1966, thus making the Argentine Air Force the last user of the Lincoln operationally by quite a margin. At least one has been preserved, B-010 in very much its original form externally; in fact, the Argentine Lincolns appear to have changed very little over the years; another one at least may still lurk at one of the remote Air Force bases we are told. The Lincolns were replaced by another British-made bomber, the Canberra.

Regrettably, despite years of research, and despite personal introductions through senior officers, air attachés, Avro's representatives, etc, little information has come out of the Argentine, but one day we may unearth a cache of photos and historical information on its Lincolns and Lancasters.

Above: Showing her age is B-017 of *Grupo de Bombardes V Brigada Aerea*, snapped at Comoradora Rividavia April 1963, by Paul Cullerne, Hawker-Siddeley Aviation photographer, from the shelter of an Avro 748 wing. Note serial number painted on starboard wing. She appears to be in the same colour as the later RAF scheme (black, with grey upper surfaces) compared with the standard bomber camouflage in which she was delivered./*Paul Cullerne*

In Civil Guise

Very little use was made of the Lincoln in civil guise. Apart from the two Napier icing trials machines, G-APRJ and G-APRP, only one Lincoln, G-ALPF (ex-RE290), appeared on the civil register. It was purchased in May 1949 by one of AVM Donald ('Pathfinder') Bennett's Companies, Airflight Limited, of Langley, Bucks, and was used for a few weeks towards the end of the Berlin Air Lift as a carrier of diesel fuel, the actual operating company being listed as Surrey Air Services Ltd. AVM Bennett had wanted to buy a whole fleet of Lincolns, many of which were known to be standing idle in storage around the country, obviously surplus to requirements. He calculated that a specially modified Lincoln could carry a better payload across the Atlantic than any of the aircraft of the day, such as the Constellation and the Avro Tudor IV. Unfortunately, the powers that be would not release any Lincolns for civil use, and the only one the AVM could get hold of was RE290 because, having been used by Rolls-Royce on engine development trials, it was 'non-standard' and therefore disposable.

It was bought for a relatively modest sum (said to be £2,000) and a ventral pannier extending under the bomb bay was built by Airtech Limited to the AVM's basic design requirement to accommodate up to 2,000 gallons of fuel, giving it a payload of nearly 15,000lb, about the same as a full bomb load.

The modified Lincoln flew well enough, though on one or two of the early test flights, with AVM Bennett himself at the controls, a few odd pieces of pannier flew off rather disconcertingly. The biggest battle was in getting a C of A, and involved the AVM in one of his almost customary wrangles with red tape and officialdom. For civil use the Lincoln was decreed to have insufficient rudder control when an outer engine was cut, though it had a perfectly acceptable military record in this configuration. After many months, and at a cost of nearly ten times the original purchase price, a C of A was acquired (shades of the ex-RAF Britannias!). Because of the long delay, G-ALPF was not delivered to Wunsdorf to take its place on the Berlin Airlift until 24 June 1949; and after only 12 'aircraft days' involving 118 hours' flying she was withdrawn from the airlift with the rest of the civil registered tankers on 12 July. As a fuel carrier, the Lincoln had proved ideal, but its limited cubic capacity made it unsuitable and uneconomic for dry cargoes.

A month after its withdrawal from the airlift, G-ALPF was sold to Airtech Limited for reasons undisclosed. There is no record of it having been used by that company and in May 1951 its civil registration was cancelled as 'withdrawn from use'. It was restored to the register in August 1951 by Fairtravel Ltd (Blackbushe) and sold to Fairflight Ltd (Southend) in December 1951, both

Flown by Surrey Air Services at the tail end of the Berlin Air Lift, G-ALPF was destined to be the sole example of her type. *Below:* The former RE290 at Langley before the addition of the pannier by Airtech. /E. J./R. T. Riding

Below right: G-ALPF coming to a halt at Southend after a freighting run to the Continent./R. Nicholls

companies owned by AVM Bennett. The Lincoln operated out of Southend on sundry and occasional freighting contracts, but by then there was little or no demand for the carriage of fuel by air. The registration was cancelled in October 1952, and the aircraft broken up for scrap at Southend some time later.

Meat Freighters

In 1956/7 a South American air charter firm was provisionally awarded a contract by the Peruvian Government to fly 84 tons of fresh meat a week from Asuncion in Paraguay to Lima in Peru, a distance of 1,350 miles over uncharted and largely unexplored central South America. There was at that time a chronic shortage of fresh meat in Peru, whose people were becoming increasingly unwilling to accept the frozen beef brought in by land and sea, journeys taking weeks because of the natural barrier of the Andes standing between Peru on the coast and the meat producing plains to the east.

The charter firm put forward the idea of flying the fresh meat into Peru over the Andes, the heights involved (up to 30,000ft) being quite enough to take care of the refrigeration without any equipment being needed. The firm's operations manager, a Captain Paul Buhler, ex-wartime RCAF bomber pilot, heard of the Lincolns at Langar, decided they would be the ideal air-

craft if suitably modified, and negotiated the purchase of three with an option on seventeen more. The Lincolns had stood in the open at Langar for some years, having finally become surplus to requirements on cancellation of the U5 (pilotless drone) project.

A conversion contract was placed with Field Aircraft Services, Tollerton, (part of the Hunting Group) and a working party was sent to Langar to prepare the three chosen Lincolns for flight. Fortunately they had been inhibited when first delivered to Langar, and although they had been in open storage for a considerable time, no real problems were encountered once the mice, cobwebs and birds had been swept from the insides. They were nicknamed 'Faith', 'Hope' and 'Charity' by the ground crews. A special one-flight certificate was issued for the eight mile 'hop' to Tollerton, to be flown without retraction of flaps or landing gear. The first, RE376, was ferried across without incident on the evening of 28 July 1957 by a Rolls-Royce (Hucknall) test pilot, Cliff Rogers (white gloves and all!) and his regular flight engineer, Cliff Holehouse, assisted by Field's own resident test pilot from Tollerton, Freddie Cronk, who unfortunately lacked a 4-engined rating. For this spare time task, the two Rolls-Royce men were paid the princely sum of £5 between them. The other two Lincolns followed soon after, and Fields quickly got down to the job of converting the first machine to enable the

charter firm to meet the deadline set by the Peruvians for delivery of the first load, 1 December 1957.

The work was extensive, especially the construction of the pannier, or 'hold', which was created by removing the bomb doors and extending the side ribs of the fuselage downwards and under to make a large compartment which was double-skinned inside for insulation. The 125 quarters of beef were to hang vertically, hooked onto special rails fitted along the bomb bay roof. The nose, too, was extensively modified to provide a proper flight deck for pilots and radio/navigator, with a bulkhead behind them. The autopilot gyro unit was moved into the faired nose, and additional radio equipment was installed.

In the event, only one Lincoln was completed at a reported price of £12,000 (presumably excluding cost of aircraft purchase). This was ZP-CBR-97 (RE376, which had, during its service days, been flown by 61, 617, 57 and 100 Squadrons). Of the other two, RF417 (ex-57, 44 and 138 Squadrons) to be ZP-CBG-96, was sanded down to bare metal and given a coat of blue preservative; but no work was done on RF458 (ex-44 Squadron) which was destined to have become ZP-CBS-98. The converted aeroplane did not fly because a certificate of airworthiness could not be obtained. It is reported that its issue depended on certain assurances from Avro's on the stressing of the new structures, but that these were not forthcoming due (it is suggested) to some ill feeling which existed because Avro's themselves had not been given the conversion contract. An official of the potential operators turned up with a foreign C of A and some ferry pilots were said to have been engaged, but the Ministry threatened action against any pilot who flew the Lincolns without a British C of A. And so the whole thing fell through, without a penny being paid on the aircraft. The three Lincolns stood forlornly at Tollerton where they were auctioned on 14 September 1959, the two unconverted machines fetching a total of £1,950, and the converted one £1,025. They were soon dismantled as scrap, finding their way to International Alloys at Aylesbury for the melting pot, and possibly to re-emerge as meat pans, who knows! A case of what might have been.

The prototype Paraguayan meat freighter ZP-CBR-97, which as RE376 had served with several bomber squadrons, was the prototype of an intended fleet of 20 meat freighters for a Paraguayan operator.

Above: The aircraft during early stages of conversion by Field Aircraft at Tollerton. /P. H. Plater

Right: In the event, the converted machine never flew again, and she is seen here at Tollerton shortly before disposal by auction for scrap in September 1959. Finish was natural metal with white top sufaces and maroon cheat line. The insignia depicted a winged, snorting bull, appropriately named *El Toro*. /Authors Collection

Swansong

Hemswell

Perched high on the rich farmland ridge of western Lincolnshire, Hemswell was to become the last Bomber Command station to see the Lincoln in front line use. Still unfinished when World War II began, it became a 5 Group Hampden station, and the local people, at first suspicious of the blue invasion, soon accepted their new neighbours and formed the first of many lasting friendships, some still intact over 30 years later, due in part to inter-marrying.

It was Hemswell which suffered the first of Bomber Command's many set-backs, the loss of five Hampdens and crews of No 144 Squadron on a daylight armed reconnaissance patrol on 29 September 1939, with the war less than one month old. With the departure of the Hampdens in July 1941 the station welcomed the first of the Polish Wellington squadrons within 1 Group's framework, destined to remain for two years. Then a period of training new crews until, in November 1944, it returned to the operational role with the arrival of two Lancaster squadrons, Nos 150 and 170. A year later saw both disbanded and all was peace at Hemswell for nine months, broken when the first Lincoln squadrons, 100 and 83, flew in during October 1946, closely followed by 97.

Little was to change over the next nine years, though 100 Squadron, a Main Force unit, left for Waddington in March 1950, leaving Hemswell with the two Marker, or Flare Force squadrons, 83 and 97, continuing their roles of the later war years, aided by Nos 139 and 109 Squadrons with Mosquitos. To this select specialist band was added No 199 Squadron in April 1952, bringing in its Lincolns from Watton, modified for use in the rapidly developing role of electronic countermeasures.

No 199 Squadron had been reformed at Watton in July 1951 as part of the Central Signals Establishment in 90 Group. Its role was the training of operators in radio and electronic countermeasures (RCM/ECM), in short, listening, monitoring and jamming of radio and radar. Its training role extended to ground as well as air operators. When operating from Watton in its early days the squadron was often called upon to work against the Royal Navy, with additional special equipment installed in its Lincolns which were able to sit aloft outside the Navy's radar and plot every move. So effective was the jamming that the Navy reached the stage where it would sometimes call off the exercise, particularly in the Med, if it was known that 199 was to participate. The Navy stood no chance with the Lincolns about.

On one exercise the squadron operated against a fighter control station in the south of England. The Lincolns put it and the whole of the southern radar defences 'out', including London Airport, whose controllers had for long boasted of the complete immunity of their system. In 1951/52 many in authority could not believe the claims of 199 Squadron, until a demonstration was laid on to convince them. Watton used to send observers to ground radar stations when the Lincolns were flying on exercises against them, and would sometimes send back reports of controllers actually in tears. While flying on one jamming sortie, the squadron inadvertently blotted out Princess Margaret's aircraft in a Purple Airway, and nothing was heard from it for nearly half an hour, before it was realized what was happening and the Lincolns received a curt message to return to base. Someone at Group had omitted to advise the Watton Ops centre of the Royal Flight!

Working under a first-class intelligence officer at Watton (Sqn Ldr Gale), the Lincoln crews could dupe the fighter defences almost at will, the Lincolns often having landed back at base before the fighters had even reached the bombers' last reported position. The squadron also co-operated very successfully on exercises with the RN against the American Navy in the Med, using Malta as a base. On one such operation, Flt Sgt Bob Nash, (a Canadian in the RAF, and a former wartime Lancaster pilot with a DFC) had a nasty experience in RF337, his regular Lincoln which was 10kts slower than any other on the squadron, and which set the pace at which the others always flew. He described it as 'a lemon of an aeroplane', and

Evocative scenes at Hemswell, 1954 at a time when the station's three Lincoln squadrons were engaged in the widely differing roles of RCM/ECM (No 199) and the training of V-Force navigators (Nos 83 and 97). From April to September, however, an additional task was to provide facilities and crews for the filming of *The Dam Busters*.

Above: A panoramic view taken during July, and in which can be seen two of the Lancaster 7s brought out of storage for the film, BCBS Varsity WJ920 used as the photograpic mount, and Wellington T10 MF628 which appeared in the film, and is now preserved./*M. J. Cawsey*

Top right: The signpost bearing names once familiar to many wartime and postwar air and groud crew immediately identifies this exposed dispersal as the 'erks' arrive to prepare for an early morning sortie. /*M. J. Cawsey*

tells his own story of its demise at Gibraltar on 17 November 1951:

'I was on the original programme for going out to Gib from Watton on an exercise but went sick, so another crew took 337 instead. They suffered a cracked block on No 1 engine while out there so I ended up flying the new block out. I was told to stay out there, as I was scheduled to be on the exercise in the first place, then bring the problem aircraft (RF337) back. We did the job, air tested her on the Friday (16 November), and then on the Saturday morning were due to come back to UK. The crew was: Nav: Flt Lt MacLeod; Sig: Flt Lt Hayter; F/E: Sgt Preston; plus eight ground crew (one being Jack Barnard an engineer).

'Hurtling down the runway I got to take-off speed when No 1 engine went on me. We were too close to the end of the runway to even think of pulling up the undercart because off the end of the runway was a drop down on to boulders 6-7 feet across. I wasn't going to drop onto those! So we just sailed off the end and into the Med. I timed it just right; when I thought the wheels would hit the water I pulled back on the stick and ripped both undercarts out from their nacelles. We went on another 150 yards or so and flopped on to the water. When we hit there was a solid sheet of water which came up over the cockpit and I thought, hells bells we're going under! I wrenched open the side windows and it was a case of no sooner opening it than I was through the gap like a cork from a bottle and stood on top of the aircraft. There was no-one else in sight but I saw old MacLeod inside the cockpit with his helmet on, a pencil in his mouth and swimming like mad. I shouted to him "hey Mac, pull your helmet plug out first, you'll never get anywhere the way you're going!" The ground crew in the back

didn't even know anything was wrong until water came up the window chutes and then they decided something must have happened. They all got out the back door and saw me standing on top up front. On the take-off I couldn't hold her to stop the swing.

'I had broken all the rules and regulations as I was supposed to be strapped in, but I only had my lap strap on, for with shoulder straps on it was not possible to go through the gate with the throttles, so essential at Gib. If anything happened you just could not reach your starboard outer throttle and it was only through me not having shoulder straps on that I could pull back on the starboard outer to stop the swing and avoid crashing into the rifle butts. As it was I left part of one rudder in the butts. I ripped it off and the Navy boys fled. They cleared out of there so fast that when we came to rest and looked back, there they all were standing on the shore watching us. A Spanish fishing boat rescued us, for by the time the RAF launch was ready round the bay it would have taken 20 minutes.

'From someone's point of view it was the luckiest thing to happen for we had a special piece of freight on board. Navy aircraft (at least 20) had come into Gib with engines missing badly through contaminated petrol. It came under A class freight and it was coming back to UK for analysis. They lost all their evidence when the kite went to the bottom, some 15ft down, having floated for about five minutes. This was the first Lincoln to be ditched and as nothing was done according to the book a top level court of inquiry was organised. I was there and some squadron leader running it cleared me of all blame. At one point things looked sticky, but an officer inside a control caravan insisted that he heard the engine go and had im-

Centre left: With full flap on, No 83 Squadron's RF539 crosses the boundary fence at Hemswell on 'finals' for a normal powered touchdown Note the original 8in serial still in place on the rear fuselage, something apparently peculiar to Hemswell aircraft. This Lincoln was later destined to come to grief at Hemswell on 13 May 1955 when flg Off Tony Lock and crew were caught in a 60°, 10-knot crosswind drift on the take-off run. The landing gear collapsed and she finished up on her belly straddling a hedge and the Harpswell/Kirton-in-Lindsey road, fortunately without injury to the crew. She was scrapped in situ./*R. C. H. Poynton*

Bottom left: Looking like a Lincoln rally is this scene at Hemswell, Lincs, circa June 1956 with most of the surviving Bomber Command machines lined up on the grass in front of the hangers for inspection by th AOC, Air Vice Marshal John Whitley. Foreground are those of Arrow Squadron (formerly No 97), No 199 centre (identified by striped spinners) and, top, Antler Squadron (formerly No 83). The Canberra B2 (WJ616), looking somewhat out of place, represents the beginning of No 199's conversion to jets and subsequent transfer to Honington./*S. A. Nunns*

Above: During practice for the September 1958 Battle of Britain Day, Flt Lt Bill Youd, captain of BCBS Lincoln RF563 and Sqn Ldr Peter Hubbard flying a Vulcan of No 101 Squadron from nearby Finningley, formate over Lindholme. Because of the great difference in speed, the Lincoln has its nose down, throttles well open, while the Vulcan, with nose needing to be kept well up, sits like a giant preying mantis. /P. U. Hubbard

mediately phoned Air Traffic and reported me in trouble.

'All the crew were still at their positions, the engineer sitting beside me, Jack Barnard sitting on the step and the seven lads in the back. There was no time to shout though I may have uttered a brief word or two like "we're going in". The initial inquiries were cut short before the court of inquiry and I wondered why. Some fellow told me a little later that they were trying to raise the Lincoln. "They got it to the surface", he said, "but it broke adrift and went down again". I later learned they had a signal from Air Ministry warning that under no circumstances was it to be raised or even touched. In any case the salt water would soon ruin the gear and, so far as I know, the Lincoln is still there on the bottom. One engine was ripped off when they tried to lift her, incidentally. I went out with a diver and he went down to her. Even though in only 15ft of water he could not stand upright due to the tide. Incredibly he had to go down into her and he didn't even know what the inside of a Lincoln was like! He had to ask me for pointers. It caused a great giggle on the squadron and the lads enjoyed it all.'

No 199 was transferred from Watton to Hemswell in April 1952 as No 1 Group, Bomber Command specialists in the countermeasures arts. Its training role continued, both of air operators and testing reactions of ground operators to jamming. The run of the mill work consisted mainly of practice jamming of the UK fighter control centres on the east and south coasts. Normally a Lincoln would do two stations in a day, one in the morning, an hour off for lunch (airborne

sandwiches, of course), then another in the afternoon, which added up to an 8-hour sortie, each crew averaging one a week. The squadron also did work for others, such as the Scandinavian countries, particularly Norway, and also Germany. The detachments to the Med and North Africa (eg Idris) also continued.

On one training sortie over Germany, on 26 June 1955, the squadron lost one of its Lincolns and crews, when WD131 flown by Flg Off Hughie Honor was hit by a USAF jet fighter which shot up out of cloud right underneath the Lincoln, slicing off one of the bomber's wings, giving its crew no chance. The fighter pilot ejected safely.

It was on Main Force exercises, however, that 199 came into its own, doing some very good work, particularly on voice-jamming, preceding and providing countermeasures cover for the ·Marker and Main Force squadrons.

But the age of the piston-engined bomber was drawing to a close. Both 83 and 97 Squadrons had lost their Flare Force role, and had switched to the training of V-Force navigators. As 1955 ended, both squadrons lost their identities, their numberplates being earmarked for V-bomber squadrons. The remnants soldiered on with new titles, 'Antler' and 'Arrow' Squadrons, the names being derived from the motifs in the respective squadron badges, an action believed unique in RAF annals.

From March 1956 the first Canberras appeared on the scene at Hemswell to join 199 Squadron, and start the takeover of the RCM/ECM role from the Lincolns which could fly neither high nor fast enough for the

Above: Resplendent in glossy under surfaces, grey top decking and blue spinners stands WD143 of Bomber Command Bombing School, Lindholme, on a summer day in July 1960. This was the twilight of the Lincoln's long and varied career, Bomber Command saying goodbye to a worthy servant with a ceremony at Lindholme 6 October 1960 and culminating in WD143 taking off for 23 MU Aldergrove, Northern Ireland with the Air Officer Commanding, Air Marshal Sir Kenneth Cross on Board. /*B. Goulding*

Left: One can almost smell the early morning freshness as a Lincoln of Bomber Command Bombing School runs up her engines at Lindholme prior to taxying out for a photographic sortie to Cherbourg, the last shrouds of mist still lingering in the background. Substitute a Lancaster and this is a scene enacted countless times at dispersals on wartime airfields. Only one month after this superb picture was taken (8 September 1960) the Lincolns had left Lindholme, their final Bomber Command stronghold./*G. S. Waterfall*

new V-bombers. The two types operated side by side for a time until, on 1 October 1957, the Lincoln element of 199 combined with Antler and Arrow Squadrons to form 1321 Flight under the command of Squadron Leader S. A. Nunns, DFC, continuing in the former specialist roles for another six months, before 199 Squadron itself moved to Honington to re-equip with Valiants. One other small Lincoln unit also remained at Hemswell: the Lincoln Conversion Flight, whose crews moved to BCBS, Lindholme, with the departure of the last Lincoln from Hemswell on 2 April 1958.

Soon the men, and women, were posted away, leaving behind a host of memories, some to recall pleasant summer days, aloft for the sheer joy of flying; or lying on the newly mown grass enjoying a quiet spell; others to shudder and bring to mind chilling winds and bleakness in winter, the low lying mists so treacherous to man and machine. It was not quite the end of Hemswell but it was the passing of an era. The once proud station became, successively, a missile base, Air Cadet gliding school, home of the Lincoln Flying Club until 1975, and even a temporary home for displaced Ugandan Asians. It now stands abandoned, boarded up and over-grown, a rather sad sight, with the ghosts of Lincoln engines no longer booming round the airfield and between the hangars.

Central Signals Establishment

The Lincoln was used at Watton by the CSE for at least 15 years, probably longer than any other unit or station. Its Lincolns played a most important part in the early development of electronic equipment, some of which is still widely used in modern combat aircraft. Its speciality became the use of radio and later electronic countermeasures, commonly referred to as RCM and ECM.

CSE was part of 90 (Signals) Group, RAF, and one of its major tasks was the monitoring and calibration of radio navigation and landing aids. Its Calibration Squadron started to receive Lincolns as replacements for Lancasters in the late 1940s/early 1950s, and they, too, became familiar sights at RAF airfields at home and abroad while checking the accuracy of landing aids like Eureka/BABS and ILS. Its other tasks included periodic checks of British weather ships in the north Atlantic, ASV nav aids, the Gee chain and, significantly, the British early warning radar chain. This latter task was to become increasingly important as the radar chain was hurriedly rehabilitated following the Korean war scare after the post-1945 run-down. Calibration Squadron was eventually divided into two separate parts, with Calibration N Squadron remaining responsible for nav aids, and an enlarged Calibration R Squadron for radar. Subsequently, N Squadron became No 116 and R Squadron No 527, both continuing at Watton. The former retained a number of Lincolns for a time,

but 527 continued as a large user of the type. It was composed of three flights, each of 10 or 11 aircraft, thus making it the largest squadron in the RAF at that time (and probably since). A Flight flew the Lincolns on the radar calibration work, B Flight Ansons (later Varsities), and C flight Mosquitos, (later Meteor NF 11s and 14s).

Whilst the work may not have sounded as glamorous as that of Bomber Command, at least the squadron's Lincolns were doing a full time job, while the bomber squadrons were spending their time in rather soul destroying training in the knowledge that the jet-age just around the corner would make them obsolete.

Also reformed at Watton, in July 1951, was 199 Squadron specialising in RCM work, flying Lincolns, but transferred out to Hemswell in April 1952 under the control of Bomber Command for RCM/ECM training duties. Towards the end of 1951, No 192 Squadron was also reformed at Watton for secret RCM work, its Lincolns including SX980, SS715 and WD130 in A Flight and SX952 and 942 in C Flight. A number of the Lincolns used by Watton's various units were delivered virtually new, some spending their whole working life there. Some also passed from unit to unit at Watton itself.

The introduction of the Queen's Colours for squadrons completing 25 years service caused an unseemly switch round of numbers in order to preserve the identities of certain squadrons to enable them to qualify for the

Below: Aerial view of No 151 Squadron's veteran Lincolns from the Central Signals Establishment, Watton – the last in use in the RAF – lined up at sunny Idris June 1962 during an exercise. Within 12 months most would go to 27 MU Shawbury, Salop, leaving WD132 to the tender mercies of the Watton fire section. Reading from left to right RF398, RA685, RF505, RF461 and WD132 display a wide variety of serial and marking styles./*D. Dacre*

award. In this rather bewildering rush, in August 1958, 527 became 245, and 116 changed its number to 115; and shortly afterwards, both took their aircraft from Watton to Tangmere, 115 its Varsities and 245 its Canberras.

However, by mid-1956, it appears that most of the Lincolns had been regrouped within the Research & Development Squadron which, from October 1956, became known as Development Squadron, with B Flight operating Lincolns and A Flight Canberras. The Lincolns had by then become concerned almost exclusively with the development of RCM/ECM jamming/sensing/listening equipment, a role in which they were to continue until the end of their days.

Most of the Lincoln crews were highly experienced men, especially the special operators (spec ops) most of whom were tour-expired signallers. Theirs was a new and vital role, in which they spent hundreds of hours at a specially installed forward-facing position aft of the main 'step' of the fuselage just by the H2S cupola-top. After take-off, they would see no other crew member for a whole sortie of up to 10 hours. It was lonely, noisy and cold, and they wore electrically heated flying suits. The rest of the crew would sometimes have no idea what the spec op's task was, so secret was the work; they would merely fly as per their instructions.

For several years, development of new listening/jamming equipment preoccupied the Lincolns and their crews, the main item being Indigo Bracket, a very high powered centimetric jamming device using such high voltages that, in its early stages, the Lincolns were restricted to flying at 500ft in case of arcing in the set. Eventually, it was cleared up to 15,000ft and from that height could put out the whole east coast radar chain. It has been reported that four Lincolns could virtually neutralise the whole of the North West Europe radar system. On exercises the Lincolns would go out at low level, and some 200 miles away from the coast, (at the radar horizon) turn, start to climb and switch on the jamming devices at full power as the V-Force flew in over the top, often undetected by the fighter controllers.

Other tasks included similar exercises in the Middle and Near East and numerous Cianis, Kingpins, and Groupexs with other RAF Commands, plus the Army and Navy. In September 1959 IB was used outside the UK for the first time, when SX942 and RA665 flew a special demonstration from Nicosia. There were also frequent exercises with the Army anti-aircraft radar units along the south coast of England and at Manorbier in Wales.

The Lincolns dispensed vast quantities of window for radar jamming purposes, a special dispenser being installed in the rear of the fuselage behind the flare chute and operated by a winding handle which chopped up the bundles. For security reasons, much of the detail must remain unpublished.

Below: Led by Flt Lt Roy Matthews and crew in SX942 'L', CSE's Lincolns peel off for a stream landing at Watton on completion of the annual AOC's flypast, 6 June 1958. The watch tower, 'blood wagon' and windsock give the airfield very much a wartime appearence under the summer sky./*R. L. Matthews*

The operational development of radio and navigational aids, radio ranges and radar homing beacons, approach and blind landing systems, jamming and listening to potential enemy transmissions – all were the province of the Central Signals Establishment. Based at Watton, Norfolk, this specialist unit was named the Radio Warfare Establishment until 24 September 1946. At varying periods several squadrons operated Lincolns within the unit's framework and shown are two representative machines; RE405 '60' (*above*) and SS715 'Q' (*above right*) both showing external evidence of their special duties. With additional 'window' chutes and ventral aerials, etc; SS715 was one of the rare SS batch of six built at Yeadon.
/P. Clifton; M. C. Gray

B Flight Development Squadron

Not all the duties or flights were entirely routine. Sometimes the crews undertook overseas trips to keep them in current practice in long-range limited-aid navigation, and operational flying in North African, East African and Middle Eastern conditions. In February 1959 it was decided to send a Watton Lincoln on a long navex to Kenya, the double-headed crew to include Sqn Ldr C. D. C. Briggs who had then recently become CO of Development Squadron. Sqn Ldr Briggs was a Canberra pilot who had converted to the Lincoln locally a few weeks previously. The other pilot was Flt Lt Roy Matthews, with a flight engineer (M/Eng Tom Milligan), two navigators (Flt Lts Bill Watkin and Colin Bachelor), one signaller (Flt Sgt Steve Walker), plus a ground crew Flt Sgt. It was to be the longest overseas flight undertaken with a Lincoln for some years.

On the morning of 26 February WD148 left Watton with Flt Lt Matthews flying the first leg of 10hr 45min to El Adem (Libya) by a roundabout route. On approaching for the night landing at El Adem, the pilot decided to go round again off the first approach, not an unusual occurrence. The Arabs had stolen all the wiring and fittings from the approach lights situated outside the airfield boundary, leaving just the runway lights seemingly suspended in a huge black bowl, with no horizon, and approach angle difficult to judge. The second attempt was successful.

After resting up during the following day, it was planned to leave El Adem at midnight for the long leg to Nairobi. With few aids available, the navs had to spend some time computing and cross-checking their astro calculations, causing some interest among two transitting Valiant crews who were fascinated by the oldfashioned methods, especially the hand-held bubble sextant which was to be used. Sqn Ldr Briggs flew this next leg, but three hours after take-off, high cirrus cloud obscured the sky and stars, and the navs had

to resort to DR. They did a good job, because as dawn broke, visual checks showed the Lincoln to be almost on track. Nairobi was approached over the Aberdare Mountains, a sight well known to some of the crew from their Mau Mau Lincoln days. On the downwind leg at Eastleigh, a large bird, commonly known as a Kyte Hawk (or some similar name), hit the No 3 engine spinner, and on landing, both spinner and backplate were found to be broken beyond repair, and would have to be replaced. There were no spares available locally and a signal to base brought the response that it would take 10 days to get one flown out from the UK, a pleasant prospect for the crew who had no objection to being stranded in such a delightful spot. One or two had friends in the area, quickly arranged visits, and dispersed up-country, the rest being put up at the best hotel in Nairobi. After only two days, telegrams were sent out recalling them all to the airfield, where they gathered somewhat disconsolately to find that some bright corporal engine fitter had remembered seeing a Lincoln spinner assembly lying in an old store-shed, dating back to the days when the Lincolns were operating locally. He had replaced the damaged one by using a Hastings propeller kit, and the poor chap, having used considerable initiative, could not understand why the Lincoln crew gave him such cold looks as they inspected his handywork.

On 4 March, Roy Matthews flew the 6hr 25min leg from Nairobi to Khormaksar (Aden) without incident, the plan being to night-stop, then press on to El Adem the next day, non-stop. This was to be a long flight of up to 12 hours, as Egypt had long since denied the RAF overflying rights, so the forecast average headwind of 15kts would necessitate an overnight refuelling stop at Khartoum. The navs suggested the appropriate request signal be sent, as it took two days to obtain diplomatic clearance for a landing at Khartoum. By this time, however,

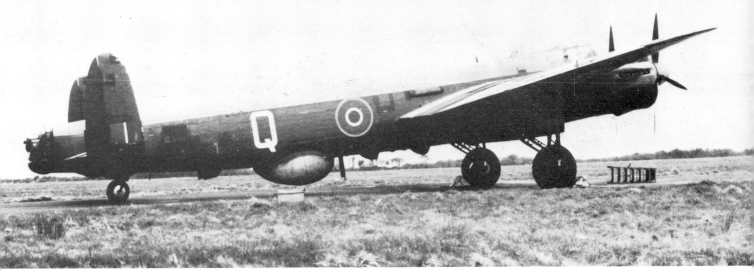

the squadron leader, having already suffered one unscheduled delay at Nairobi, was anxious to get back to Watton, and was perhaps beginning to suspect that some of the crew were wanting to spin out the stay in Aden, so a decision was put off until next day. The following morning, the expected headwinds were still put at 15kts, but Sqn Ldr Briggs, who was to fly the stage, decided they should go, and risk a possible diversion to Khartoum as an emergency, if need be.

On 5 March, as WD148 lifted away from Khormaksar, there was a great bang from No 3 engine and the control tower reported a trail of black smoke. The Sqn Ldr asked the engineer what he thought had happened, and was told it was a 'blow back'. He got the same answer from the co-pilot sitting in the nose. It was suggested by the two more experienced Lincoln men that in view of the long desert crossing, it would be advisable to burn off fuel for 2/3 hours and return to Khormaksar. To jettison the fuel would probably damage the tanks. Still in the circuit, the pilot decided that as the engines appeared to be running well enough, they should continue the flight to El Adem as planned, not a welcome prospect an 11/12 hour flight over totally barren and un-inhabited terrain. So, press-on it was, right across Ethiopia, towards the Sudan, with Flt Lt Matthews map reading in the nose, finding the features on the maps getting progressively fewer, until the almost wholly light brown area was marked by a single dotted line and no more, this tracing the route of some British expedition of the mid-1800s. On over the Sudan, hour after hour; at one point a discreet note on the back of a cigarette packet from the nav was passed into the nose via the engineer. On it was written 'ETA El Adem now outside fuel endurance'. No comment was made, and it was on in silence, past 'Nasser's Corner' at the southern end of Egypt, across the most barren of deserts, where for many miles the only mark on the map was a black area which denoted

the largest 'town' – three stone dwellings; then a little further north was marked 'a mushroom shaped rock' which stood out clearly for many miles across the otherwise featureless desert.

Eventually, El Adem was reached after $11\frac{1}{2}$ hours, and a safe landing made. On taxying in, however, No 3 engine would not throttle back, so it had to be stopped on the mag switches. The Flt Sgt crew chief took a look inside the cowling and found the air intake trunking had split open from front to back like a sardine can by the force of the blow back, which had also bent the throttle linkage to the carburettor. In the bottom of the intake trunking was a pile of broken supercharger blades, and the crew gave silent thanks to the reliability of the Merlin which had performed so perfectly for $11\frac{1}{2}$ hours with its rpm and oil pressure remaining perfectly steady the whole time. There were only 200 gallons of fuel remaining, of which less than half might have been usable.

The CO signalled base for an aircraft to come out to collect him, and departed for Watton, leaving Matthews with Colin Bachelor and Steve Walker (his regular nav and signaller) plus the engineer, Tommy Milligan, to get the aircraft back. After five days, a Beverley arrived from the UK with a replacement engine and an airman fitter, who helped the engineer to get it installed. El Adem's transit mess was not the liveliest of places and after 10 days there, the crew were glad to get 148 airborne again, on 16 March, for a quick air-test, then on to Luqa (Malta), a short hop of only 4hr 15min up the Med. for a day's stop. A midnight take-off was planned so as to reach Marham in time for the early opening of customs, and on the night of 18 March, Matthews taxied 148 to the holding point. Pre-take-off checks completed, he requested 'line up' but the tower asked him to hold as they had a Canberra downwind. As it came in on finals over the sodium lights it was obviously in trouble, with nose well up and a

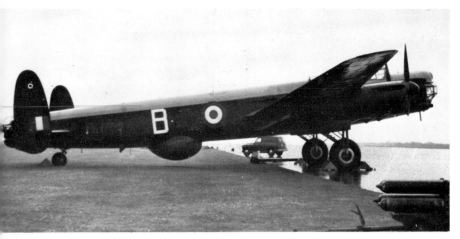

Above: 'Lancaster Bravo'.
/*A. J. Jackson*

wing well down as it disappeared down the runway, passing out of sight behind the Lincoln's port wing. A few moment's silence, and the tower reported that the Canberra had crashed on the active runway, fortunately with no loss of life or injury. On its way to 'finals' it had also knocked off the tails of two parked Canberras. It seemed that 148 and its crew never would get back to the UK, but after a 30 minute delay, the Lincoln was cleared for take-off on another runway. On opening up to take-off power, however, all the lighting inside the Lincoln came up very bright then went out with a crack as the bulbs burst. The master regulator had failed. A quick crew check showed that all were ready to manage: the nav had a torch, the signaller could sort out the problem in the air. The pilot had a battery operated emergency light on the control column, so off they went, and with the aid of occasional VHF bearings and visual fixes from lighthouses, etc, the French coast was crossed on track.

North of Paris, it was usual to pick up the Gee cover for navigation round London, but the jinx persisted, the Gee was u/s. Over the Channel, a descent through cloud brought the Lincoln round to the east of the London complex. Heading northwards for East Anglia, in and out of cloud at 900ft, the pilot, by then rather tired, suddenly saw a large RAF airfield below, not the healthiest of places to be at that height without clearance. Flt Lt Matthews called up the nav to ask 'Where the bloody hell is this place below?' not realising that in doing so he had pressed the transmit button with the VHF already set on the common airfield frequency. As quick as a flash came the tactful reply from the ground 'Lincoln aircraft is overhead Stradishall'. Marham was reached after 7hr 10min in the air. The crew opened their bags for the customs men only to find that while at Luqa, the Maltese aircraft cleaners had rifled their luggage and robbed them of clocks, cigarettes and other gifts bought on the trip. As if that was not enough, on trying to start up for the short flight from Marham to Watton, No 2

engine would not come to life. It was something to do with heat expansion which jammed starter motors, and which would only correct itself after the engine cooled down, which took four or five hours.

So, the gremlins persisted to the end, and the crew returned to Watton, and home, by 'bus. What should have been a five or six day sortie had taken $3\frac{1}{2}$ weeks, the crew having encountered just about every imaginable difficulty.

Flt Lt Matthews and crew were involved in another eventful overseas flight in December 1959, this time a navex to Malta and Idris, which by then was about as far afield as the Lincolns were permitted because of recovery difficulties. The crew departed Watton on 8 December in SX948 direct to Malta, 6hr 35min flying. The next night a $4\frac{3}{4}$-hour astro navex over the Med to Idris, where the same trouble was encountered as at El Adem previously, no approach lights, and an overshoot necessary from the first attempt.

On 11 December, an early morning take-off from Idris for what should have been a straightforward leg to Gibraltar, along the Med, round the Tunis 'bump'. The French had declared certain areas off the North African coast as prohibited zones as a deterrent to gun-runners supplying the Arab terrorists in Morocco, and extra care was taken with the flight plan. The forecast was bad, and sure enough, 948 was soon in thickening cloud which eventually became solid cumulo nimbus. Few radio bearings were obtained, and for five hours, the crew flew on dead reckoning.

Suddenly the Lincoln emerged from the heavy cloud to find itself surrounded by Vampires of the French Air Force which 'buzzed' it several times across the bows. One Vampire drew close alongside and kept putting its wheels up and down, the rest swooping round the Lincoln, waggling their wings. Flt Lt Matthews called up his nav, Flt Lt Colin Bachelor, who confirmed his fears that these were the 'follow us or be shot down' signals. A quick request for advice was made to Gibraltar on the radio by Flt Sgt Steve Walker, the signaller, and the answer came back to the effect that the Lincoln crew should comply with the Vampires' signals, reluctant though they were to divert. Matthews duly altered course to the left and followed the fighters. As he did so the two special operators in the rear fuselage of the Lincoln were busily dumping their secret material overboard into the sea.

Walker recrystallised one of the VHF sets to the French area frequency, and, sure enough, the crew immediately heard the French controller calling 'Lancaster Bravo, Lancaster Bravo, you are under arrest', the 'Bravo' being from the white code letter B still carried on the fuselage. The French, though knowing full well there were no Lancasters left serving in the RAF, would be unlikely to know either the difference between a Lanc and Lincoln or of the existence of the few remaining Lincolns in any case. The appearance, therefore, of a rather elderly black bomber had aroused their suspicions and they had scrambled the Vampires, being convinced they had found a 'hostile'.

On landing at Oran, the Lincoln was followed along the runway by two armoured cars, both with gun turrets turned menacingly towards it, and on coming to a stop at dispersal, the Lincoln was surrounded by French soldiers in camouflaged capes, all pointing their sub-machine guns directly at the cockpit in the most unfriendly fashion. Ordering his crew to remain in their places, Flt Lt Matthews removed his flying overall so as to reveal his RAF uniform, and went to the rear door where he was greeted by a French Army captain in the pouring rain. The appearance of an RAF uniform seemed to do the trick and after a short discussion the French troops relaxed, and a 'bus was provided to take the Lincoln crew to lunch, over which their host, the French captain, disclosed that a tip off had been received about an attempted arms drop, and they were convinced it was the Lincoln, which would certainly have been shot down had it not followed the fighters' orders to land. Over lunch, relations became extremely cordial and the Lincoln crew were invited to spend the weekend on the French base, but had to decline.

The only slight difficulty was in explaining away the additional person in civilian clothes not included in the crew list which had been supplied to the French captain. This eleventh passenger was Duggie Haig, one of the Kings Lynn Customs Officers, who had become well known to the Lincoln crews over the years, and had always treated them most fairly at Marham. He was about to retire, and had been brought along semi-officially as a farewell gesture. The French captain was good enough to turn a blind eye, perhaps as Duggie himself probably had done on occasions, and his presence passed off without further comment. As it happens, before the Lincoln was cleared to leave, a signal had been received by the ops centre at Oran that two French Air Force aeroplanes had diverted to Gibraltar in the bad weather. Gib had signalled: 'We have two of yours: you have one of ours. Game and set to us'. The message was repeated back at Watton where it left everyone completely mystified.

It was later discovered that whilst the Lincoln had strayed slightly south of track, its flight plan, filed at Idris, had not been passed forward because of a strike by Air Traffic Controllers there, so the unannounced penetration of French airspace was perhaps excusable.

B-Baker duly left Oran and completed its scheduled flight to Gibraltar, where its crew spent the rest of the weekend, treating Duggie Haig to a tour of the nightspots of La Linea before returning to Watton in $7\frac{1}{4}$ hours by the long way round sea route on 14 December. For the retiring Mr Haig, it had been a most exciting send off.

The last Lincolns soldiered on at Watton until March 1963, doing sterling work on radio/electronic listening, detection, jamming, etc. From the eight on charge in October 1959, the final number dwindled to six by the end of 1962. Whilst they were perhaps becoming a little 'tired', the opinion was that they still had plenty of life left.

In 1959 several of the aircraft had undergone extensive rebuilds by an Avro's working party who had renewed engine nacelles, bomb doors, flaps, wing leading edge nose ribs and skins, etc. Spares were certainly becoming a problem, and in June 1960, for example, SX942(L) received two replacement engine drive shafts, scavenged from RF564 at Hullavington. In January 1961 RF461 was newly delivered from 23 MU Aldergrove, but in March of the same year, two of the old faithfuls, WD130 and SX948 (our old friend "Lancaster-Bravo") were found to have spar cracks and were certified as Cat 5 – ie, scrap. Every removable item was used elsewhere, even the fuel. The plugs from 130 went to RF505 and 948's props to RF461 which at one stage in 1960/61 was flying with dayglo-painted fins and rudders. Another long service Lincoln, WD148(P), was certified Cat 5 with cracked wing spars, and withdrawn in July 1961, and RF398 (now preserved) was brought in as a replacement from 23 MU.

Strangely, when delivered to Watton, RF398 still retained its original hand-priming equipment mounted in the starboard undercarriage bay, but it received WD148's electric cockpit-priming system before the latter was removed for scrap in October 1961. There were no drawings available, and the modification (No 1715) was a long job carried out single-handed by SAC George Jiggins.

Participation in Command and Mediterranean area exercises continued throughout the year, and in August RF461 flew out to Malta, Idris and Nicosia, its bomb bay loaded with panniers of supplies for 51 Squadron. It had all sorts of mechanical problems, giving rise to opinions at one stage that it never would get back to the UK. It eventually returned safely from Idris with a length of 3in rubber tubing replacing its static line, a temporary modification which was to remain until it was withdrawn from

use. Never a popular aircraft, the crews claimed 461 needed 4lb of boost more than normal just to get it round the circuit, and avoiding flying it whenever possible.

On 1 January 1962 a parade was held, at which Development Squadron became No 151 Squadron.

Later that month, another ex-BCBS aircraft was collected from 23 MU, RF570. It was airtested over Loch Neagh in appalling weather by Flt Sgt Jack Wynne and his Flight Engineer, M/Eng Roy Ives – weather so bad even the 202 Squadron Met Flight Hastings crew had declined to take off – but had so many snags the crew had to leave it at Aldergrove. The props were out of track, the compass was well adrift, not having been swung, etc, etc. A week later, another try, this time VHF failure, again in bad weather, and delivery to Watton did not take place until 21 February, still with a number of snags which Watton's experts soon put right.

During the summer of 1962 there were a number of detachments to Mediterranean bases for exercises, and in August five of the Lincolns took part in a large exercise with the fleet. En route from St Mawgan to Gib a search was made for US Navy ships in the Bay of Biscay, resulting in RA685 landing after a flight of 11 hours with only 15 min fuel remaining, while another Lincoln, RF461, had to land at Lisbon to refuel.

Whilst the usual problems associated with piston-engined aircraft continued to be encountered, the Lincolns were still performing well in expert hands, both in the air and on the ground. There was little excuse to be found at station level for scrapping them. There was no doubt, however, among the

crews that excuses were being sought to scrap the Lincolns: for example WD132 went before the end with a twisted wing, which upset her regular pilot, Flt Lt Don Dacre, and she ended her days on the Watton fire dump. Then the very bad winter of 1963 curtailed flying considerably for nearly three months. Early in 1963 RF398 flew out to Akrotiri and Idris, but that was just about the last time a Lincoln went abroad. And then on 12 March 1963 came the 'final' flypast, though the Lincolns actually continued in use until the end of the month, RF505 having done a Thorney Island-Gutersloh sortie as late as the 25th. Flt Lt John D. Langley flew the last three out of Watton; RF461 and RA685 to Shawbury for scrapping on 18 and 19th April respectively, then RF398 to Henlow for preservation on 30 April 1963, thus ending the days of the Lincoln in service with the Royal Air Force.

When the time finally came to say goodbye to the Lincoln, three of the last five still operating from Watton flew a farewell tour of towns and areas associated with the type since the war. Pictured are two of the final five. *Above:* WD132 pictured at rainsoaked Hucknall, wearing the ultimate CSE livery./*Rolls-Royce*

Top: RF505 in her earlier days on radar trials with TFU Defford (from April 1956 until transfer to CSE, June 1958). /*Royal Radar Establishment*

Pots and Pans

Above: It may seem a crime to deliberately burn an aircraft but RA711, seen here, well ablaze, is providing a firecrew with valuable experience in the event of a crash. Fireman Derrick 'Ginger' Hine makes a hasty exit at Lindholme 24 May 1962, from a Lincoln which had been a long-serving member of the station's Bomber Command Bombing School's fleet./*D. S. Hine*

Centre left: Still bearing evidence of No 83 Squadron's operations in Malaya is RE358 being dismantled by a working party in the snow at Hemswell, January 1955, looking decidedly 'Cat 4' to use the official term. Her days of usefulness over, she is a far cry from the Lincoln pictured on p77 when she was the regular mount of Flt Sgt Joe Kmiecik and crew. /*M. J. Cawsey*

Bottom left: The breakers in action at Lindholme, Yorks, 18 July 1957./*C. S. Waterfall*

Above: Future pots and pans in the International Alloys yard at Aylesbury, Bucks, in 1958. /*P. R. Arnold*

Centre left: SX958 at 15 MU Wroughton, 29 April 1957. /*B. Goulding*

Bottom left: Honourable retirement comes for the Tyne Lincoln G-37-1, shown here at Hucknall with the tethering gantry for the 'Flying Bedstead' in the background. /*Rolls-Royce*

Top right: A long period in the history of No 10 Squadron Maritime Squadron based at Townsville came to an end on Monday 30 July 1962. Five MR31s, including A73-61 seen here were towed away to a nearby paddock, there to be broken up by their new owner, Mr Peter Hookway. Price for a once front line aeroplane – a mere £400. /*Townsville Daily Bulletin*

Right: Appeals to preserve an Austrailian Lincoln were sadly ignored. Far from ending up in a museum, A73-65, flown from Townsville to Darwin on 14 June 1961 by Plt Off Robert Stewart RAAF and crew (the final sortie by an Australian-built Lincoln) slowly fell apart as firemen learned and practised their essential task. Here she is seen some months later shorn of engines and equipment but still with nose windows virtually intact. /*J. L. Laming*

Survivors

Right: A void on the British aviation scene for too many years was a National Royal Air Force Museum. Happily this has now been rectified and Hendon has already become an institution. This is RF398 pictured at Henlow (the museum's main store) during the summer of 1964, following delivery from the Central Signals Establishment, Watton, on 30 April 1963 by Flt Lt John Langley. In the background is Lancaster PA474 being painted up as a No 83 Squadron machine for the film *Operation Crossbow*. At the time of writing RF398 is held at Cosford, Staffs, due to lack of space at Hendon. First public appearance of 398 as a preserved machine was as a static exhibit at the RAF's 50th Anniversary Pageant at Abingdon, Berks, in May 1968. For this event a mid-upper turret was installed./*M. Parkinson*

Centre left: With little ceremony G-APRJ (alias RF342) climbs away from Cranfield for the last time, 9 May 1967, just 40 minutes flying time away from her final resting place, Rochford Airport, Southend, Essex, to take her place in a private museum. Though stripped of test equipment her new owners were allowed to keep the nose probe and ventral blister, while the wing silhouettes (carried both sides of the nose) bear testament to her service in the field of aviation research.
/*College of Aeronautics*

Bottom left: A memorial to the Argentine's first – and last – strategic bomber force stands B-010, handed over to the National Museum at Aeroparque, Buenos Aires, in 1968 and beautifully restored. The picture was taken in August 1975. Originally built by Avro and allocated the RAF serial RE408, she bears the insignia of *Grupo 1 de Bombardes V Brigada Aerea*. It is suggested that another Lincoln may be preserved at one of the Argentine bases in the south of the country, but is not confirmed.
/*Denir Lima da Camargo*

Appendices

RAF LINCOLN BOMBER SQUADRONS AT A GLANCE

	Lincolns	Converted Straight to	Disbanded	Reformed	To Convert to
7	8/49-12/55		1-2/1/56	1/11/56	Valiants
9	7/46-5/52	Canberras			
12	8/46-4/52	Canberras			
15	2/47-10/50	Washingtons (1/51)			
35	9/49-2/50		23/2/50	1/9/51	Washingtons
44	10/45-5/46	(Retained Lancasters)			
	12/46-1/51	Washingtons (2/51)			
49	10/49-8/55		1/8/55	1/5/56	Valiants
50	7/46-1/51		31/1/51	15/8/52	Canberras
57	8/45-3/51	Washingtons (5/51)			
61	5/46-7/54	Canberras			
83	7/46-12/55		1/1/56*	21/5/57	Vulcans
90	4/47-9/50		1/9/50	4/10/50	Washingtons
97	7/46-12/55		1/1/56*		
100	5/46-4/54	Canberras			
101	6/46-6/51	Canberras			
115	9/49-3/50		1/3/50	13/6/50	Washingtons (8/50)
138	9/47-9/50		1/9/50	1/1/55	Valiants
148	1/50-7/55		1/7/55	1/7/56	Valiants
149	10/49-3/50		1/3/50	14/8/50	Washingtons (11/50)
207	8/49-2/50		1/3/50	29/5/51	Washingtons (7/51)
214	2/50-12/54		30/12/54	2/3/56	Valiants
617	9/46-1/52	Canberras			
199	also included as it formed part of 1 (Bomber) Group 7/51-10/57 Canberras and Valiants				

* Nos 83 and 97 Squadrons renamed 'Antler' and 'Arrow' respectively on this date. Both absorbed into 1321 Flight 1/10/57

LINCOLN PRODUCTION SERIAL LIST

Serial	Mark	Manufacturer	No.
PW925, PW929, PW932	Prototypes	Avro's, Chadderton/Ringway	3
RA628-RA655	Mk I	Metrovick, Trafford Park/Woodford and Vickers Armstrongs, Chester (640-645 and 651-655)	17 / 11
RA656-RA658 RA661-RA693 RA709-RA724	Mk II	Metrovick, Trafford Park/Woodford	52
RE227-RE268 RE281-RE288	Mk I	Avro's Chadderton/Woodford	50
RE289-RE325 RE338-RE380 RE393-RE424	Mk II	Avro's Chadderton/Woodford	112
RF329-RF332	Mk II	Armstrong Whitworth Baginton/Bitteswell	4
RF333-RF334	Mk I	Armstrong Whitworth Baginton/Bitteswell	2
RF335-RF370 RF383-RF427 RF440-RF485 RF498-RF539 RF553-RF577	Mk II	Armstrong Whitworth Baginton/Bitteswell	194
SS713-SS714	Mk I	Avro's Yeadon	2
SS715-SS718	Mk II	Avro's Yeadon	4
SX923-SX958 SX970-SX993	Mk II	Armstrong Whitworth Baginton/Bitteswell	60
WD122-WD133 WD141-WD149	Mk II	Armstrong Whitworth Baginton/Bitteswell	21
		Total British/RAF	**532**
B-013-B-030	Mk II	Armstrong Whitworth Baginton (for Argentine)	18
FM300	Mk XV	Victory Aircraft, Malton, Ontario (Canada)	1
A73-1-A73-54	Mk 30	Government Aircraft Factories Fisherman's Bend, Melbourne, (for RAAF)	54
A73-55-A73-73	Mk 31	Government Aircraft Factories Fisherman's Bend, Melbourne, (for RAAF)	19
		Total Built	**624**

LINCOLN SPECIFICATION

B1
4 x 1,635/1,705bhp* Rolls-Royce (British built) Merlin 85s or 85As.

B2
4 x 1,635/1,705bhp Rolls-Royce (Packard, USA built) Merlin 68As.

B30 and early Mk 31
4 x 1,635/1,705bhp Rolls-Royce (British built) Merlin 85Bs (some B30s also fitted outboard with 2 x 1,580bhp Merlin 66s).

B30A and Mk 31
4 x 1,650bhp Rolls-Royce (CAC, Australian built) Merlin 102s.

Dimensions
Span	120ft
Length	78ft 3½in (Mk 31:85ft 4in)
Height (tail down)	17ft 3½in (Mk 31:19ft)
Wing area	1,421sq ft
Wing loading	52.77lb/sq ft

Weights
Main structure (empty)	23,112lb
Power plants	14,590lb
	37,702lb
Fixed military equipment	6,486lb
Removable military equipment	3,828lb
7 crew (incl parachutes)	1,400lb
	49,416lb
Combination of fuel, oil and bombs	32,584lb
Total max auw	82,000lb
Normal maximum bomb load	14,000lb
Normal maximum range with full bomb load at 20,000ft/215mph	2,640 miles
at 15,000ft/200mph	2,800 miles
With 4,000lb of bombs, range could be stretched to over	4,000 miles

Performance
Normal service ceiling	28,000ft
Speeds—Take-off (82,000lb)	125/130mph
—Climb	165/170mph
—Cruise	167mph
—Maximum level	310mph
—Diving	350mph
—Stalling (u/c and flaps up. 82,000lb)	132mph
(u/c and flaps up. 56,000lb)	100mph
(u/c and flaps down. 56,000lb)	81mph
—Landing	105/110mph

* Range of power ratings (bhp) are for take-off (+18) and combat (+18, MS, at 5/6,000ft)

97 Squadron, Hemswell.
/R. C. H. Poynton